RISK AND SOCIETY

THE RISKS AND HAZARDS SERIES

RISK AND SOCIETY

Studies of risk generation and reactions to risk

Edited by

Lennart Sjöberg

Department of Psychology, University of Göteborg, Sweden

London
ALLEN & UNWIN
Boston   Sydney

Allen & Unwin (Publishers) Ltd,
40 Museum Street, London WC1A 1LU, UK

Allen & Unwin (Publishers) Ltd,
Park Lane, Hemel Hempstead, Herts HP2 4TE, UK

Allen & Unwin Inc.,
8 Winchester Place, Winchester, Mass. 01890, USA

Allen & Unwin (Australia) Ltd,
8 Napier Street, North Sydney, NSW 2060, Australia

First published in 1987

ISSN 0261–0507

British Library Cataloguing in Publication Data

Risk and society : studies of risk
generation and reactions to risk.—(The
Risks and hazards series; ISSN 0261-0507)
1. Risk perception—Social aspects
I. Sjöberg, Lennart II. Series
302   H91
ISBN 0-04-604001-3

Library of Congress Cataloging-in-Publication Data

Risk and society.
(Risks and hazards series, ISSN 0261-0507 ; 3)
Includes bibliographies and index.
1. Risk management. 2. Risk—Social aspects.
3. Risk—Evaluation. I. Sjöberg, Lennart. II. Title:
Risk generation and reactions to risk. III. Series:
Risk & hazards series ; 3.
HD61.R566 1986   306   86-17235
ISBN 0-04-604001-3

Set in 10 on 11 point Times and Typeset by Mathematical Composition
Setters Ltd., Salisbury, UK and printed in Great Britain by Mackays of Chatham

Foreword

The *Risks & Hazards Series* is designed to make available to a wider readership the research results and intellectual developments arising from current concerns with hazards in the environment, and the associated risks to human health and wellbeing. Scientific as well as public concern about hazards has reached a new peak but the changes occurring are more than a matter of degree.

There is in all Western industrial societies a new element of public anxiety about hazards, which threatens to erode the confidence and trust that people place in the most powerful institutions. Because of this anxiety and the common policy and management questions that arise, hazards are being studied for the first time as a set of related phenomena. This generic approach is leading to an erosion of the commonsense distinction between natural and man-made hazards. Across a wide spectrum of risks, many people are no longer content to accept the inevitability of adverse effects as being natural or to be expected. Each event requires an explanation, and often the search for explanation is linked to a search for the locus of responsibility – someone to blame. These new circumstances have been in part generated by intellectual enquiry, but in their turn they are now posing new questions for research and giving rise to a demand for more effective policies.

Two decades ago systematic enquiry into the causes and consequences of natural hazards was conducted in disciplines and professions that worked to a considerable degree in isolation from each other and from the public. Beginning in the 1960s a much broader interdisciplinary approach to hazards developed, strongly influenced by geographers (natural hazards research) and by sociologists (disaster research). This research has shown that the consequences of floods and droughts can no longer be explained away as "Acts of God" but are often the result of the misapplication of technology. More recently the realisation is emerging that the technical shortcomings of particular human agencies are not the whole story either. To understand fully the problem of environmental hazards we must delve deeper into man's relationship with nature and the nature of human society.

The time seems opportune therefore to launch a new series that will provide more effectively for the substantial development and presentation of the empirical and conceptual advances that may be expected. In keeping with the nature of the subject matter, the series is planned to be international and interdisciplinary in scope and will deal with both natural and man-made hazards. As a vehicle for major contributions from scholars and practitioners the series is intended to meet needs in three directions: (a) professional managers, (b) research workers, and (c) students and teachers.

The social and scientific problems associated with environmental hazards now command the attention of a large group of management professionals in public and private organisations at local, national and international levels. The series is expected to help identify new directions in research and policy as the understanding of the causes and consequences of hazards deepens.

The interactions between hazard theory, research and management practice are now being incorporated into the content of university-level courses in the natural and social sciences as well as a number of interdisciplinary fields such as environmental studies and planning.

The common theme of the series is the concept of hazards and their management, and the orientation will be largely towards practice and policy. More theoretical works, and 'critical science' approaches are not excluded, and the series will be especially pleased to consider manuscripts that arise from interdisciplinary work; that consider more than one hazard; or that study hazards in a multinational or cross-cultural context; and present a broad human-ecological approach to environmental hazards.

Preface

This book contains a selection of reports written for a project on risk generation and risk evaluation which has been supported by the Swedish Committee for Future Research. The purpose of the project was to review research of relevance to physical risks, how risky decisions are made, and how risks are evaluated and reacted to. It is mainly the social sciences that are represented in the volume, but some humanistic and natural science work is also reviewed.

When I accepted to serve as the director for the project, I did not quite anticipate how many and intricate problems are involved in such an endeavor. The field was to be covered with the help of many scientific disciplines which usually work rather independently. It was not obvious how they should be selected and how their work should be coordinated. What, indeed, is involved in a study of how "society" generates and reacts to physical risks?

I have chosen to present the work in three broadly defined sections, viz. generation of risks, reactions to risks and communication about risks. Of course, there is some overlap between the sections and the placement of some papers seemed fairly difficult. The sections are also somewhat unevenly covered. I found it much more difficult to obtain good material on the generation of risks than on the other topics.

The papers presented are review articles, often with a speculative orientation. The nature of the project was to generate ideas and to stimulate further research. Still, neither I nor the other authors could always abstain from drawing some conclusions; we do so at the risk of being criticized for having too little data in support. The field of physical risk involves one both morally and emotionally, and it is hard to stick to the ideal of the disinterested and objective scientist. This is especially true because the papers were orginally written at the end of the 1970s which was a period of intense risk debate in Sweden, culminating in the nuclear power referendum on March 23, 1980. I can only hope that what has been lost in scientific purity and completeness of coverage is gained by readability.

Any scientist facing an interdisciplinary problem such as risk is immediately faced also with learning about the limits of his own competence. I, being a psychologist, received great help in the project work from a Steering Committee consisting of an expert in statistics, Thorbjörn Thedéen, and an expert in cultural geography and social planning, Philip Moding.

The work on this book was carried out when I was on leave from the University of Göteborg for two years in 1980–82. The first year was spent at the Netherlands Institute for Advanced Study. During the second year I was associated with the Faculté Universitaire Catholique de Mons (FUCAM), Belgium, and my work was also supported by the European Institute for Advanced Studies in Management, Brussels. I thank these institutions which made it possible for me to work on the book while I stayed in the Netherlands and Belgium. I also thank the Committee for Future Research for their support of the work.

Two of my children spent some time with me abroad while I was doing this work; but Hans, my son, did not. I dedicate my work to him.

LENNART SJÖBERG

Acknowledgments

The publication of this book was supported by a grant from the Swedish Council for Planning and Coordination of Research, Stockholm, Sweden.

Chapter 14 is reprinted from *Journal of Communication* 31 (2), 85–96, with the permission of the School of Communications, University of Pennsylvania.

Contents

List of tables

List of contributors

Lennart Sjöberg
Department of Psychology, University of Göteborg, Sweden

Mats Björkman
Department of Psychology, University of Uppsala, Sweden

Sören Bergström
Department of Business Administration, University of Stockholm, Sweden

Michael Mussachia
3271, Caminito Ameca, La Jolla, California 92037, USA

Kajsa Friedman
Department of Social Anthropology, University of Lund, Sweden

Anna-Christina Blomkvist
Ericsson Information Systems, Stockholm, Sweden

Hampus Lyttkens
Department of Theology, University of Lund, Sweden

Birgitta Juås
Department of Economics, University of Karlstad, Sweden

Bengt Mattsson
Department of Economics, University of Karlstad, Sweden

Eva Selin
Department of Physics, Chalmers University of Technology, Göteborg, Sweden

Lennart Nordfors
Department of Political Science, University of Uppsala, Sweden

Hollis Routledge
Nova Scotia Forest Industries, Port Hawkesbury, Nova Scotia, Canada

Ron Aurell
Nova Scotia Forest Industries, Port Hawkesbury, Nova Scotia, Canada

Margareta Cronholm
Audience and Program Research Department, Swedish Broadcasting Corporation, S–105 10 Stockholm, Sweden

Rolf Sandell
Department of Psychology, University of Stockholm, Box 6706, S–113 85, Stockholm, Sweden

1 *Introduction*

LENNART SJÖBERG

Risk has become an urgent social concern since the 1960s. Decision makers are faced with the intense concerns of various individuals and groups regarding what they see as potential dangers in the environment, dangers often associated with the development of advanced and complex new technology. The mass media are often quite eager to spread such information about risks and to carry on with the debate. Demands for participation in the decision-making process are voiced, and politicians and administrators find their sphere of action considerably constrained, caught, as they are, in the midst of intense social conflicts and controversy over risks.

It is natural that this situation stimulates research on risk. One early approach is due to Starr (1969) who presented some actuarial data on risks and benefits of various activities. He suggested, on the basis of these data, that greater risks are increasingly accepted if the benefits also increase and the greater risks are more acceptable for voluntary activities than for involuntary ones. It was also clear that risks decrease over time when a technology becomes better developed.

Several groups initiated research on risk in the 1970s. Here I need mention only books by Lowrance (1976) and Rowe (1977), the extensive programs carried out at Clark University (Kates 1977), UCLA (e.g. Okrent 1977), the Battelle Institute of Frankfurt (e.g. Conrad & Krebsbach-Gnath 1980), the IAEA-IIASA group in Vienna and the very influential group of psychologists at Decision Research in Eugene, Oregon (e.g. Slovic *et al.* 1979). The initial enthusiasm over the findings by Starr has weakened over the years. Methods for deciding on the acceptability of risk were reviewed by Fischhoff *et al.* (1980) and they came out with rather negative conclusions for the "revealed preference" approach by Starr. Earlier, Otway and Cohen (1975) voiced several critical comments about the quality of the data that Starr utilized. Many (e.g. Juås & Mattsson, Ch. 8 in this volume) have been critical about the distinction between voluntary and nonvoluntary forms of behavior. It is probably fair to say that the question of what is an acceptable risk is not a very good or profound question. There is no such thing as an absolute level of acceptability. Besides, it is typically impossible to attain agreement on what the risk is, how large is the probability and what are the consequences of, say, a core melt-down in a nuclear power plant?

Research has, therefore, become quite diversified and more empirical. The present risk project (first presented in Sjöberg 1978) sponsored reviews of risk perception (Sjöberg 1979) and risk debates (Sjöberg 1980); it included a special review of risks in highway traffic (Svenson 1981) and historical risk studies (Odén 1977). Some of the work in the project is also available in a book in Swedish (Sjöberg 1982b).

Vlek and Stallen (1980, 1981) have undertaken further work, the former paper giving an up-to-date review of the field. The Battelle Institute held a conference which was published in book form (Conrad 1980) and so did the Energy Research Institute of the Swedish Academy of Sciences (Goodman & Rowe 1979). The importance of risk to social decision making is exemplified by the risk-evaluation committee which was appointed by the Swedish government to provide material for the March 1980 referendum on nuclear power; the experience of the present author as a member of this committee has been briefly described elsewhere (Sjöberg 1980).

The present book contains 13 chapters dealing with various specific aspects of risks and a final chapter of conclusions. The papers are divided into three main sections dealing with generation of risks, reactions to risks and communication about risks. They will be briefly summarized here.

Generation of risks

Björkman (Ch. 2) gives a review of psychological research in which time is the independent variable. He argues that cognition and involvement both decrease as a function of time distance. In other words, things distant in the past and the future concern us less and are badly remembered or anticipated. Because of this pervasive trend, which can be seen as functional to everyday adjustment, there is little reason to expect, according to Björkman, that politicians really can make skilful decisions about events in a distant future, and it is also unlikely that they are really all that involved. Björkman's analysis is at the individual level.

Bergström (Ch. 3) takes a more organizational approach. His problem is how risky products come to be marketed. He points out that commercial motives and morals may lead to a neglect of the safety of the consumer, as may certain organizational factors. The organizational factors are, in turn, different for firms of different sizes. The consumer is protected by a net of factors, the mass media being one of the more potent (and unpopular). When times become harsh, as they are today, the safety net probably becomes less efficient and the commercial motives stronger; hence more risk taking is enforced on the consumer.

Mussachia (Ch. 4) takes the angle of the theory of science. Risks are produced, in his analysis, by research and technological development. He divides the analysis into three phases: basic research, applied research and practical application programs, which is the point where he makes contact with Bergström's analysis in Chapter 2. Mussachia points to several components that account for risks being produced. There may be unknown side effects due to the extensive application of technology and its wide-ranging effects on the ecology; planners tend to lack concrete and specific knowledge; benefits are evident and short term whereas costs and disadvantages are obscure and long term. Feedback about risks is therefore slow and ambiguous. These arguments are well in line with some of the other chapters in the book, for example Björkman's Chapter 2 and Selin's Chapter 9.

Friedman (Ch. 5) applies a much more global perspective to risk. She discusses the "rise and fall" of civilizations and relates it to shifts in center—periphery relations. Industrial production and know-how will be moved from the center to the periphery because of increasing costs and intense exploitation of resources in the center and the increasing availability of skilled labor in the periphery. The center will be shaken by internal conflicts and loss of morale; the eventual shifts of political and military supremacy being only a question of time. Applying this model to the present world economy, Friedman finds the prospects for the West to be bleak. The movement of industrial production to the periphery has begun; the center is shaken by economic decline and political unrest. Computer technology is, of course, a new factor but it may, according to Friedman, speed up the process by decreasing the demand for education of the work force rather than supporting and sustaining present power relations.

Risks will become more frequent and stronger as the economic conditions and the social climate continue to deteriorate; the tie to Bergström's analysis of business decisions (Ch. 3) is clear. The very conditions that maximize risk production according to Bergström are just around the corner according to Friedman. Increasing pressure on researchers may also bring about a still more short-sighted perspective, in line with Mussachia's views (Ch. 4). Björkman's analysis of the time perspective is of importance here, too. The decline and fall of civilizations are rare events of a nature hard to imagine while life around oneself goes on more or less, as usual. The prediction of historical development, even within a generation, seems to be tremendously difficult. Somehow, although tomorrow is going to be almost the same as today, the world is transformed in unanticipated ways in 20 years. Who, at the turn of the century, could have been even somewhat right in guessing at, for example the rise of the Nazis and World War II or the development of the computer?

The development and exploitation of science is both a cause of increased wealth and population and an effect thereof. In the process, risks are produced and taken, often quite blindly, because the temptation of short-term advantages is irresistible.

Reactions to risks

People react to the risks that they come to believe exist. These reactions are important because they feed back into the political decision-making process whenever society is open to communication and feedback; the result is, of course, that smaller risks are taken. We discuss here only the open societies of the West. Risk taking in authoritarian, closed societies, such as those of Eastern Europe and the Soviet Union, constitutes a highly important topic because disasters do not recognize national boundaries, but it was outside the scope of the the project.

Risk reactions partly reflect values (Blomkvist, Ch. 6). The concept of value has been treated, in psychology, in a somewhat uneasy manner. Are values the causes of preferences or are they merely used to justify them? (cf. Zajonc 1980). It is particularly important to discuss moral values and moral indignation when risks are considered. Risks concern very central, and morally significant, human values; the values of health and life itself. Such values are hard to compare with more mundane dimensions without running the risk of being seen as cold-hearted and cynical. There have been attempts at the measurement of the value of human life within an economic frame of reference (see Juås and Mattsson, Ch. 8), but there are indications that responsible decision makers do not like to come out in public as endorsing any such measures. Moral indignation is probably also a factor underlying much of the power of mass media (see Ch. 13 for some examples); pure and simple fear of death may, of course, be another factor adding to their ability to influence politicians. An opinion aroused by the existence of a mortal threat demands political action. Few democratically responsible politicians can afford to neglect it.

Blomkvist also discusses the opposition to the industrial growth society with its emphasis on materialistic values. The alternative, which she calls the life necessities society, is a society trying to achieve ecological balance. However, such a society is not necessarily less risky.

The technology for a safe and reasonably comfortable life for the present world population is not yet available; it is debatable if it can ever be. The debate is here, as usual (cf. Sjöberg 1980), one-sided. Maybe Blomkvist is right in her conclusion that one-sidedness is an unavoidable consequence of, and a precondition for, efficient societal action and change.

Lyttkens (Ch. 7) draws a broad picture of the unrest and anxiety that is characteristic of much contemporary life. The question is how it should be explained. The beginnings of economic decline, as Friedman (Ch. 5) described them, are quite recent. Fear of war has always been more or less realistic, even if it has obtained especially lugubrious proportions in the modern nuclear age. Lyttkens favors the approach of viewing anxiety as a reaction to the eternal, tragic dimension of human existence. Death is always there as a reality, our own and that of those who are close to us. Since death takes us out of time and space, it seems logical that the anxiety it creates can be met most efficiently with metaphysical or religious beliefs which answer the existential questions "Why am I here?" "What happens after death?" and give comfort and stability. In the secularized Western societies, and Sweden is a prime example of secularization, rationality has largely destroyed religious belief, and indulgence in material wealth has, at least temporarily, replaced the search for existential closure. However, wealth and pleasure can only be obtained in limited amounts and always at a price; frustration follows and anxiety remains.

The reaction to modern society so described is partly reality oriented. The frustration in the search for material wealth is quite real, the ecological limits are met more and more often and intense scientific exploitation of the environmental resources creates quite real risks to the life and health of everyone. It is, however, also possible that some concerns over risky technology are scapegoats. It is true that science is directly responsible for the very real risk of a nuclear holocaust and it would be strange if such a rôle were not met with some aggressive reactions, no matter how much it may be argued that the real responsibility lies with the political and military leadership.

In Chapter 8, Juås and Mattsson discuss the measurement of the value of life within an economic framework. They distinguish between explicit life values, as sometimes used in planning, and implicit values which may be estimated from decisions that involve physical risks but which are nevertheless kept covert in the decision-making process. They derive a utility model of life value which they use to explain why one should, in general, expect that life values will differ across different activities. Their chapter also includes a section in which they report data obtained with the help of a questionnaire sent to planning authorities in various countries.

As may be expected, Juås and Mattsson find that life values vary greatly across different spheres of activity. They, and others, have found that life values seem especially high in certain forms of advanced technology, most notably the nuclear power industry. It may be very low, on the other hand, in traditional and risky activities such as fishing (see Sinclair *et al.* 1972). It is likely that life values reflect several different kinds of reactions to risks. One type of reaction is, of course, the wish to increase safety. However, if this were to be the whole story, life values should not differ between various sectors. It is very plausible that life values also reflect the attempts by decision makers to cope with moral indignation (cf. Ch. 6) and to decrease fears, rather than risks – a distinction discussed further in Blomkvist's chapter on public transportation (Ch. 10). It is debatable just how ethically defensible such differentiations are; after all, all human lives should be of equal value. The intricate discussions of the value of human life are beyond the scope of this book, however; the reader is referred to the book by Glover (1977).

Selin (Ch. 9) discusses the threats to the environment and to health caused by modern large-scale technology. She is especially concerned with the concept of collective risks, i.e. risks to a group, a society or even mankind. The vulnerability of the organism to a host of small, but possibly significant, environmental disruptions, such as the decreased availability of certain trace elements, is little known. The question arises whether we would really be willing to take those risks if we were to be fully informed about them, especially since there is a potential threat to the collective, not only to the individual. It seems likely that we have here, again, a case of a remote and somewhat abstract risk matched against a number of short-term benefits. As pointed out by Björkman (Ch. 2), it is hard to obtain knowledge about, and to get involved in, such remote and seemingly unlikely events. If there is really a quite concrete threat to a society it is, on the other hand, plausible that the collective risk is seen as being of utmost importance. The collective-risk aspect that Selin brings into the discussion has rarely been attended to in the risk debate and it is important to analyze it further, both from a normative point of view and in further empirical research.

In Chapter 10, Blomkvist gives a review of public transportation in which she draws a contrast between risk and fear. Some fears are more or less irrational, the most extreme examples being given by phobias. It is conceivable that some of the reluctance to use public transportation is due to phobias; witness, for example, the widespread fear of flying. Even today, a sizable proportion of the Scandinavian population has not even once traveled by air.

These notions are related to the ones put forward by Lyttkens in Chapter 7, although Lyttkens suggested an existential rather than a neurotic background to anxiety, and was concerned with a more broadly spread anxiety. The question is to what extent the phobic and existential reactions are related. Human misery may, of course, have several different causes, and neurotic reactions may reflect more of a personal experience than the more general existential reactions.

It is, at any rate, plausible that phobic reactions may be at the root of some people's avoidance of public transportation with its crowds, lack of personal control, etc. They opt for the use of private automobiles in the belief that they are better drivers than most other people (Svenson 1981). In so doing, they take, in fact, increased risks and contribute to traffic congestion and air pollution.

It is therefore important to design public means of transportation so as to minimize the likelihood of avoidance reactions. It seems likely that such design criteria would also lead to positive evaluations from the majority of travelers who are not phobic, but still feel a certain unease at conditions that provoke phobic reactions among a minority of people.

The section on reactions to risk is concluded with two case studies. In Chapter 11, Nordfors describes the dramatic events that led, in Sweden, to quite restrictive legislation concerning the use of asbestos. The authorities were on the verge of introducing less restrictive regulations in the fall of 1975 when data on possible carcinogenic effects were given wide publicity. Although only a few cases were documented, the demands for drastic measures were adamant. The authorities were forced to prohibit the use of asbestos on a wider scale than planned. The second example is from Canada. In the mid-1970s, The Nova Scotia Forest Industries faced severe threat from attacks by the Spruce budworm which they saw as likely to destroy an important part of their timber supply. Spraying of the forests became a hotly debated issue; Chapter 12 gives the company's view. The fierce opposition to spraying was based on fears that it might be detrimental to the health of the population. Some medical doctors gave important support to these suspicions and politicians conceded. The company was frustrated in its attempts to preserve the basis of its operations, and Routledge and Aurell argue that the decision, not the spray, was entirely irrational.

The two case studies have many similarities. In both cases, medical reports caused a tremendous public response and politicians were forced to follow through even when the scientific basis was shaky, as it seems to have been at least in the Spruce budworm case. The mass media played, of course, a very important rôle in the process, a rôle that will be further discussed in the third section of this book. The Nova Scotia Forest Industries wanted to apply a cost –benefit approach to spraying, whereby the tangible benefits to be obtained by spraying were compared to the more or less unlikely health risks. Such an analytical approach met with little understanding and approval. It is, however, quite typical that opponents paint black and white pictures of the pros and cons (cf. Sjöberg 1980) and, in this way, they produce cases where the espoused option (spray or no spray) is dominating other options. Montgomery (1983) has suggested that people employ these tactics to get desired dominance structures that can be used to justify decisions and to persuade others. Sjöberg (1982a) studied the interaction between beliefs and values and showed that it increased as a function of involvement. People tend to see only advantages in what they like and disadvantages in what they dislike, and this tendency seems to be little affected even by the emotional state that they find themselves in; it is prevalent also in neutral moods (Sjöberg & Biel 1983). Of course, this tendency is likely to lead to factual inconsistencies and errors which are particularly offensive to the experts, who can point to the weak parts of the argument. They thereby come to see the opposition as emotional and incompetent and they tend to take too lightly the limitations of their own knowledge and problem analysis.

It is possibly significant that medical doctors played such an important rôle in the cases. Lyttkens (Ch. 7) pointed out that concerns about health and the body have come to occupy a central rôle among the concerns of modern man. Also, the cases illustrate the rôle of moral indignation. It is simply very difficult to argue in favor of economic values when people perceive their lives as threatened, even if the threat is tenuous and speculative. People do not like to take chances on their health, and they oppose such "gambles" if they get a chance to know about them and to influence the decisions. There are exceptions, of course, to this rule, but they bring in new factors such as the thrill of adventure, the chance to excel in "macho" showing off, fatalism, etc.

Those who produce the risks do so as side effects of other activities and they tend to pay less attention to them than those who are directly concerned; see Bergströms and Mussachia's, Chapters 3 and 4, respectively. The availability of credible medical expertise may be necessary for a powerful opposition to develop. One of the cases described below, in Chapter 13, illustrates how a premature concern about risks of a food-stuff ingredient was quickly forgotten, lacking, apparently, such backing by medical experts.

Communication about risks

Blomvist and Sjöberg (Ch. 13) discuss the rôle of the mass media in reports about accidents and risks, as illustrated in several case stories. The media are, in some cases, quick to react, but it is not always easy to understand the reasons for the distribution of attention that they apply. Take, by way of illustration, two recent train accidents in Sweden treated by Blomkvist and Sjöberg. Both accidents were disastrous, but the first one was given much more attention, and had some political consequences for the safety work of the railroads. It is enigmatic why the media reacted so mildly to the second accident, having displayed, a year earlier, such intense concern with a similar incident.

The strategy of media reporting is frequently to give individualized and concrete information. This may take the form of interviews with people at the scene of an accident, with the locally responsible authorities, with victims and their families, etc. Since major accidents frequently have complex and multiple causes, the views elicited, more or less immediately, by the media are not likely to be entirely correct. The media seek explanations, however, and they want them quickly. They also frequently look for any responsible persons who may be blamed for what happened. Chapter 13 also discusses media coverage of environmental and food-stuff risks in a few selected cases. The rôle of medical expertise appears, as noted above in the Nova Scotia case, to be crucial. Premature "scares" quickly vanished from the media if they found no expert backing. On the other hand, the local opinion and the media succeeded, in one of the cases discussed (BT Kemi), to expose negligent behavior by a firm and enforced the discontinuation of dangerous dumping of poisonous substances. Again, moral indignation played a major rôle.

Chapter 14 by Cronholm and Sandell is a review of work on scientific information in the mass media. Scientific information, especially about environmental issues, has become more frequent. Still, many journalists lack scientific education and errors in the reporting of scientific news are quite common. Also, when scientific news becomes important news items, the responsibility tends to shift from science journalists to general reporters who have still less background in the sciences. In Sweden, separate schools of journalism have been created fairly recently and they apparently make it still less likely that future journalists will obtain a good scientific education and respect for the importance of factual accuracy. On the contrary, some schools of journalism have been known to subscribe to the very "trendy" notion that truth somehow does not exist, so it is up to everyone to be as subjective as deemed necessary in order to favor the "cause" (of, usually, socialism).

Politicians read newspapers and base their ideas on what are important political questions and constraints at least partly on what they read. The media have a tremendous impact by setting the agenda of social debates, and by influencing the public and presenting "reality" to the politicians. Cronholm and Sandell, noting the problematic nature of mass-media communication, finish by bringing up the perspective of person-to-person communication but, of course, this is simply impractical no matter how efficient it may be when it can be carried out.

Another set of problems is connected with the audience. Scientific television programs are not very popular, to take an example. Decreasing interest in the natural sciences in secondary schools may also result in less well-prepared audiences in the future. The audience is frequently faced with opposing views by experts; in the intense media coverage of nuclear power prior to the referendum in Sweden it was, as a rule, impossible for experts to agree on anything. Since the audience can seldom evaluate the strength of the arguments on factual grounds, other factors, such as professional affiliation, titles, personal charisma, etc., probably affect the perceived credibility of the expert.

The final chapter of the book is a chapter of conclusions, where an attempt is made to point to some areas for future research and to draw some preliminary conclusions from the project.

References

Conrad, J. (ed.) 1980. *Society, technology and risk assessment.* New York: Academic Press.

Conrad, J. and C. Krebsbach-Gnath 1980. *Technologische Risiken und Gesellschaftliche Konflikte.* Politische Risikostrategien im Bereich der Kernenergie. Technical Report, Battelle – Institut e. V. Frankfurt: Frankfurt.

Fischhoff, B., S. Lichtenstein, P. Slovic, R. Keeneg, and S. Derby 1980. *Approaches to acceptable risk: A critical guide.* Oak Ridge National Laboratory, NUREG/CR-1614.

Glover, J. 1977. *Causing death and saving lives.* Harmondsworth: Penguin.

Goodman, G. and W. Rowe (eds.) 1979. *Energy risk management.* London: Academic Press.

Kates, R. W. 1977. *Managing technological hazard: Research needs and opportunities.* Institute of Behavioural Science: Univerity of Colorado.

Lowrance, W. W. 1976. *Of acceptable risk. Science and the determination of safety.* Los Angeles: Kaufmann.

Montgomery, H. 1983. Decision rules and the search for a dominance structure in *Analysing and aiding decision processes*, P. Humphreys, O. Svenson and A. Vari (eds.), pp. 343–70. Amsterdam: Marsh-Holland.

Odén, B. 1977. Historiskt perspektiv på riskparnoramat i ett föränderligt samhälle. Projektet Riskgenerering och riskbedömning i ett samhälleligt perpektiv. Samarbetskommitén för langsiktsmotiverad forskning.

Okrent, D. and C. Whipple 1977. *An approach to societal risk acceptance criteria and risk management.* Los Angeles: UCLA, School of Engineering and Applied Sciences.

Otway, H. and J. Cohen 1975. Revealed preferences: comments on the Starr benefit-risk relationships. *Research Memorandum 75–5.* Laxenburg, Austria: International Institute for Applied Systems Analysis.

Rowe, W. D. 1977. *An anatomy of risk.* New York: Wiley.

Sinclair, C., P. Marstrand and P. Newick 1972. *Innovation and human risk: The evaluation of human life and safety in relation to technical change.* London: Centre for the Study of Industrial Innovation.

Sjöberg, L. 1978. Risk generation and risk assessment in a social perspective. *Foresight* **3**, 4–12.

Sjöberg, L. 1979. Strength of belief and risk. *Policy Sci.* **11**, 39–57.

Sjöberg, L. 1980. The risks of risk analysis. *Acta Psychol.* **45**, 301–21.

Sjöberg, L. 1982a. Beliefs and values as components of attitudes. In *Social psychophysics*, B. Wegner (ed.) pp. 199–218. Hillsdale, N. J.: Erlbaum.

Sjöberg, L. (ed.) 1982b. *Risk och beslut. Individen inför samhällsriskerna.* Stockholm: Liber.

Sjöberg, L. and A. Biel 1983. Mood and belief-value correlation. *Acta Psychol.* **53**, 253–70.

Slovic, P., S. Lichtenstein and B. Fishhoff 1979. Images of disaster: perception and acceptance of risks from nuclear power. In *Energy risk management*, G. Goodman and W. Rowe (eds.), pp. 223–45. London: Academic Press.

Starr, C. 1969. Social benefit versus technological risk. *Science*, **165**, 1232–8.

Svenson, O. 1978. Risks of road transportation in a psychological perspective. *Acc. Anal. Prevent.* **10**, 267–80.

Svenson, O. 1981. Are we all less risky and more skilful than our fellow drivers? *Acta Psychol.* **47**, 143–8.

Vlek, C. and P. J. Stallen 1980. Rational and personal aspects of risk. *Acta Psychol.* **45**, 273–300.

Vlek, C. and P. J. Stallen 1981. Judging risks and benefits in the small and the large. *Org. Behav. Human Perf.* **28**, 235–71.

Zajonc, R. B. 1980. Feeling and thinking. Preferences need no inferences. *Am. Psychol.* **35**, 151–75.

Part I

GENERATION OF RISKS

2 Time and risk in the cognitive space

MATS BJÖRKMAN

Introduction

There are two circumstances connected to the dimension of time, one is psychological and the other epistemological, which seem relevant to decision making and should be mentioned at the outset.[1] In combination, they form a kind of past–future dilemma. First, the past, the present and the future, i.e. "time", are associated with a psychological mechanism of the following kind. The past "lies there", invariably the same, and fragmentarily known. We are facing completed facts and are inclined to believe that history could not have been otherwise (Fischhoff 1975, Fischhoff & Beyth 1975). Moreover, we are fairly unaware of this being wisdom after the event: we have an unconscious tendency to believe that past events have a higher predictability than they in fact had. Our knowledge about the past, which forms the basis for decisions about the future, appears more structured and valid than it is.

Second, our answers to how, when and why concerning past events are guesses and interpretations in hindsight. Historians cannot arrange the conditions and wait and see what will happen. Neither do the conditions repeat themselves, and it is not possible to investigate whether invariant conditions give invariant outcomes. Casual explanations are not as accessible in history and social sciences as they are in experimental research. Such explanations (see e.g. Hempel & Oppenheim 1971) require that conditions C_1, $C_2 \ldots C_n$ in combination with general laws L_1, $L_2 \ldots L_m$ make it possible to infer logically the occurrence of an event E. Furthermore, if one considers that C_1, $C_2 \ldots C_n$ exist at time t_1 and one wants to infer *when* E occurs (t_2), time must enter into the laws. Stringent laws of this kind are extremely rare for political and social courses of events, and absent also from the context of most personal decisions (compare, however, statistical predictability as discussed below). Extrapolations from the present to the future are highly uncertain, simply because we lack the general laws and often the relevant facts needed for such extrapolations. Hitherto, judgment and choice have primarily been investigated in static environments. However, Hogarth (1980) has analyzed judgment heuristics in dynamic environments and shown that judgments which are considered as biased in a static environment may be functional in a dynamic one.

These circumstances bring to the fore a dilemma of the following kind. We have to use our present knowledge for making predictions and taking actions, for example to minimize future risks which might accompany a decision. But we are over-confident in the predictability of the past, that is, in our present knowledge, and this knowledge is unreliable for making inferences about the future. Decision makers are thus faced with a double handicap. Moreover, we do not live in a stationary world. Conditions of life are changing, and to a great extent the changes are due to our desire to make the world better. All this makes it impossible in principle to predict the future from the past and the present: "The past is the determined, the present is the moment of 'becoming' when events become determined, and the future is the as-yet undetermined" (Whitrow 1961, p. 295). It is "time" in all these aspects that decision makers have to handle.

Perhaps the reader is of the opinion that my description is unnecessarily pessimistic. To avoid misunderstanding, it should be said that lack of lawfulness, between the present and the future, does not imply a defeatist unwillingness to act. Thoughts and acts are directed towards the future and are most important: we take measures to get control over the course of events and thus run counter to unpredictability. Quite often we find that things do not turn out as we expected − "the past−future dilemma" is confirmed. However, this does not curb us too much. Thoughts and acts are dominated by the idea of a better future, the content of which is determined by what is done here and now; the alternative would be a stoic fatalism. In other words, we act now as if decisions and measures determine the future course of events. They certainly do to a certain extent, but this decreases the longer the time-perspective is.

Against this background, issues of decision making and time may appear fairly unamenable to closer scrutiny and structuring. Perhaps they are. At least this is the impression one gets from the fact that a comprehensive research on decision making has left the time variable almost untouched. However, instead of putting off the issues of time and decision making as inaccessible and diffuse, I have chosen to continue and will state the following reasons and excuses.

(a) Any decision is time dependent in a simple and obvious way. First, decisions are based on information collected during the past. This information is affected by various psychological factors like personal experiences, memory, selective attention and attitudes. These and other factors may lead to biases, for example the over-confidence mentioned above. Second, decisions result in outcomes in the future. Among other things this raises the question of learning. Can people learn about their decisions from experiences of the outcomes? As will be argued later, this possibility is very limited.

(b) Important psychological phenomena vary with time in characteristic ways. Their most interesting feature is precisely their relation to time. Three processes of this kind will be discussed: (i) involvement in future events, (ii) knowledge about the past and the future and (iii) time discounting, which means that the present value of a commodity decreases as a function of time until consumption.

(c) Although we lack laws connecting present conditions to future events, several areas permit statistical predictability, for example air and road traffic, public health and education. For sufficiently long periods the same holds true for certain natural phenomena (e.g. earthquakes, droughts and avalanches).

(d) The insight that lawfulness is lacking and predictability far from perfect might say something about appropriate strategies in decision making.

The question of strategy becomes especially important in situations involving risk, that is large negative effects with small probabilities of occurrence. Such effects may be small per unit of time and difficult to detect. However, the accumulated effect over a period of time may be considerable, although it does not have the instantaneous character of a catastrophe. Insidious risk effects (e.g. slow cultural deterioration and gradual pollution of the environment) may accompany social, medical and technological reforms. All too often they remain hidden in the pale gleam surrounding "the good purpose".

The aim of this paper is not to examine the conceptions and images people may have about time in general (e.g. its beginning and end and its direction), but to explore how values and involvement in events, and a knowledge of them, are related to the time dimension, and how these psychological factors may affect decisions. Knowledge, value and involvement affect inferences from the past and judgments about the future. Therefore an important question concerns how diagnosis (of the past) is related to prediction (of the future).

Thus, man's ideas and inferences about occurrences in the past, and above all in the future, is of main concern. It is this "world of thoughts", the cognitive space, that determines how a person will decide and act. Explorations of the cognitive space cannot of course be put into "rules of thumb for decision makers". However, some progress can perhaps be made if people increase their awareness of the cognitive limitations in connection with decisions. For example, decisions are dependent on hypotheses about environmental changes over time. Thus, the optimality of decisions is "conditional on certain environmental assumptions and a specified time horizon" (Einhorn & Hogarth 1981, p. 55). Both environmental assumptions and time horizons belong to the cognitive space and as such they are bounded cognitively.

Various aspects of time

PHYSICAL TIME

In current usage we find expressions like "time is short" and "time is up", which indicate that time is represented by spatial relations. In other phrases, time is expressed as motion "time passes", "the course of time" and "time has come". Change and motion have always been natural indicators of time. Cyclical motions, for example the orbits of the moon and the earth, have been the basic ways of measuring time. By its practically uniform motion the rotation of the earth has been a fundamental time meter.

REALISM AND IDEALISM

Among philosophers, a dividing line sometimes appears between those who argue that time is a kind of illusion which lacks reality and exists only in our conciousness, and those who advocate that time is a fundamental property of nature, as real as the dimensions of space. Kant was a true representative of the former opinion, idealism. According to Kant, time and space do not belong to the external world but exist only in consciousness. They function as frameworks (references) for localization of courses and occurrences of events. Kant was influenced by Newton and his idea of absolute time, which has an idealistic touch: "Absolute, true and mathematical time itself, and from its own nature, flows equally without relation to anything external" (Newton's Mathematical Principles).

Representatives of realism argue that time is a fundamental and nonreducible property of nature. Time is a part of nature that cannot be derived from nontemporal phenomena. The decisive aspects are before, concurrently and after, which are relations that can be applied to events in the external world.

A modern advocate of realism is Popper (e.g. Popper 1969, pp. 179–83, Popper 1974, p. 1144). He made the important observation that "A realist theory of time is thus as absolutely essential for ethics as it is (in my view) for physics. Idealism, which once could be disregarded as a harmless fancy of philosophers, has been vaunted as a reason for not taking one's responsibilities seriously" (Popper 1974, p. 1144). This remark is worthy of attention in connection with decisions, in particular those that may lead to long-term risk effects.

As long as experimental psychology has existed, psychologists have investigated the relation between subjective time and physical time, between our experience of time and time on the clock. Subjective time is related to physical time, but it has its own independent status in the same way as experiences of light, color and distance.

For reasons given below, it is important to distinguish between two kinds of subjective time, which will be termed experienced time and cognitive time. It is primarily the latter that comes into focus when judgments and decisions are considered in a time perspective.

EXPERIENCED TIME

It is a common observation that time intervals of equal length can be experienced as long or short depending on the circumstances. Time may pass slowly while waiting for someone, but in pleasant company time passes quickly. Time may appear slow in passing but short in retrospect. The phenomenology of time was aptly described by William James (1890): "In general, a time filled with varied and interesting experiences seems short in passing, but long as we look back. On the other hand, a tract of time empty of experiences seems long in passing, but in retrospect short". The word "empty" should not be taken too literally. At other places in his brilliant chapter on time, James states that "empty time" cannot be experienced at all: experienced time is a function of "the mental content" filling the time interval.

Experienced time, or rather experienced duration, has been studied in psychological laboratories for more than a hundred years. The majority of the studies have investigated short durations, from seconds (or parts of a second) to a few minutes. A common focus has been the relation between experienced duration and physical duration, the psychophysical function. A compilation of psychophysical studies of duration has been published by Eisler (1976).

The psychophysical function can be described as a power function, $T = t^n$, where t is physical time, T is experienced time and n is a constant. From Eisler's review (see also Eisler 1975) it appears that n is usually somewhat less than one. Subjective duration grows more slowly than physical duration.

In psychophysical investigations of subjective time, the subject has an immediate and direct experience of a duration, for example the interval between two flashes of light. He or she estimates this interval on a subjective scale (modern psychophysics has developed several methods for scaling subjective magnitudes). The time intervals that are brought to the fore in connection with decision making do not usually have the character of "experienced time". First, it is "time to come" that matters and by definition this time cannot be experienced. Second, the time intervals are of a quite different magnitude compared to those used in psychophysical studies. We have to exchange seconds and minutes for days, years, decades and even generations. Third, although decisions concern the future they are based on information collected during the past. Decisions are made in "the moment of becoming" but they are founded on the past and have effects in the future. Thus, judgments and the acts contingent on them must be viewed in a bi-directional time perspective (see below on prediction and diagnosis).

COGNITIVE TIME

A notion is needed that separates experienced time from imagined time, or time thought. Let us take this into account by introducing cognitive time. This notion is meant to cover firstly the apprehension of the past, including events beyond our memory experiences, and secondly, the apprehension of the future. The two aspects included in "cognitive time" differ in a decisive and obvious way. The past, in particular recent experiences, appears more or less clear and distinctive, sometimes in a way that reminds one of pictures or photographs. Quite naturally, a feeling of empirical evidence accompanies memories of the past. The future, on the other hand, is void of empirical content. What is to come must be guessed or extrapolated from present information and inferred from previous experiences, plans, ideologies and wishes. This, of course, does not prevent us from thinking of the future in the sense of having considerations for it. The uncertainty is itself an incentive to be worried about the future. Planning, whether individual or collective, is a way to attain control over the future course of events. Such planning activities may, for example, concern family planning, education, work, insurance against unemployment and disease. Hogarth and Makridakis (1980) have reviewed studies of judgment from the view of forecasting and planning. They showed that many biases (e.g. "the illusion of control") can induce errors in forecasting and planning activities.

The fact that people are anxious to plan their future does not contradict what was said earlier about the difficulty to predict events. But often the planning activities can give an exaggerated feeling of control of future events. Several studies (e.g. Cohen 1960, Howell 1971, 1972) have shown that people are over-confident in their own control when they take an active part in the course of events (the illusion of control). The need for control over environmental uncertainty is of very primitive origin. Regular rites have the function of providing man with protection against awkward surprises. In primitive cultures cognitive time and risk were also associated! Rites, worship of gods and saints with one god being responsible for each risk category (e.g. wild animals, fertility, disease, rain, etc.) were the means available to con- ciliate nature. Worships and rites indicate that primitive man conceived nature to be more regular and less random than it in fact is. Modern man also functions in exactly the same way (e.g. Kahneman & Tversky 1972, Tversky & Kahneman 1973, Kates 1962). Shweder (1977) argued that magical thinking is characterized by an inability "of normal adults to draw correlational lessons from their experience, coupled with a universal inclination to seek symbolic and meaningful connections (likeness) among objects and events". Likeness (resemblance) instead of covariation forms the basis for our impressions of what goes with what in our environment. This way of thinking is not limited to primitive cultures (as shown by Shweder's study of personality judgments): "Resemblance, not co-occurrence likelihood, is a fundamental conceptual tool of the everyday ('savage?') mind. Most of us have a 'savage' mentality much of the time" (Shweder 1977, p. 638).

Involvement in future events

In the middle of the 1960s Ekman and Bratfisch (1965) started investigations of involvement in events. As expected, they found that involvement decreased with increasing distance to the place where the event was assumed to occur. For example, if you live in Sweden, a catastrophe in China or Australia is of less concern to you than a catastrophe in Norway. A few years later analogous studies of involvement and time were started (Bratfisch *et al.* 1971) and, during the last decade, researchers at the psychological laboratories in Stockholm and Turku have developed the methods further and broadened the framing of the questions (Ekman & Lundberg 1971; Lundberg, 1972; Lundberg & Ekman 1973; Lundberg *et al.* 1974, 1975a,b; von Wright & Kinnunen 1976a,b; Lundberg & Ellonen 1976).

In these studies, events and the time of their occurrence are described, for example an accident at a nuclear power plant occurring in 2010. For each item the subject's task is (a) to estimate on a subjective scale the length of the time from "now" to the occurrence of the event, and (b) to assess his or her per- sonal involvement in the event. These data can be used to study the relation between cognitive time and physical time, and the relation between involve- ment and either of the time variables (cognitive time and physical time). These relations vary somewhat depending on scaling method, type of events and longest time period occurring in the questionnaire. However, the general pic- ture is fairly clear-cut and can be summarized as in Figure 2.1.

Figure 2.1(a) shows that cognitive time is not perfectly linearly related to physical time. The curve shows a slight negative acceleration and in this respect it agrees with the psychophysical function for duration (see Eisler 1975, 1976). Similar results have been reported by Cohen (1967) and Gorman *et al.* (1973).

More interesting, and more important for our purpose, is the relation be- tween involvement and time (Fig 2.1b). Involvement decreases rapidly to begin with and then more slowly. This decelerated decay of involvement with time

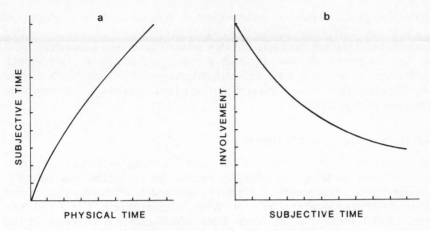

Figure 2.1   The functions relating (a) subjective time to objective time, and (b) involvement to subjective time.

is the common finding. In some studies, however, it has been observed that involvement is quite stable over a couple of decades and then falls rapidly to zero (Lundberg *et al.* 1975a). A study by von Wright and Kinnunen (1976) indicated that this form of the relation, positive instead of negative acceleration, occurs when the events concern personal rather than global matters (e.g. their own health and employment). The realism and importance attached to personal events is greater than for global events, which may appear abstract and diffuse. There is a distinct difference in becoming ill yourself than in imagining a global nuclear war! The latter is probably judged both unlikely and unreal in comparison with illness and unemployment which strikes oneself.

The results of the involvement studies are not surprising. We can all affirm that involvement decreases both with spatial and temporal distality. More interesting is the form of the function, which can be described as an exponential decay function (i.e. a rapid decrease for the intervals close to zero and then slow approach to an asymptote). This is significant in view of the fact that there are several other time-dependent processes that obey the same trend (see below).

There is no reason to believe that the results of these studies should not be valid for decisions and decision makers in general. From this broadened outlook the results are somewhat discouraging. People seem unable to get involved in and evaluate future events other than those that are very close in time and space to themselves. This holds true for catastrophes like a nuclear war as well as for beneficial events like the invention of effective methods to obtain food from the sea. The cognitive limitations demonstrated in studies of involvement might be interpreted as the combined effect of two factors. First, time gradually loses its realism as the time perspective becomes longer. The cognitive time continuum is limited. Second, future events appear unlikely, and increasingly so the farther away from "now" it is assumed that they will occur. This leads to the reflection that risk factors, negative effects with a low probability of occurrence are underestimated. Indirect support for this belief can be found in Bayesian studies of probability revision which have shown that people's conservatism increases for rare events (Slovic & Lichtenstein 1971, pp. 695–6); people do not attribute enough information to rare events. Limitations of cognitive time and underestimation of risk probabilities may have the effect that decision makers overlook long-term risk effects which are small per unit of time.

DISTALITY AND COGNITIVE SPACE

An important aspect of events in the world around us is their cognitive distance from ourselves. Let distality denote the compound psychological variable for the distance of an event in time, space, relationships, political affiliation or emotional involvement. What happens here and now and concerns oneself ("ego") is an origin from which events are located in the cognitive space. The studies of involvement can be viewed as showing that distality, in time and space, is inversely related to involvement in events.

The terms distal and distality have been preferred to distant and distance for the following reasons. First, we have to deal with distances in respects other than time and space. Distality is a function of several "separate distances" for example time, familiarity, and emotional involvement. Second, distality is a general notion that can be applied to events of entirely different content. It becomes possible, for example, to compare personal and global events along the continuum of distality. Third, and most important, distality, in contrast to "distance," always refers to distance from an origin, which can be described by the words here, now and ego. The cognitive space is genuinely egocentric.

The notion of cognitive space can be viewed as a coalescence of Tolman's (1948) "cognitive map" (see also Neisser 1976) and Brunswik's (1939) "regional reference." The cognitive space is like a multidimensional map though with a peculiar property: it can be read off only from the origin (here, now and ego). This, of course, means that the subject's cognizance of the world is highly circumscribed. The proximal origin is surrounded by layers of varying distality, "regional reference." For most purposes we assume that distality, in contrast to distance, is finite. The subject is encapsulated in his own unique cognitive sphere.

Knowledge of the past and the future

Among various psychological processes occurring over time, we are constantly reminded of one in particular: what has been learned has a tendency to disappear. Many elementary textbooks of psychology present a curve, the retention curve, showing how much of what was learned is retained as time passes. The curve drops rapidly immediately after learning and then declines more slowly.

KNOWLEDGE OF THE PAST

Instead of starting from the time when learning occurred and then measure retention after various time intervals, let us turn things over and ask: how much is retained "now" of what was learned yesterday, two days ago or a year ago. This means that the ordinary retention curve is reversed. We start from "now," instead of the learning occasion, and go backwards in time. Obviously this curve should have its highest value at "now" and then decline along the negative time axis. It is advantageous to look upon retention in this way because "now" is the origin of the cognitive space.

The left part of Figure 2.2 illustrates the reverse retention curve. Note that nothing has been added to or subtracted from the ordinary retention curve; it is only looked at from a different position. Knowledge acquired close to "now" is better retained than knowlege acquired far away from "now." Increased distality into the past means decreasing knowledge. It is probably not too imprudent to believe that the function is approximated by an inverse exponential decay function (for experimental support, see e.g. Björkman 1958). Knowledge is located in the center of the cognitive space (at "now"); the cognitive capacity is limited.

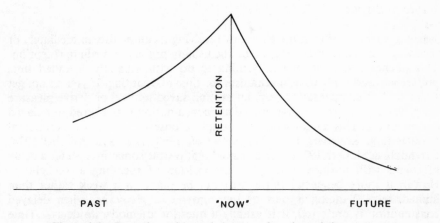

Figure 2.2 Retention of knowledge as a function of time (see text).

KNOWLEDGE OF THE FUTURE

How great is the retention now of the amount of knowledge a person has tomorrow, next week, in a year? The question may appear strange, but it is precisely this aspect of knowledge, extrapolated or "imagined knowledge," that decision makers are facing. They would like to know, for example, the environmental conditions that will prevail in a few years time, and they would like to have this knowledge when the decision is made ("now and here" in the cognitive space). The question is not peculiar at all if it is phrased in economic language. Economists are used to considering the present value of a commodity which is received at some later time. Expressed in economic terms we would say that knowledge is time-discounted. This is the same as saying that the present amount of knowledge is smaller the farther away the point of time it concerns. Knowledge about the future decreases along a retention curve that is turned right-way round (the right-hand curve of Fig. 2.2). A reasonable guess is that knowledge about the future decreases more rapidly than knowledge about the past; yesterday's events are more available cognitively than the events of tomorrow.

Comment. What has been done in Figure 2.2 is simply that the retention curve has been used to illustrate how the amount of knowledge "discounts" in both directions of time. The curves are strikingly similar to those for involvement and time. Perhaps it is somewhat premature to conclude that the degree of involvement is the same as the amount of knowledge. On the other hand, it is difficult to imagine how one can get involved in events without having some knowledge of them. Exceptions may occur, but in general the above examination seems to permit the following conclusion. Involvement is proportional to the amount of knowledge and both decrease according to an exponential decay function.

Value and time

When a person is offered the choice of receiving a commodity immediately or receiving it at some later time, he or she usually prefers immediate reception. This phenomenon, which has nothing to do with inflation, is called time preference, and is the basic mechanism for time discounting. If you do not get some kind of compensation (e.g. interest on saved money) or derive pleasure from waiting, the rule is that immediate consumption is preferred to delayed consumption. This agrees with commonplace observations and experimental findings (e.g. Klineberg 1968, Mischel *et al*. 1969, Lee 1972, Mischel 1974, Örtendahl & Sjöberg 1979). Lee observed that people sometimes prefer a delay of events with positive value. The proposition of spending a weekend in Hawaii is more beneficial if the trip can be made in a week rather than immediately. Planning is part of the enjoyment. However, when delayed consumption is preferred, it is usually a question of moderate delays. Time preference is the general rule.

Studies of time preferences are sometimes afflicted with methodological shortcomings that make them difficult to interpret. For example, children's choices between a small immediate reward and a large delayed reward cannot be interpreted unequivocally as long as the amount of reward and the delay have not been varied in a non-confounded manner. It is also noteworthy that psychologists have done relatively little work on time discounting at the same time as economists have worked on axiomatic formalization of discounting theory (Koopmans *et al*. 1964, Bell 1972).

The studies of Nisan and Minkowich (1973) and Jones and Johnson (1973) are particularly interesting because the tasks contained alternatives with risk and because of their background in psychological theory. In both studies it was found that the tendency to take risks increased if the consequences of the decision were delayed. The theory behind these studies was Miller's (1959) conflict theory, which was developed and tested in a quite different context. Miller's theory concerns behaviour in the presence of a goal that contains both an attractive and a repulsive component. Thus, a conflict arises between the tendency to approach the goal and the tendency to avoid it. Important postulates in Miller's (1959, p. 205) theory are (a) "the tendency to approach a goal is stronger the nearer the subject is to it," (b) "the tendency to avoid a feared stimulus is stronger the nearer the subject is to it," and (c) "the strength of avoidance increases more rapidly with nearness than does that of approach."[2] The "goal" in decision making is the consequences of the decisions, consequences that may be more or less delayed from the time of the decision. Although Miller's theory is developed for spatial relations between subject and goal, here, as in the two studies mentioned above, we apply it to time. According to the third postulate, "the gradient of avoidance" is steeper than that of approach: far from the goal the tendency to approach is strongest, near the goal the tendency to avoid is strongest. Transferred to the risk–time context this means that the tendency to avoid negative consequences is weaker the more distant from the decision the consequences are. A person's willingness to take a risk would be stronger the farther away from the decision the risk effects are assumed to occur. This was the result found in the studies already discussed. If we allow ourselves to "translate" behavior to cognition it could be said that both positive and negative consequences are "more salient" (see the first two posulates) the nearer the subject is to the goal. But the negative consequences are more salient that the positive ones. Thus, people would be more sensitive to risks, with a tendency to avoid them, when the consequences are close in time to the decisions.

Miller's work, anchored as it is in psychological theory (Hull, Lewin) and experimental research, provides a promising approach to further study of risk –time issues. Jones and Johnson (1973, p. 635) remark: "Although the present results tell us not to look for nice linear functions in this area, it seems probable that some form of monotonic function between delay interval and riskiness would obtain in a wide variety of decision situations. We would expect the present hypothesis[3] to be highly general then, as long as linearity is not implied and as long as the hypothesis is not committed to a particular temporal threshold."

RATIONAL MAN

It has been common in decision theory to view decision making as a choice between well-defined alternatives A_1, $A_2...A_n$. To each alternative there belongs a set of outcomes E_j, $j = 1...N$ which occur with probability $p(E_j)$. Each outcome has a consequence X_j the utility of which is $U(X_j)$. The subjective expected utility (Edwards 1954, 1961) of alternative A_i is:

$$SEU_i = \sum_{j=1}^{N} p(E_j) U(X_j) \tag{1}$$

Both positive and negative $U(X_j)$ values may enter into the sum. Risk, as viewed here, refers to those contributions to SEU_i that derive from large, negative $U(X_j)$ values with small $p(E_j)$ values.

According to the classic rule the decision maker should choose the alternative with the largest expected utility (the principle was formulated by Pascal in 1669 and stated more precisely by Bernoulli in 1738). This norm tells how "rational man" should act. However, as will be discussed below, many decision situations are not of the well-defined character that is needed for man to act rationally.

Typically enough, decision theory uses notions like "expected utility" and "expected value." These expressions show that the choice of an alternative and the outcome of it are separated by a time interval. Thus, decision makers naturally have expectations about the consequences of their decisions. It is somewhat paradoxical then that decision research has neglected time both in theory and experiments. In their classic work von Neumann and Morgenstern (1953, p. 19) wrote: "it would be an unnecessary complication as far as our present objectives are concerned, to get entangled with the problems of preference between events in different periods of the future. It seems, however, that such difficulties can be obviated by locating all 'events' in which we are interested in one and the same standardized moment, preferably in the immediate future." Most experimenters have been content with a "standardized moment," . . . "in the immediate future." Exceptions, however, can be found. An example is the study by Örtendahl and Sjöberg (1979). They performed experiments in which the subjects were offered lotteries that varied with respect to (a) the probability of winning ($p(E_j)$ in Eqn. 1), (b) the size of the prize ($U(X_j)$ in Eqn. 1) and (c) the time of the lottery. The shortest time interval was zero (the lottery took place immediately) and the longest was two weeks. Clear time discounting was found in these experiments. If the subject had to choose between lotteries with equal expected value, he or she preferred the one that was nearest in time.

Time discounting is a well-documented phenomenon. The natural next step is to ask: what kind of mathematical function is adequate to describe discounting? Brumet (unpublished paper 1969, quoted by Moskowitz & Hughes 1973) stated the following axioms: (a) time preference – immediate payoffs are preferred to delayed payoffs; (b) scaling – discounting factors are independent of the size of payoff; (c) transitivity – if A is preferred to B and B to C, then A is preferred to C; and (d) stationarity – discounting factors depend on time intervals but are otherwise independent of time. The only function that fulfils these conditions is an exponential decay function (Moskowitz & Hughes 1973, p. 1). Let us therefore introduce exponential discounting in the *SEU* model:

$$SEU_i(t) = \sum_{j=1}^{N} p(E_j) \, U(X_j) \, a^t \tag{2}$$

where a represents rate of discounting ($a < 1$). The product $U(X_j) \, a^t$ express future utility, "subjective expected utility," at the time of the decision. This quantity decreases exponentially along the time continuum of the future. It follows that the variance of the distribution of $SEU_i(t)$, (where i = 1...n) decreases and approaches zero. Note that the distribution of $SEU_i(t)$ contains both positive and negative values. The alternatives $A_1, A_2...A_n$ become less salient and harder to discriminate the farther in the future their consequences are expected to occur. The outcomes of various alternatives become shrouded in mist. Rational man has nothing to be rational about.

Again we find that the cognitive space is bounded. Our decisions are captured in a proximal sphere around the center of the cognitive space ("here," "now," "ego") with slight possibilities to foresee the distal consequences of various alternatives. The cognitive spaces of "ordinary people" are not like those of prophets and seers. This state of affairs can only be accepted and decision strategies developed accordingly (some aspects on decision strategies will be discussed at the end of the paper under "concluding remarks").

Converging results: some generalizations

The three phenomena considered above, involvement, knowledge and value, behave in similar ways when they are related to time. The magnitude of each of them decreases with negative acceleration along the time continuum. It is pertinent then to ask if the three processes may have something in common, if they may be regarded as different expressions of the same underlying process. I will try to approach this question by first assuming, as was indicated above, that involvement in events is proportional to the knowledge about them. If, in the empirical studies of involvement, one had also scaled people's amount of knowledge, the relation between knowledge and involvement would have been linear according to this assumption. Involvement and knowledge would decrease with cognitive time according to the same function; they would differ only with respect to a constant of proportionality.

Second, it can be noticed that knowledge, like value, expresses a subject–object relation which has the quality of belonging and ownership. When subject X has the knowledge Y (i.e. X believes that a certain statement Y is true), then Y belongs to X. Should Y disappear because, for example, it is forgotten, X feels that he or she has lost something that previously belonged to him or her. Notice also that knowledge is "acquired" and "possessed" and that "retention" is a term with economic connotations. From this "economic view" of knowledge it doesn't seem too strange to believe that time discounting also characterizes knowledge. A kind of test of this reasoning is to apply the four axioms of time discounting to knowledge, for example "immediate knowledge is preferred to delayed knowledge," and ask if they appear "natural" when "pay-off" is substituted for knowledge. To the author it seems adequate to regard knowledge as a quantity that obeys the principle of time discounting.

According to the first hypothesis, involvement and knowledge follow the same function. According to the second one, knowledge is time-discounted in the same way as value. Thus, at the origin of the cognitive space, where all decisions are made, involvement, knowledge and value decrease (exponential decay) the farther away the events to which they refer are located. The idea advocated is thus that all three processes are different sides of essentially the same basic phenomenon. Since they are thoughts concerned with the future, the term distal cognition seems adequate.[4] As this term is used here, it has a quantitative connotation; it refers to the amounts of involvement, knowledge and value. Distal cognition exists here and now and decreases with the cognitive future (Fig. 2.3).

Figure 2.3 generalizes results from the three research areas according to the above reasoning; first involvement is proportional to knowledge and second, knowledge discounts. What it says is hardly surprising. Its message is simply

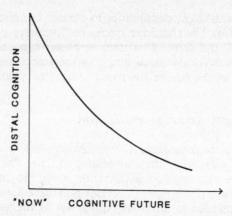

Figure 2.3 A generalization: distal cognition, that is involvement, knowledge and value, decreases (exponential decay) along the cognitive time continuum.

that man's cognitive capacity is limited. Cognitive limitations make man captured in a narrow sphere around the cognitive origin (here, now and ego)[5]. Cognitive limitations may too easily be interpreted as severe mental handicaps. Therefore it must be strongly emphasized that time discounting is a biological principle so fundamental that it is hard to imagine how organisms would have survived at all if the values of consumption were independent of time. Imagine for a moment a line parallel to the x-axis in Fig. 2.3 instead of the decay function. At every moment of life, man would be totally indifferent to whether events with some personal value, positive or negative, ocurred now, in a week, or in a few years. He or she would be as much, or as little, concerned with events that are expected to occur in the future, as with events here and now. It is easily seen that saving, planning, reproduction and finally evolution and life itself would collapse if the principle of time discounting was brought out of play.[6]

Cognitive limitations *vis-à-vis* time are biologically indispensible and no more remarkable than perceptual limitations, for example limited visual accuity, limitations as regards lights and sounds of extreme wave lengths and limited attention and memory. This fact, the biological significance of cognitive limitations, does of course not imply that they should be only noticed and left without consideration in the context of decision making. Cognitive limitations must certainly be accepted, but the awareness of them may give hints about appropriate strategies and heuristics.

A second generalization concerns the relation between willingness to take risks and distal cognition. It was established above that "risk willingness" increases the more delayed the risky consequences are. Or, in Miller's terminology, and in the reverse direction: "the tendency to avoid a feared stimulus is stronger the nearer the subject is to it." This means that risk willingness – the tendency here and now to make decisions with future risks – increases along the cognitive time continuum. The inevitable, and perhaps regrettable, consequence is the following: The less we are involved in, know of and value the consequences of our decisions the greater is our willingness to make decisions with future risks. This generalization is based on the relation between distal cognition and time (Fig. 2.3), and the relationship between risk willingness and delay. It shows in a sharp light both how time may facilitate decisions that otherwise would have been postponed or not made at all (e.g. the decision to pay a visit to the dentist), and how time may seduce us to make decisions, the disastrous consequences of which are so far away that they are entirely neglected.

Diagnosis and prognosis: learning from experience?

The world is seldom like a menu with a specified set of ready decision alternatives to choose among. Very often, both in personal business and in societal affairs people simply experience that the situation (e.g. the job, the family situation, the unemployment in a country) is unsatisfactory and that "something needs to be done." However, the situation is unstructured and it is not immediately clear what precisely are the reasons for the disequilibrium between what is aspired to and the actual state of affairs. Before decisions can be made and actions taken, the factors responsible for the disequilibrium must be diagnosed, much in the same way as a physician establishes a diagnosis before deciding about a treatment. Diagnosis may be viewed as the initial stage of what Kahneman and Tversky (1979, p. 274) called the editing phase in their prospect theory: "The function of the editing phase is to organize and reformulate the options so as to simplify subsequent evaluation and choice."

The need of diagnosis prior to decisions about appropriate measures is self-evident. This fact needs to be emphasized, however, because the success or failure of decisions and their outcome in the future, is highly dependent on the accuracy of the diagnosis. Acts are directed towards the future, they are *prognostic* and the outcome aimed at can only be as good as the accuracy of the diagnosis (Björkman 1981). Sometimes, the decision maker can observe the outcome of an action taken at some earlier time. This fact immediately raises the question of learning from experience: can people learn about their diagnostic and prognostic judgments by observing the outcome of their actions? Is there reason to believe that intended goals have a greater chance of being achieved by learning through outcome feedback? The question of learning about one's judgments from the outcome of actions was addressed in a recent paper by Einhorn and Hogarth (1978). Specifically, they focused on the question why people persist in having high confidence in their judgments in spite of the fact that the judgments are fallible ("persistence of the illusion of validity"). The significance of their paper, the results of which are worth much consideration, derives from the fact that the authors developed a formal model in which judgment, action and outcome feedback were considered simultaneously: actions are contingent on judgments and actions lead to outcomes.

Among various factors, all due to the structure of the task and its environment, that make learning difficult, the following one will be mentioned as an illustration. Consider a judge who has to decide which job applicants to reject or accept. He or she uses a cut-off point on the judgment continuum and only those who are above the cut-off limit are accepted. At some later time those who were accepted can be observed with respect to success or failure in the job (outcome feedback). This implies that disconfirming information, "by which is meant the information that can be gained by the nonoccurrence of an action or prediction" (Einhorn & Hogarth 1978) cannot be used. Criterion information for those who were rejected is not available. The observer thus notices that "accept" and "success" go together (confirming information). Because people have a tendency to attend to confirming information and to neglect disconfirming information, the confidence in one's judgment will persist. Furthermore, if the cut-off is such that only a few applicants are selected, the judge's prognostic ability can be fairly low and still a high percentage of those accepted will be categorized as successful. Lack of disconfirming information, in combination with a low selection ratio, will strongly support the judge's confidence in his or her fallible judgments.

Besides difficulties in using disconfirming information, Einhorn and Hogarth pointed out that people are usually not sufficiently aware of environmental factors (e.g. base rates) that affect the contingency of action on judgment. Moreover, people have to code and store outcome information without memory aids. Altogether, the consequences of these environmental and task factors result in a fairly pessimistic view concerning the possibilities of learning about judgments from the outcome of actions, and revising one's confidence to be in better agreement with one's ability to make diagnoses and prognoses. This pessimistic view is reinforced by other writers (e.g. Brehmer 1980). If we exclude laboratory studies and school teaching, the environments are such that we do not know what there is to learn and how it should be learnt. The natural environment does not present itself in company with an experimenter, or teacher, who first "knows the truth" and second informs one that this or that should be practised and learnt. Brehmer also emphasized that we even have difficulties in knowing that we have learnt and, if we have, what in fact was learnt.

Another reason why it may be difficult to learn about one's judgments is directly related to the length of the time interval between the decision and the outcome. Two points of time have to be considered: first, the occasion when the decision is made (t_1) and, second, some later occasion when the consequences of the outcome are observed and evaluated (t_2). According to the general principle of distal cognition and time (Fig. 2.3), the consequences occurring at t_2 cannot be fully assessed at the time of the decision, t_1, and this is more true the longer the interval between t_1 and t_2. The situation is no better at t_2 because now the expected consequences exist only in memory, and should be compared to the actual consequences as they are assessed by direct observation. Thus distal cognition (t_1), in combination with imperfect memory (t_2), makes it difficult to draw the correct conclusions from observations of the outcome and its consequences. Besides, emotional and motivational factors may make the judge reluctant to go back and examine the initial judgment and perhaps find that it was in error.

Concluding remarks

THE IRRATIONALITY OF BEING RATIONAL

In general, decision makers do not face well-defined problems. They have to deal with unstructured environments with ill-defined problems. The conjunction of ill-defined problems and cognitive limitations makes it difficult to act according to the principles of rationality, for example the maximizing of expected utility.

Besides limited distal cognition, people have biased conceptions of probability, randomness, regression, causality and correlation (Kahneman & Tversky 1973, Slovic et al. 1974, Slovic et al.1976, 1977, Tversky & Kahneman 1977, Einhorn & Hogarth 1981). In this connection, however, it is important to note that the notion of "error" or "bias" presupposes that we know what is normatively correct. And this is perhaps more complicated than one might believe (see Einhorn & Hogarth 1981, for a discussion of optimality). For example, Lopes (1980) showed in a stimulating paper that randomness cannot be unambiguously defined. Precise logical criteria of randomness do not exist, and it is quite impossible to tell what is erroneous and what is correct in people's conceptions of randomness. Thus, the very basis for rationality is in doubt.

In the SEU model, and all its relatives based on probability and expected utility, probabilities and utilities refer to distinct and well-defined outcomes. As mentioned earlier, the consequences of concern to decision makers do not always have this distinct and well-defined character. Examples are air and water pollution, side effects of drugs and insidious negative consequences of societal reforms. The limitations of distal cognition prevent people from being fully aware of such nondistinct effects which are delayed and accumulate slowly. This circumstance is particularly serious when there are decision alternatives, the positive utilities of which are large, distinct and immediate, whereas the negative utilities (the risks) are small, nondistinct and delayed. Owing to the way distal cognition functions (Fig. 2.3), such alternatives will appear unduly attractive; the long-term effects cannot be fully assessed. For the same reason, alternatives with the inverse structure, immediate negative consequences and delayed positive ones, will appear unattractive and will seldom be chosen. We can conclude that man's limited cognition, i.e. poor distal cognition, may sometimes lead to decisions with disastrous consequences in the future.

Ill-defined problems, cognitive limitations and nondistinct outcomes make the SEU model and its relatives fairly useless as a norm for practical decisions. A somewhat more realistic alternative, which is closer to how people think and act, is the recent prospect theory developed by Kahneman and Tversky (1979). This theory, however, preserves some of the basic tenets of expected utility theory, for example that man faces an environment with well-defined decision alternatives and is able to choose the prospect with the greatest value. Some fundamental issues of expected utilities theory, for example the multiplicative combination of utility and probability, were critically examined in a recent paper by Lopes (1980). Lopes concluded (Lopes 1980, p. 385), and the present author agrees: "I have no doubt that a revision of the conception of rationality along the lines I have described will be displeasing to some because of its inelegance, its vagueness, and its essentially inductive character. But this is the price that will have to be paid if we are to have the kind of useful decision technology that *captures and clarifies the concerns of real people in real environments*. I do not believe that the decision sciences can afford the luxury of clinging to any theory of rational choice that is simply not sensible" [italics mine].

Simon (1955, 1956, 1957) has criticized the notion of maximizing (value, utility, profit) or minimizing (time, error) and suggested an alternative decision criterion called *satisficing*. This strategy, bounded rationality, means that individuals and organizations "live on" by keeping to acceptable goals instead of maximizing (or minimizing) some criterion value. Instead of conforming to a statistical norm, decisions may aim at outcomes that exceed a certain level of aspiration. "Satisficing" is a way of adapting to the uncertainties and complexities of the environment which can be regarded as functional and rational, although in a different way from that prescribed by expected utility theory. March (1978) argued that behaviour may be intelligent though it violates statistical (analytical) norms ("calculated rationality") and he continued: "If behavior that apparently deviates from standard procedures of calculated rationality can be shown to be intelligent, then it can plausibly be argued that models of calculated rationality are deficient not only as descriptors of human behavior but also as guides to intelligent choice."

Closely related to Simon's "bounded rationality" is the notion of *quasirationality* (Hammond 1980, 1981), which refers to the fact that cognition contains both analytical (rational) and intuitive components. Cognition varies along a continuum where the one end is represented by "intuitive thought" and the other by "analytical thought". The latter is very similar to March's "calculated rationality". Our thinking is usually not perfectly analytical and logical, nor is it perfectly intuitive. It is characterized by compromise between analysis and intuition and varies along the cognitive continuum depending on characteristics of the task we deal with. A chess game or an algebraic problem may induce more analytical than intuitive thinking, whereas, say, prediction of the future trend of the stock market may induce more intuitive than analytical thinking.

In conclusion, the notion of rational man is of little use, or rather it is mistaken, both as a norm for acting and as a description of human behavior. It is deficient as a norm because, as March emphasized, behavior can be intelligent ("functional") without following "the standard procedures of calculated rationality." It is deficient as a description because, as Hammond has shown, cognition is both analytical and intuitive.

QUASI-RATIONALITY AND DISTAL COGNITION

A perfectly analytical way of solving a problem or making a decision presupposes the following requirements as a minimum. (a) The facts, the premises, must be known, (b) the decision maker must know the analytical rule which should be applied to the facts, and (c) he or she must be able to execute the rule. The limitation of distal cognition has the consequence that the decision maker, or judge, is not very familiar with the facts and that he or she has no analytical rule readily available. These circumstances will induce a quasirational mode of thought with more intuition, and less analysis, the more distal cognition is. But, and this is important, the covariation between distality and intuition gradually disintegrates. The facts lose their character of genuine facts and quasi-rational thought has no material to operate on.

For example, political decision making illustrates both how politicians usually get around the consequences of limited cognition (quite surely without any conscious consideration) and how they sometimes seem to be entirely unaware of their cognitive limits. In his studies of political behavior, Lindblom (1959, 1968) has found that politicians try to find their way by slowly and cautiously settling problems. Their activity is characterized by "muddling through." The decisions taken are typically short-term and do not have outcomes that deviate too much from the *status quo*. The decisions do not have thorough consequences and can often be modified by later decisions. Successive small changes with flexibility preserved is characteristic of political decisions. In this way, politicians avoid the most disastrous consequences of limited cognition. On the other hand, "successive small changes" may lead to uncontrolled negative effects in the long run. The sneaking growth of an inefficient bureaucracy accompanying societal reforms is an example.

A characteristic and well-known expression of the politicians' attitudes toward the future − their "muddling through" attitude − is their consistent refusal to discuss any issues that may arise in the future as a consequence of decisions taken "now". The typical reaction is "this is a hypothetical question", which means that the issue at hand should not be discussed. The day-to-day activity among politicians is a perfect example of enclosure in the center of the cognitive space. Political activity is proximal-oriented rather than directed towards distal goals. However, there are exceptions to this rule. In sharp contrast to their usual "muddling through", politicians are also involved in problems the solution of which have far-reaching consequences in the future. And in these situations they seem to be totally ignorant of their cognitive limitations.

Nowadays it has become popular among politicians to talk about their responsibility to coming generations. This kind of alleged concern was, for example, quite common in the public debate that preceded the 1980 referendum concerning the extension of nuclear power in Sweden. It is also quite common in the present (1981) discussion of the economic situation; the next generation should not be forced to "inherit" large debts to foreign countries. Of course nobody, not even the most clairvoyant politician, can know about, value, not to say get involved in, problems that the next generation, say 20 years from now, will encounter. It is thus sheer nonsense when politicians speak about their concern for future generations. Such concern is beyond the limits of man's cognitive capacity.

It is something of a paradox how politicians who cannot get into the nearest hypothetical future ("hypothetical questions") can participate in risky decisions the consequences of which are wrapped in obscurity. It should be recalled, however, that people have a preference for decision alternatives with immediate positive effects and delayed negative ones.

In conclusion, the limitations of distal cognition induce quasi-rational thought. However, "facts of the future" rapidly dissolves and neither rational nor quasi-rational decisions can be made in a cognitive space that is empty, or at best filled with speculations and fantasies.

ARE THERE STRATEGIES THAT CAN COMPENSATE FOR LIMITED COGNITION?

The most significant consequence of the limitations of distal cognition is that *people are ignorant of the future effects of their decisions*. They are aware of the effects in the immediate future but unaware of more distal consequences. During the last few decades we have witnessed a variety of measures, mostly infringements in ecological systems, which have resulted in serious unexpected side effects. Are there any possibilities to guard oneself against undesirable outcomes? Goldberg (1975) approached this question by means of system theory. He showed by examples, from the use of insecticides against malaria to modern road traffic, how a *narrow focus* (in the first case to get rid of malaria, in the second one to increase the transportation capacity) may lead to unexpected and undesirable side effects. After an analysis of the stability of socioecological systems, their resistance to external disturbances, Goldberg laid down the following guiding principles for decisions. They ought to:

(a) be small in scale and implemented slowly;
(b) acknowledge ignorance and uncertainty explicitly;
(c) be wary of success and the arrogance it can breed;
(d) be more concerned with avoiding disaster than with achieving success;
(e) maintain decision options for the future, maintain and encourage diversity and complexity, and avoid simplification of the system or its subsystems;
(f) be implemented with a hierarchy of responses, each appropriat· o the hierarchy of perturbations posed by the system's environments.

Goldberg, who criticized the narrow focus of "maximizing" on the grounds that it presupposes a constant environment, was of the opinion that these points should serve as general norms for decision making. Goldberg's criteria can be viewed as rules of conduct intended to compensate both for the instability of socioecological systems and the cognitive limitations of the decision makers.

The theme of this chapter is "Time and risk in the cognitive space." From various points of departure it has been demonstrated that evidence converges toward the fact that distal cognition is limited. It is limited to the "surroundings" close to "now." Beyond this narrow sphere, ignorance dominates. There is thus every reason to be aware of the risk of living beyond one's cognitive means.

Explanatory notes

1   This paper concentrates on risky decisions in a context of time. For a recent, more general, review on risk see Vlek and Stallen (1980).
2   Note the parallel between approach–avoidance gradients and the value function in prospect theory (Kahneman & Tversky 1979). The pain associated with losing a sum of money is greater than the pleasure associated with gaining the same amount. Thus, the value function for losses, corresponding to avoidance, is steeper than for gains, corresponding to approach.
3   In this quotation "present hypothesis" refers to the approach–avoidance theory.
4   The term "distal cognition" has been chosen instead of the more common "distal knowing." This is because, in addition to knowledge, value and involvement are included.
5   Compare Plato's story about the prisoners in the cave and Popper's (1969) critique of the thesis that the truth is manifest.
6   Man as a "biological being" is discussed by Goude (1977).

References

Bell, D. 1972. *A utility theory approach to preferences for money over time.* Technical Report No. 72. Cambridge, Mass.: Massachusetts Institute of Technology.

Björkman, M. 1958. *Measurement of learning.* Stockholm: Almqvist & Wiksell.

Björkman, M. 1981. *Predictive and diagnostic inference: cues, causes and cognitive strategies.* (Unpublished manuscript.)

Bratfisch, O., G. Ekman, U. Lundberg and K. Krüger 1971. Subjective temporal distance and emotional involvement. *Scan. J. Psychol.* **12**, 147–60.

Brehmer, B. 1980. In one word: not from experience. *Acta Psychol.* **45**, 223–41.

Brunswik, E. 1939. The conceptual focus of systems. *J. Unified Sci.* **8**, 36–49.

Cohen, J. 1960. *Chance, skill and luck*, pp. 178–88. Harmondsworth, Middlesex: Penguin.

Cohen, J. 1967. *Psychological time in health and disease.* Springfield, Ill.: Thomas.

Edwards, W. 1954. The theory of decision making. *Psychol. Bulletin* **41**, 380–418.

Edwards, W. 1961. Behavioral decision theory. *An. Rev. Psychol.* **12**, 473–98.

Einhorn, H. J. and R. M. Hogarth 1978. Confidence in judgment: persistence of the illusion of validity. *Psychol. Rev.* **85**, 395–416.

Einhorn, H. J. and R. M. Hogarth 1981. Behavioral decision theory: processes of judgment and choice. *An. Rev. Psychol.* **32**, 53–88.

Eisler, H. 1975. Subjective duration and psychophysics. *Psychol. Rev.* **82**, 429–50.

Eisler, H. 1976. Experiments on subjective duration 1868–1975: a collection of power function exponents. *Psychol. Bull.* **83**, 1154–71.

Ekman, G. and O. Bratfisch 1965. Subjective distance and emotional involvement: a psychological mechanism. *Acta Psychol.* **24**, 446–53.

Ekman, G. and U. Lundberg 1971. Emotional reaction to past and future events as a function of temporal distance. *Acta Psychol.* **35**, 430–41.

Fischhoff, B. 1975. Hindsight and foresight: the effect of outcome knowledge on judgment under uncertainty. *J. Exp. Psychol. Human Perception and Performance* **1**, 288–99.

Fischhoff, B. and R. Beyth 1975. "I knew it would happen". Remembered probabilities of once-future things. *Organ. Behav. Human Perf.* **13**, 1–16.

Goldberg, M. A. 1975. On the inefficiency of being efficient. *Env. Plan. A* **7**, 921–39.

Gorman, B. S., A. E. Wessman, G. R. Schmeidler, S. Thayer and E. G. Manucci 1973. Linear representation of temporal location and Steven's law. *Mem. Cogn.* **1**, 169–71.

Goude, G. 1977. *Man – a biological being or a technological mistake?* (unpublished manuscript.)

Hammond, K. R. 1980. *The integration of research in judgment and decision theory.* Center for Research on Judgment and Policy, Working Paper, No. 226, University of Colorado.

Hammond, K. R. 1981. *Principles of organization in intuitive and analytical cognition.* Center for Research on Judgment and Policy, Working Paper, No. 231, University of Colorado.

Hempel, C. G. and P. Oppenheim 1971. The logic of explanation. In *Readings in analytical philosophy*, H. Regnell (ed.) pp. 100–38. Stockholm: Läromedelsförlagen.

Hogarth, R. M. 1981. Beyond discrete biases: functional and dysfunctional aspects of judgmental heuristics. *Psychol. Bull.* **90**, 197–217.

Hogarth, R. M. and S. Makridakis 1981. Forecasting and planning: an evaluation. *Man. Sci.* **27**(2), 115–38.

Howell, W. C. 1971. Uncertainty from internal and external sources: a clear case of overconfidence. *J. Exp. Psychol.* **89**, 240–3.

Howell, W. C. 1972. Compounding uncertainty from internal sources. *J. Exp. Psychol.* **95**, 6–13.

James, W. 1980. *Principles of psychology*. New York: Holt, 1980 (originally published in 1890).

Jones, E. E. and C. A. Johnson 1973. Delay of consequences and the riskiness of decisions. *J. Person.* **41**, 613–37.

Kahneman, D. and A. Tversky 1972. Subjective probability: a judgment of representativeness. *Cognitive Psychol.* **3**, 430–54.

Kahneman, O. and A. Tversky 1973. On the psychology of prediction. *Psychol. Rev.* **80**, 237–51.

Kahneman, O. and A. Tversky 1979. Prospect theory: an analysis of decision under risk. *Econometrica* **47**, 263–91.

Kates, R. W. 1962. *Hazard and choice perception in flood plain management*. Chicago: University of Chicago, Department of Geography, Research Paper, No. 78.

Klineberg, S. L. 1968. Future time perspective and the preference for delayed reward. *J. Person. Social Psychol.* **8**, 253–7.

Koopmans, T. C., P. A. Diamond and R. E. Williamson 1964. Stationary utility and time perspective. *Econometrica* **32**, 82–100.

Lee, W. 1972. Temporal and contextual effects on utility (manuscript).

Lindblom, C. E. 1959. The science of muddling through. *Public Admin. Rev.* **19**, 79–88. [Also in W. J. Gore and J. W. Dyson (eds) 1964. *The making of decisions*, New York: Free Press.]

Lindblom, C. E. 1968. *The policy-making process*. Englewood Cliffs, N.J.: Prentice-Hall.

Lopes, L. 1980. *Doing the impossible: a note on induction and the experience of randomness*. (Unpublished manuscript.) Department of Psychology, University of Wisconsin, Madison.

Lopes, L. 1981. Decision making in the short run. *J. Exp. Psychol. Human Learn. Memory* **7**, 377–85.

Lundberg, U. 1972. *Psychological distance and emotional involvement*. Reports from the Psychological Laboratories, The University of Stockholm, Supplement 11.

Lundberg, U. and G. Ekman 1973. Individual functions of subjective time distance and emotional reaction. *Scand. J. Psychol.* **14**, 29–33.

Lundberg, U., J. M. von Wright, M. Frankenhaeuser and U. J. Olsson 1974. Note on involvement in future events as a function of temporal distance. *Percep. Motor Skills* **39**, 841–2.

Lundberg, U., J. M. von Wright, M. Frankenhaeuser and U. J. Olsson 1975a. Involvement in four future events as a function of temporal distance. *Scand. J. Psychol.* **16**, 2–6.

Lundberg, U., J. M. von Wright and U. J. Olsson 1975b. *Scaling of involvement in desirable and undesirable future events*. Reports from the Department of Psychology, No. 449. The University of Stockholm.

Lundberg, U. and E. Ellonen 1976. *Involvement in potential future events estimated by males and females*. Reports from the Department of Psychology, No. 469. The University of Stockholm.

March, J. 1978. Bounded rationality, ambiguity and the engineering of choice. *Bell J. Econ.* **9**, 578–608.

Miller, N. 1959. Liberalization of basic S-R concepts: extensions to conflict behavior, motivation and social learning. In *Psychology: a study of science*. S. Koch (ed.) pp. 196–292. New York: McGraw-Hill.

Mischel, W. 1974. Processes in delay of gratification. In *Advances in experimental social psychology*, L. Berkowitz (ed.), Vol. 7. New York: Academic Press.

Mischel, W., J. Grusec and J. C. Masters 1969. Effects of expected delay time on the subjective value of rewards and punishments. *J. Person. Social Psychol.* 11, 363–73.

Moskowitz, H. and J. Hughes 1973. *The descriptive validity of the stationarity assumption in time discounting: an exploratory study*. No. 417. West Lafayette: Krannert Graduate School of Industrial Administration.

Neisser, U. 1976. *Cognition and reality. Principles and implications of cognitive psychology*. San Francisco: W. H. Freeman.

Nisan, M. and A. Minkowich 1973. The effect of expected temporal distance on risk taking. *J. Person. Social Psychol.* 25, 375–80.

Örtendahl, M. and L. Sjöberg 1979. Delay of outcome and preference for different courses of action. *Percep. Motor Skills* 48, 3–57.

Popper, K. R. 1969. *Conjectures and refutations*. London: Routledge and Kegan Paul.

Popper, K. R. 1974. Replies to my critics. In *The Philosophy of Karl Popper*, P. A. Schilpp (ed.) LaSalle, Ill.: Open Court Publishing Co.

Shweder, R. A. 1977. Likeness and likelihood in everyday thought: magical thinking in judgments about personality. *Curr. Anthropol.* 18, 637–48.

Simon, H. A. 1955. A behavioural model of rational choice. *Q. J. Econ.* 69, 99–118.

Simon, H. A. 1956. Rational choice and the structure of the environment. *Psychol. Rev.* 63, 129–38.

Simon, H. A. 1957. *Models of man*. New York: Wiley.

Slovic, P. and S. Lichtenstein 1971. Comparison of Bayesian and regression approaches to the study of information processing in judgment. *Org. Behav. Human Perform.* 6, 649–744.

Slovic, P., H. Kunreuther and G. F. White 1974. Decision processes, rationality, and adjustment to natural hazards. In *Natural Hazards. Local National, Global*, G. F. White (ed.), pp. 187–205. New York: Oxford University Press.

Slovic, P., B. Fischhoff and S. Lichtenstein 1976. Cognitive processes and societal risk taking. In *Cognition and social behavior*, J. S. Carroll and J. W. Payne (eds), pp. 165–84. Potomac, Md.: Lawrence Erlbaum.

Slovic, P., B. Fischhoff and S. Lichtenstein 1977. Behavioral decision theory. *Ann. Rev. Psychol.* 28, 1–39.

Tolman, E. C. 1948. Cognitive maps in rats and men. *Psychol. Rev.* 55, 189–208.

Tversky, A. and D. Kahnemann 1973. Availability: a heuristic for judging frequency and probability. *Cognitive Psychol.* 5, 207–32.

Tversky, A. and D. Kahnemann 1980. Causal schemata in judgments under uncertainty. In *Progress in social psychology*, M. Fishbein (ed.), pp. 49–72. Hillsdale: Lawrence Erlbaum Associates.

von Neumann, J. and O. Morgenstern 1953. *Theory of games and economic behavior*, 3rd edn. Princeton, N. J.: Princeton University Press.

Vlek, C. and P. Stallen, 1980. Rational and personal aspects of risk. *Acta Psychol.* 45, 273–300.

von Wright, J. M. and R. Kinnunen 1976a. *Scaling of involvement in personal and global future events*. University of Turku: Psychological Reports, No. 22.

von Wright, J. M. and R. Kinnunen 1976b. On scaling of future time. *Percep. Motor Skills* 43, 1235–41.

Whitrow, C. J. 1961. *The natural philosophy of time*. London: Thomas Nelson.

3 Business decisions and consumer risks

SÖREN BERGSTRÖM

Introduction

Products are not self-evidently evil, of course not. But they might threaten life and health; they might constitute a risk to the consumers. That is my point of departure.

I take for granted that no business firm by pure "ill will" will spread dangerous products over the market. If that should be the case it is outside my discussion here. The basic issue in this chapter is to discuss possibilities to explain consumer risks by analyzing conditions for and within business firms.

It should also be said in the beginning of this chapter that my theoretical claims here are quite modest. The kind of connections between different factors might be described as "tendencies" or "possibilities." There is no room for law-like propositions. The kind of relations observed, depends on the observer's perspective and theoretical way of reasoning. I use a consumer perspective and mainly an organizational theory-like language. This kind of discussion does not aim to solve any very specific problems. On the other hand, I do hope that I can contribute to some understanding of the dynamics in a mixed economy. That understanding ought to be valuable to academic colleagues, politicians and actors in the market.

The concept of consumer risk

I talk about consumer risks when there is some threat to the life and health of consumers. "Life and health" is a medical question on the one hand and a very subjective question on the other. Here I prefer to denote the concept by a list of examples. I think the following list is an illustration of the fact that some products may be injurious:

- dangerous microbes or poisonous substances in groceries
- tobacco, alcohol and narcotics
- bad construction in cars, sailing boats, safety equipment and other things you as a consumer usually rely upon
- products that can cause accidents when they are used without appropriate knowledge and training (e.g. tools for do-it-yourself work)
- bicycles for children
- shoes for children so constructed that they cause life-long damage to their feet

38   BUSINESS DECISIONS, CONSUMER RISKS

- radioactive materials in houses
- drugs with damaging side effects

Forces behind business behavior

Most people working with product development and marketing want to do a good job. That is a reasonable point of departure for analysis of what is going on within firms. With that view, the focal point will be the conditions for "doing a good job." What you are allowed to do, what you must do, what is a normal way of thinking and acting and what kind of "self-evidences" you work within. That is how my argument will proceed here. But it might be clearer if I turn it upside down.

My analysis is quite cynical. We cannot trust the "good will" of people forming business behavior to be sufficient to prevent consumer risks. I think we will get a more comprehensive picture if we look at these people's working conditions, i.e. what they are allowed to, can, know and must do. I want to point out some such conditions because they can be seen as forces that, to some extent, make it intelligible that injurious products are on the market and are bought. I will concentrate especially on the following three forces:

(a) What you are allowed to do. For almost every behavior there is a morality that justifies that behavior. Here I want to emphasize the morality that justifies commercial behavior. I will call that "commercial morality."
(b) What you can do. Here I will concentrate on the circumstances that delimit the firms' possibilities to adapt to known information (i.e. about consumer risks).
(c) What you know. I think that consciousness and the opposite – unconsciousness – in many situations can explain the discrepancies between market supply and consumer needs.

WHAT YOU ARE ALLOWED TO DO: COMMERCIAL MORALITY

The concept of the consumer, and his or her relations to business firms that I am investigating here, belong to a commercial set of concepts. The basic concepts are buying and selling. A commercial morality indicates what you might and must do just because you work commercially (or competitively). When I talk about a commercial morality, it is a purification. In most practical situations there are other ethic codes working too. The commercial morality does not say anything about social decency, for example. If you look at the competitive system with a pure consumer perspective, and that is rather rare, the picture might be a little ugly. The commercial morality is tolerant towards many honorable acts but also towards acts of gangsters. (Maybe that is a good definition of a "gangster": a person following no other morality than the commercial one.) It is hard to understand the workings of a commercial system without having insight into its ethical underpinnings. Without that insight we might attack details and symptoms in vain.

If you simplify the theory and practice of the commercial system to its ethical foundations, you might find the following four commandments:

- that which is demanded may be sold
- demand may be influenced
- competitors may be restrained
- you are responsible only for your own profitability

That which is demanded may be sold   Basically the consumer has himself or herself to blame. That is the fact in practice. Neoclassical economic theory and the marketing literature work as a legitimizing body. Marketing textbooks seldom make any judgment according to the product quality from a consumer's point of view. As long as the products are sold, they are good. Even injurious products need good marketing, they say. Kelley (1965, p. 96) related the classic case of how firms found extended markets: it was when "the cigarette manufacturers who in the 1930s persuaded women that smoking was socially acceptable. With this accomplished the market potential for cigarettes doubled." It is possible that the cigarette producers in the 1930s did not know anything about smoking and cancer. Anyway, when the book was written, that relation was very well known.

Demand may be influenced   This is a commercial variation of a very general moral code: you may influence others. That is an ethical cornerstone for teachers, educators and preachers. By changing words the rule becomes: you may seduce. In the commercial setting, several circumstances, such as advertising, salesmanship, supermarket layout, product exposition, packaging, unfair product information, fashion and fads fit into this framework.

Once again we can recognize reality in the advice given in marketing literature. Kotler (1972, pp. 164–665) claims that advertising is most important in marketing processes where the buyer's knowledge is small and when the products have qualities that are difficult to observe. In a critical discussion Galbraith (1967, p. 228) concluded: "It is possible that people need to believe that they are unmanaged if they are to be managed effectively."

I do not need to argue this point here. You know the situation from the supermarkets: you find milk at the back and candy, toys and comics at the front. That is the rule. What people need they look for themselves, what they do not need, or in some way are hurt by, must be accompanied by acts of seduction. Of course, seduction can help consumers to overcome thresholds, for example attaining knowledge about new products, but in the commercial setting it might be a way of manipulation that shows no respect at all towards the integrity of the consumer as a person.

The competitors may be restrained   In the marketplace you have a general right to restrain others. Some people say it is a duty to try to demolish one's competitors. In most societies, there are restrictions on this third commercial commandment spelled out in criminal law. What business firms do to restrict each other may not have primary consequences for consumer risks. But an obvious consequence, at the consumer level, is ways and means to make you unaware of alternative products. Brand merchandising is aimed at instigating your buying without reflection, and that is a consumer risk, since your deliberations may be very valuable to you.

You are responsible only for your own profitability   This ethical standpoint is the very fundament in many an economist's picture of society: egoism as the elementary drive. In the border zone between a moral commandment that legitimates how business firms in practice behave and psychological theory about human beings many economists get lost. Joan Robinson is one who did not get lost. She claims that the offspring of neoclassic economic theory was to raise profits to the level of moral dignity that was already attributed to wages (Robinson 1964, p. 57). Still, it is the standard opinion among neoclassical economists that almost nothing could do more harm to a free society than if employees in business firms elected to take any other social responsibility than earning as much money as possible for their shareholders.

Richard Titmuss (1970) once undertook an investigation of altruism. He compared the "markets" for human blood in the UK and the USA. In the USA there is a commercial market for blood which does not exist in the UK. In the UK, it is a question of "pure giving." Titmuss' conclusion is, first, that altruism is possible. Second, he claims that the UK system is working better than the American one.

You could say that this fourth commandment is a mirror of the first: both say that the consumer has himself to blame and that business firms just have to solve their own problems. This reasoning has been used as an active argument for continuing to produce and sell products that are obviously dangerous to those who buy them. Generally, you could say that in cases of products where consumers can not judge qualities and risks for life and health this attitude is one of the forces behind consumer risks.

A preliminary conclusion   It is a popular standpoint to see competition among firms as the best thing for the consumer. My discussion points to the other side of the coin: the fact that firms work on commercial conditions is by no means a guarantee against consumer risks. The commercial morality accepts injurious as well as good products. As long as the consumers are the weakest part on the market, and in Sweden they are, they need protection in one way or another.

THE COMPETENCE OF LARGE ORGANIZATIONS

Many observations indicate that there is a law of sluggishness for organizations that encourage business firms to continue their operations as before, even after a point when they should know how to do better. To go on as usual is the easiest way to do business. I will not delve very deeply into this issue, since it is generally well known. Some points, though, might be worth noting. First, it is typical in big organizations that decisions that lead to practical action are built upon a vast array of compromises throughout that organization. These compromises are valuable assets, and the management is seldom motivated to destroy them. Second, as a means to raise productivity, routines of several kinds are built up. A routine makes surprising information nonexistence. That is the core of it. You could also remark that an effective control of operations prevents learning.

I could go on for a long time, noting these kinds of special qualities in large organizations. The general conclusion is, as many authors have said before, that bureaucratic organizations are very dependent on a stable environment. Since the environment is not that stable just by itself, it has to be made so. In practice that is why, amongst other things, we get heavy and aggressive marketing efforts.

A change of policies is very dependent on people with courage. It is easy for people working within these large bureaucratic firms to imagine − and I have had the opportunity to observe it several times − how much purposeful and tactical knowledge is also needed. Since all these are scarce resources, there is an obvious risk that nobody really acts on "weak information" about consumer problems before the problems increase and the information becomes dramatic. Within big firms one often needs a "crisis" to change route. If that is the case, it is quite probable that the commercial morality in practice is the dominating concern.

WHAT IS KNOWN

Some injurious products do exist on the market, to some extent because nobody knew anything about the consumer risks in question when the products were first marketed. The risks were never actualized in the development and marketing process. It is easy for such a process to work within blinkers. Sometimes that is the result of very specialized education of young people who later get jobs within an even more specialized organization unit. You could talk about "clean" unconsciousness in cases where nobody anywhere has raised the question about risks. Maybe, some of the developments within the auto business "before Nader" could be described as "clean" in that way. The unconsciousness was a little less clean when questions were raised, but these, for some reason, did not affect the development process. Conceptually, we are now in a discussion that has some kinship with what has been said before about commercial morality and other social ethics. Figure 3.1 might make the distinctions clearer.

I have treated "know nothing" and "cynicism" as ends on a continuous scale. Cases close to the right end, classified as cynicism, could best be analyzed within the commercial morality framework. Cases at the other end are what I called here "clean" ones. Cases around the middle of the scale represent different types of organizational and administrative inadequacies, partly of the general character that I have mentioned before and partly of a gate-keeper character, which I will discuss later on in this chapter.

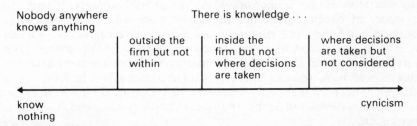

Figure 3.1 Conceptually, and in practice, unconsciousness and cynicism are intermingled in a fuzzy way.

Consumer defense systems

In simple and uncomplicated societies, people live and cooperate mostly under unwritten rules. But when society grows and becomes complicated, the unwritten rules represent too much ambiguity. That is one way to explain why the mixed economies of the Western world use so many stabilizing systems. Laws, rules, norms and several forms of public and private controls "make" the society. With the Swedish experience as an example, I will demonstrate "the defence systems" for consumers within this framework.

I distinguish four such systems, which more or less directly operate within firms. They are:

- laws and public bodies
- private industry organizations
- mass media
- a minority of critical consumers

It is beyond the scope of this chapter to discuss in detail the laws and governmental organizations in the consumer policy field. I will delimit the discussion by pointing out some central targets for consumer policy. These targets have developed over several decades, and have materialized as different public bodies. As a consequence, they are not automatically consistent. The main targets are as follows.

Target 1: The consumers should have access to useful information about products.
Target 2: Products should keep up with certain quality standards.
Target 3: Firms should not be able to misuse their power against each other.

These are preconditions for the sound working of an economic system. In the 1950s, it was generally believed that competition among firms was always to the consumers' advantage.

Target 4: Firms should not be able to misuse their power against the consumers.
Target 5: Consumers should learn to look after themselves.

If you compare these targets with the commandments in the commercial morality, you will find a total conflict. Still the public defence system is working strictly *within* the framework of the commercial morality. It seems to be a matter of circumstances how the conflicts are solved. In times of good business conditions, the authorities are a little more aggressive, whereas in times of business depression, the elementary functions of the economic system receive priority over claims from the consumers. There are many examples of this in Sweden and you can find them in other countries too. In 1981, President Reagan announced that, since times were bad, Detroit did not have to follow legislation in the interest of the consumer's (driver's) safety and environmental protection.

Private industrial organizations often take action in the interest of a "decent majority" of firms within the industry against some ruthless few. In Sweden, we have good examples within the auto-dealer industry. A problem within that industry, as well as in others, is that business conditions for big firms and small firms are so different. If the industrial organization establishes norms that contribute to "good" routines within already bureaucratic organizations, that might be good for their customers. However, the same norms can build up a heavy burden in small firms. This means that the consumer will have to pay higher prices. In fact, it has been observed that the big firms, through their influence in industrial organizations and lobbyists groups, use new "consumerist" norms as a means in their competition with the small firms. In such cases there really is no guarantee that the norms in effect eliminate any consumer risks.

The mass media has power because most firms are frightened of bad publicity and ill will. Scandalous writing in the papers is sometimes the kind of "crisis" that makes sluggish organizations quicken their reactions.

Critical consumers play a rôle too. Tibor Scitovsky (1976) says that Americans are easy-going and unsuspicious as long as they act as consumers in the market. He says: "We find it embarrassing to bargain or even to engage openly in comparison shopping; we are ready to trust the sellers' expert advice and to forget the natural conflict between his interest and our own."

In Europe, on the other hand, and especially in France, there is a deep critical tradition in the market place. For many Europeans it is almost a sport and a way of life to bargain and to try and gain an advantage and to complain when products do not come up to expectations. Scitovsky (1976) argues that a small élite of critical consumers gives the rest of us some basic security. The critical consumers see to it that lower quality also means lower prices. Then the rest of us, the unsuspicious people, can use prices as the main information. According to Scitovsky, Americans stand a greater risk than the French of buying bad and injurious products at a high price because they do not have as many critical consumers.

FEEDBACK

The safety systems so far discussed work in several different ways. Some are like absolute restrictions on the behaviour of business firms. That is the case of consumer protection laws with specific clauses and technical restrictions of several kinds. Much less definite and harder to grasp are various forms of feedback mechanisms that might work as ways of learning and correcting actions within firms. These mechanisms form the theme for the next few pages.

Here I discuss feedback as the general concept covering various information about consumer problems eventually caused by the products of a specific firm. The central questions are then:

• how soon does the feedback information arrive?
• how distinct and obvious is that feedback information?

These questions are decisive if the firm is to make full use of feedback information for action and learning. There is usually no problem with the learning process if the feedback is immediate, for example when accidents with products occur. The situation is then dramatic and might even be covered by the media. The products involved cannot be hidden. You can often get examples in the papers of this kind: e.g. poison in food, bad construction of cars, insufficient safety devices and such things. When the injurious effects appear for the first time after a long time of use, they seldom cause so much alarm. The possibilities and propensities to learn within firms are then smaller.

When talking about the second question, the distinctiveness of the feedback information, we move between different opinions about how obvious it is that the specific product is the cause behind injuries. It is not easy to find many examples where you can claim a general and unconditional connection between a product and eventual injuries. Ordinary scientific discretion prevents that. Those examples that can be used might be trivial. One is the connection between tobacco smoking and bad health. Another is the long-term health effect of poor nutrition. More often the connections between a specific product and injuries are ambiguous. The bad effects are in some ways specific and conditioned by several causes. The specific product might be one such cause. The other causes can be of different kinds, for example the involvement of other products, like special tyres on a car or certain chemicals acting together with other chemicals, or a special situation, such as extremely bad weather causing malfunctions on sailing boats. It could also be that the risks are real only for certain people who are lacking in the capacities that are needed to use the product. This is especially true when the use of the product presupposes an exact understanding of written instructions. The discussion so far can be summarized in Table 3.1.

In Table 3.1 you can see that feedback concerning risks can be described as anything from obvious and quick to ambiguous and late. The two of the four types are the least interesting; in the first case there is no problem and in the second case there is, in practice, no feedback. The other two types are more dependent on internal conditions in the firms when you want to evaluate the workings of the feedback mechanism. I think this is a good argument for a closer examination of the way such feedback is revealed in the product development and marketing processes in big firms.

I have studied several such processes, and they make me a little pessimistic concerning the effectiveness of feedback. There are so many blocks in the work of a marketing manager that prevents the reality of consumer risks from going through. There are three main blocks:

- Block 1: "Everything we do is good."
- Block 2: "We have already thought of everything."
- Block 3: "I have no time to discuss that just now."

A description of these blocks might give some insight into the dynamics of the marketing process.

Block 1: "Everything we do is good" One fundamental function that marketing people have in big firms is that of optimists. They are the people who bring information about the future to management. That information should always have the quality of showing how the future will be successful. No marketing manager gets his salary for saying: "there is no purpose in doing anything." There should always be a profitable option.

Table 3.1 Different conditions for practical use of feedback information.

	Immediate effects	Slow or late effects
injuries are quite common	quick and obvious feedback	late and obvious feedback
if there are injuries, they are conditioned and specific	quick but ambiguous feedback	no feedback

In practice, you can indicate that optimism in several ways. I am not quite sure which indicators, that I know of, are specifically Swedish and which are of a more general phenomena. Anyway, I have seen very few objections to the rule that reality never catches up with the prognoses and that marketing managers discuss their competitors as if they were not as smart as they themselves.

This professional optimism could be viewed both psychologically and as a phenomenon in a social psychological sphere; psychologically it is a basic requisite for creative work that people really believe in the goals and possibilities of the task. Socially the optimism is actively backed up by the risk to hurt the good mood within the group ("but we have all from the beginning said..."). There is a definite risk for what Irving Janis has called "group think" (see Janis 1972). Together these circumstances build up a myth of excellence within marketing groups, which might be almost impossible to overcome.

Block 2: "We have already thought of everything" In the big companies, the marketing plan is the central document controlling most marketing activities. I have seen many such plans and they have one property in common. That property is the description of the firm's situation entirely without conflicts. Marketing is a matter of technique where questions about problems and goals are solved at a general level at the beginning of the development processes. It is not hard to understand that people, working with such rational processes, do not have any special propensities to actualize new problems or new goals that might appear through the feedback channels. The thinking is done. For most of the time it is a matter of doing.

Block 3: "I have no time to discuss that just now" The extent to which work in product development and marketing is carried out under heavy stress from time schedules is astonishing. The stress arises from two main sources. First there is a general tendency in firms producing consumer goods to regularly plan for "news" in the assortment. The amount of news contributes both to the image of the firm and to its management. It is the picture of how "dynamic" they are, and often it is profitable to be seen as "dynamic".

The other source is the marketing people themselves. Earlier I mentioned the regularly too optimistic prognoses. It is not possible to present such optimistic prognoses after several earlier failures. The only way to keep the optimistic mood and still sound reasonable is to change the circumstances. In practice, that is to work with "news." Of course, there are other reasons for being in a hurry. Anyway, there is little time to discuss unexpected (feedback) information "just now."

A comment on small firms

What is said in this chapter mostly refers to large firms marketing consumer goods. In order to denote some limitations in that analysis, I will make some comments on differences when discussing small firms. Here I mean really small firms with, say, at the most 50 employees.

COMMERCIAL MORALITY

The commercial rules of the game are in many ways harder and more definite for the small firms than for the big ones. That is because the small firms are clearly dependent on their success in sales with a comparatively small assortment. They cannot spread the risks involved as well as the big firms.

CAPACITIES

I said that the big firms are typically quite sluggish, which means that, in many situations, they continue to do what they have done even after receiving information about bad aspects of their actions. In this respect the small firm is radically different; it is not sluggish at all, but the result might still be the same: continuing as before. The total resources in small firms are often severely restricted. The end effect is an absolute inability to change routines.

CONSCIOUSNESS

Among small firms we would probably find the extreme cases. On one hand there are the "idealists," people who find a quality of life by making good products and honest business and, on the other hand, we would find the cynics who do not reject the possibility of making money in ways that bigger firms, which are not anonymous and unknown, could not use. In both cases there are people knowing very well what they are doing. There are, however, cases of almost "clean" unconsciousness here. There could be small firms using a straight imitation strategy; they are making almost the same products as a dominant firm on the market. They do not care if the products are injurious in some way, their excuse being "I thought the big ones had thought about that...."

CONSUMER DEFENSE SYSTEMS

When a national policy is designed, the large companies are usually the leading model, this is also the case where the policy is to be implemented on small firms. Because of this, small firms tend to be sceptical and suspicious about central authorities. Authorities usually like firms with strict bureaucratic' systems and small firms are in business just because they manage without such systems. That is their way of keeping prices low.

People in the mass media are often objects for hatred as I have observed. Small firms are very careful to be anonymous. They are much too aware of their small chances of success if journalists become curious.

Some conclusions

This chapter is a critical evaluation of a mixed economy from a consumer point of view. It is more of an essay than a formal analysis. It is based upon my own empirical research in Swedish firms producing consumer goods. My basic way of arguing is that when firms work under stress, that is with a low profitability, they are doing what they *must* do and (hopefully) what they are *allowed* to do. That means that in hard competition and during bad times the commercial morality has some capacity to explain the occurrence of consumer risks.

It may also be worth noting that the dynamics in a mixed economy, like the Swedish one, depend heavily upon the commercial morality, and that no part of the consumer protection system that exists challenges that commercial morality.

References

Galbraith, J. K. 1967. *The new industrial state*. Boston: Signet Books.

Janis, I. L. 1972. *Victims of groupthink*. Boston: Houghton Mifflin.

Kelly, E. J. 1965. *Marketing: strategy and functions*. Englewood Cliffs, N.J.: Prentice-Hall.

Kotler, P. 1972. *Marketing management*, 2nd edn. Englewood Cliffs, N.J.: Prentice-Hall.

Robinson, J. 1964. *Economic philosophy*. Harmondsworth: Penguin.

Scitovsky, T. 1976. *The joyless economy*. Oxford: Oxford University Press.

Titmuss, R. M. 1970. *The gift relationship: from human blood to social policy*. Harmondsworth: Penguin.

4 *A theory of science view of risks in scientific research and technological development*

MICHAEL MARK MUSSACHIA

Introduction

A theory of research analysis of risk generation and assessment is the modeling of the scientific and technological systems that generate and assess risks. These systems involve various sorts of risks from research situations, from those that are physically risky for the researchers themselves to adverse environmental or social effects of the widespread application of a new technology. The risk-generating systems may be modeled as three basic types: (1) basic research, (2) applied research and (3) practical application programs. In real life, such systems often overlap in complex ways, and they are embedded within various social contexts. Our goal in this chapter, however, is to present only a "first approximation" model, one that portrays distinct and idealized systems (basic research, applied research, and practical application programs), their most general characteristics and interrelations, and the ways in which they typically generate and deal with risks. Given the complexity of the subject, we hope here to merely model its most essential structure.

Our basic perspective in this endeavor is that of "theory of science and research," in which the organizational and processal (knowledge and technique producing) characteristics of research programs are viewed in terms of the various factors influencing, or "steering," their development. Here we separate internal from external steering factors. Examples of the former are the influence of theory on experiment and vice versa and paradigmatic ideals of science. Examples of external steering factors are ideological influences, economic interests and political interests. Of central concern to theory of science and research are the ways in which the various steering factors influence the interaction of the system with its territory (i.e. some part of the physical or social world), both in epistemological and technological ways. In the past, theory of science and research has concentrated on the analysis of basic research. In this paper, the model used therein will be adapted to applied research and practical application programs.

The industrialization of "R and D"

Although scientific and technological developments have always been directly or indirectly tied to economic life, pre-World War I science was largely a craft industry. Research was carried on in small home or shop laboratories and at universities and hospitals. Staffs were small, the division of labor minimal and the research motives were not so generally directly economical as today. (For references on the industrialization of R & D see Kaplan 1965, Rose & Rose 1969, 1976, Greenberg 1969, Ravetz 1971, Mendelsohn *et al.* 1977, Krohn *et al.* 1978).

The artisan scientists of yesterday shared an ideal of science, a self-conception as scientists, and informal standards of scientific quality. Central to this ideal of science was the ethics of the search for truth, of knowledge and know-how for itself and for the general good of mankind. Knowledge was to be shared while its originator was to be acknowledged. Scientific honesty was of the utmost value, and the main form of reward for good work was a sense of accomplishment and the esteem of colleagues rather than material benefit. To the degree that scientists adhered to this ideal, it helped maintain the morals of the scientific community and the quality of scientific work. To the degree that it was not adhered to, the morale of the scientific community suffered, the quality of scientific work dropped, and opportunism became the name of the game.

In this century, scientific research has become industrialized, capital intensive "Big Science." Since World War II, science has penetrated deeply into industry as an organized "force of production" geared via "R and D" to technical developments for both productivity and product innovation. At the same time, industrial organization has penetrated into science with the establishment of large laboratories with capital-intensive research, a strict hierarchical division of labor, a proletarization of scientific workers, central planning and administration of research, and extensive interlocking relations with industry, the military and the state. The advantages of the industrialization of science are essentially those obtained in big industry *per se*, namely the economics of scale: concentration of scientific manpower and talent, rapid communication of information and more intensive utilization of resources (e.g. multiple-group use of large-scale experimental equipment, computers, etc.). Modern administrative organization and management techniques are geared toward the maximization of the productivity of research for a given investment of human and material resources.

The industrial production of knowledge and technique has been necessitated by the scale of the projects and funding required for much modern science. Modern management, administration and control are necessary for the allocation of large sums of money among competing demands and for the evaluation of research results. On the other hand, the development of "Big Science" has brought about some undesirable shifts in the attitudes of its scientific work force.

(a)   The hierarchical division of labor of big science, a business type of administration and the lack of contact with, and control over, the final products of research has resulted in a fragmented, repetitious alienated work for at least the lower, "proletarian" levels of the scientific workforces.

(b)   The socioeconomic context of at least big science in the West has resulted in the planning and designing of technologies as single-purpose instruments, and the production of knowledge as a commodity serving commodity innovation, productivity increases, industrial organization and management, marketing, military power and social control at all levels (from IQ tests and the commercial media to the data processors of the state police).

(c)   The factors mentioned in (a) and (b) have resulted in a shift in the ideal of science and the self-conception of scientists towards cynicism, careerism and monetary motivations, though the older ideals of science and self-conception persist to some degree (the less industrialized the science presumably the greater the degree).

(d)   There has been a shift from informal, consensual, qualitative criteria of scientific value to formal, administrative, quantitative criteria (e.g. number of publications and citations).

Needless to say, all of these factors and tendencies strongly influence the probability of risk generation via sloppy work, compartmentalist attitudes and materialistic values usually at variance with the "search for truth" and "the common good." If ignorance and inexperience were more a cause of risk generation within early scientific and technological developments, it is not the main problem today. With this historical perspective and these conjectures in mind, let us now turn to the organization and functioning of R and D and its applications.

The systems of scientific and technological developments

We can divide the world of scientific research and technological developments into three interdependent systems: basic research, applied research and practical application programs (Fig. 4.1; see Ravetz 1971, Krohn *et al.* 1978).

Basic research is concerned with obtaining knowledge, both empirical data and theory construction, of certain aspects of the world. Generally speaking,

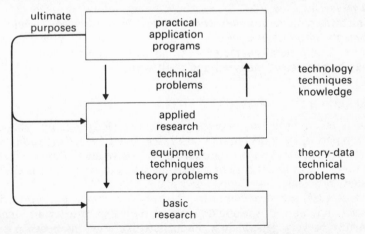

Figure 4.1 The basic interrelations of basic research, applied research and practical application programs.

basic research is directed at the more fundamental (or essential) aspect of its subject matter. Although technology is involved at all levels of basic research (laboratory equipment, computers, etc.), the ultimate goal is not a new technique (technical "know-how") or piece of machinery (technology) but rather the growth of knowledge. Basic research provides theoretical knowledge for, and receives techniques and technologies from, applied research.

Applied research is, as its name implies, the application of theoretical knowledge to practical problems. It is the endeavor to use knowledge of the general laws of the subject matter to develop means of controlling and changing certain aspects of it. The goal of applied research is a new technique, usually embodied in new technology, with prespecified functional parameters, i.e. the technical goal, a specific function, is set beforehand. (This stands in marked contrast to basic research, where the content of the desired knowledge cannot be specified beforehand except as a theoretical prediction.) In practice, some basic research may occur during the course of applied research, and applied research is usually involved at the experimental level of basic research.

The products of applied research are the central input to practical application programs in which new techniques, technology and knowledge are used on the market, in social services, in the factory, etc. Such practical applications may constitute the long-run motive or ultimate purpose for basic and applied research, as in industrial R and D, or they may be *post hoc* utilizations of available knowledge and technique. In both cases, the ultimate goal is not knowledge or technique, but rather their application to some social function (e.g. profit, education and welfare) with different degrees of predetermined specificity (e.g. profit, military advantage and a man on the moon within 10 years). On the other hand, practical application programs require their own information processing and technique development prior to and during their execution. The nature of the territory, the ways in which the technology may interact with the territory, and the techniques required for the application (and control) of the technology must all be studied in order to link the technology with the ultimate goal. In other words, technical problems arise and necessitate applied research.

Having broken up the complex world of scientific research and technological developments into these three simplified stages, we will now proceed to schematize their general characteristics and to indicate the points at which risks may be generated, analyzed and dealt with.

BASIC RESEARCH

A basic research program involves people, knowledge, equipment and a territory, a part of the world to be studied (see Bunge 1967, Törnebohn 1973). The goal of the researchers is to produce a "cognitive map" (knowledge) over the territory. The essential core of a research program involves four elements: hypotheses, problems, instruments and plans.

Hypotheses (H) are ideas about the territory, i.e. about its characteristics. Hypotheses may be very specific (e.g. about the value of a certain quantity) or they may be very general (e.g. about law-like relations between certain variables). Hypotheses may be produced in an *ad hoc* manner or they may be predictions derived from a theory about the territory. When a hypothesis is confirmed or supported by evidence and accepted as such by the community of scientists, scientific journals, or the research project's ruling committee, it becomes "public" knowledge.

Problems (P) are the research tasks at hand in relation to hypotheses, for example should a hypothesis that has been experimentally refuted or poorly supported be "junked" or modified? Problems may also pertain to instruments or to the need for a new experimental technique.

Instruments (I) are the tools used by scientists to obtain and process information. Instruments may be hardware, as with machines and objects used in experiments and data processing, or they may be software, as with statistical techniques of handling data. During the course of research, new instruments may be developed and may replace old ones.

Plans (Pl) are the formulations of how to deal with the research problems at hand, for example which hypotheses to test, what to do with a poorly supported hypothesis, and so forth. Plans in this sense constitute the short-term tactics of current research, and they are revised as the research proceeds through its various steps.

The core state of a research program consists of a set of hypotheses, problems, instruments and plans:

$$<H, P, I, Pl>$$

A current or "running" research program consists of an evolving sequence of such sets:

$$<H, P, I, Pl> \mapsto <H', P', I', Pl> \mapsto <H'', P'', I'', Pl''> \mapsto \dots$$

The development of a research program is "steered" directly and indirectly by many factors. Internal steering factors are those operating within the research program itself, whereas the external steering factors originate within the social context of the research. The most common external steering factors are: (a) general plans, interests, programs and policies held by scientific associations, industry and government, (b) external sources of funds for scientific research, (c) the interests and evaluations of various groups outside the research program (e.g. other groups of scientists), (d) secondary information and instruments available from outside sources, and (e) the dominant ideology of the social environment (e.g. social values and ideals, view of man and social relations).

Typical internal steering factors are: (a) strategic research aims (e.g. the nature of nuclear forces), (b) available knowledge and techniques within the field, (c) criteria used in internal planning, processing, evaluation and criticism of research, and (d) the "paradigm" of the researchers (i.e. their ideal of research, self-conception and preconceptions about the territory etc.). We will amplify on this.

The paradigm of the researcher consists of several components:

(i)   An ideal of research. Scientists have a view of what their field of research is and of what goals they should have (e.g. the pursuit of truth, the quantification of the data and theories of their field). There are informal or formal standards of research procedures and results (i.e. internal criteria are a part of the paradigm). Scientists typically acquire their conceptions about their field of research through their formal education and training and research experience within the field. Certain highly respected scientists and their work may constitute ideal examples for other people in their field (or in related fields).

(ii) Self-conception as scientists. Closely related to an ideal of research is the conception researchers have of themselves, of their rôle and status within science and within the society at large. The self-conceptions of scientists are at least in part ideological (e.g. scientists as a rational élite).

(iii) Ethics of research. Here one typically finds the ideals of objectivity, honesty and conscientiousness. The actual practice of researchers may, of course, be quite at variance with such ideals, especially within the world of "big science" and industrial R and D.

(iv) Preconceptions of the territory. When investigators start out on a research project they begin with a general idea about the territory based on presumed analogies with other territories, secondary information, the general world view of their scientific tradition (e.g. concepts of space, time, matter, life, society, etc.), and the ideology of their social environment. The social sciences are especially subject to the influence of ideological conceptions of man, society, social goals, etc.

The paradigm of researchers strongly influences the initial formulation and the overall development of the research program. The paradigm suggests what secondary resources and instruments might be relevant, what questions are important and where and how to begin investigating the territory. The preconceptions of the territory are adjoined with secondary information and additional hypotheses to provide an initial tentative model of the territory. These paradigmatic influences and the other internal steering factors (operating within the constraints of the external steering factors) combine to produce an initial research program state $<H_0, P_0, I_0, Pl_0>$ (Fig 4.2).

Risks in basic research   Risk assessment may occur at two points in basic research. First, the risks involved in any possible future applications of basic research may be assessed by those agencies responsible for the general planning, policy formulation and administration of scientific research. Both government scientific research planning and advisory committees and industrial concerns are involved here. National science organizations may also carry out such analyses. A case in point is that of research in genetic engineering, which has tremendous potential for misuse in military applications.

Secondly, certain risks may be involved in the basic research activities themselves. Experiments and the use of certain instruments may entail risks to the researchers themselves in the form of explosions, poisoning, electrocution, etc. The local environment may also share these risks, as in the case of the accidental release of toxic agents. The assessment of these risks and the implementation of appropriate safety measures is undertaken by the researchers and research program administrators.

It should be noted that basic research personnel rarely concern themselves with the possible long-term consequences of their research. This insensitivity is usually expressed in paradigmatic self-conception terms (e.g. "We are seekers of knowledge and we are not responsible for how knowledge is ultimately used by others in the society").

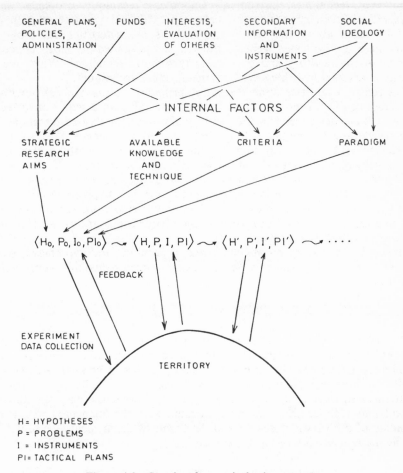

EXTERNAL FACTORS

Figure 4.2 Steering factors in basic research.

APPLIED RESEARCH

An applied research program involves people, knowledge, equipment and a
territory to be studied (see Ravetz 1971, Krohn *et al.* 1978). In this case,
however, the goal is to produce a knowledge of how to effect a certain
manipulation of the territory (i.e. technical knowledge) in order to produce a
prespecified state of the territory (i.e. a new technology, machinery). Here we
take as the territory that part of the world to be studied, manipulated and
transformed into certain objects with a specific function (e.g. the physical
world of electrical phenomena and electrical equipment, including the desired
new electrical technology). At the same time, it should be kept in mind that
technology is the physical embodiment of technical knowledge and production
technique.

The essential core of an applied research program involves six elements: hypotheses, techniques, instruments embodying technique, problems, supplementary instruments and research plans. As with basic research, hypotheses (H) are ideas about the territory, about its characteristics and how to manipulate it. Typically, general theories are adjoined to more concrete models of the territory and a concrete theory of techniques. What one is mainly concerned with here are hypotheses about techniques.

The central goal of an applied research program is a prespecified function, or technique (T). In moving towards this technical goal, a sequence of techniques (T) are developed that successively approach the desired technique T. The developing techniques will be embodied in a sequence of developing instruments (I). The end-product of this sequence is a working prototype instrument, or technology (I) embodying the desired technique T.

Problems (P) are the research tasks at hand in relation to hypotheses H, developing techniques T, and developing instruments I. Supplementary instruments (Is) are the tools used by researchers to obtain and process information and to effect techniques. Plans (Pl) are the formulations of how to deal with the research problems at hand.

During the course of an applied research program, the hypotheses, techniques, instruments, problems, supplementary instruments and plans evolve over time:

$$\langle H-T, I, P, Is, Pl \rangle \rightarrow \langle H'-T', I', P', Is', Pl \rangle \rightarrow \ldots$$

As with basic research, the steering of applied research may be divided into external and internal compartments (e.g. a corporation and its research and development division). The types of steering factors in applied research are similar to those in basic research, but with one significant difference: there is a specific technical goal. In practice, this means that the external steering factors play a closer rôle in applied research, as in the financing and general planning of a business' research and development department.

The main external steering factors are:

(a) The specific technical goal of the organization initiating and funding the research program. The technical goal in turn becomes internalized in the research program and functions as an explicit research goal.
(b) The funding of the program.
(c) The ultimate purpose of the technical goal.
(d) The general plans, interests, policies and administration of the organization controlling the research program and of any organizations influencing such programs (e.g. government regulations).
(e) Secondary information and instruments available from outside the research project, some of which come from basic research.
(f) Social ideology and world view. These factors interrelate with those in points (c) and (d). For instance, business profit lies behind an ultimate purpose of marketability, a view of man as an insatiable materialistic consumer may influence the technical goal and its ultimate purpose, and a view of humans as autonomous individuals with different birth-given abilities may influence the organisation of research.

The internal steering factors of an applied research program are:

(a) A specific technical goal.

(b) Available knowledge and techniques within the field.

(c) Criteria used in internal planning, processing, evaluation and criticism of research.

(d) The paradigm of the researchers.

The paradigm of personnel in applied research is very similar to that of basic research personnel. The paradigm consists of an ideal of research, a self-conception, the ethics of research and preconceptions of the territory. In the ideal of applied research the attainment of a technical goal replaces that of the search for truth; and, in those stages of the research program involving the development of knowledge, the truthfulness of the knowledge serves the

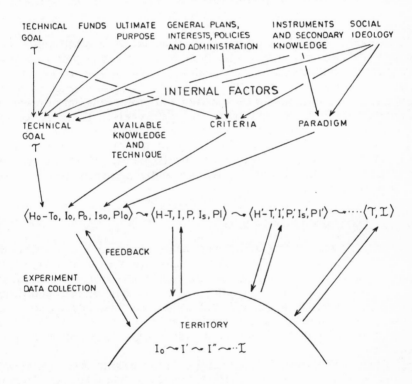

Figure 4.3 Steering factors in applied (technical) research.

technical goal. This makes it possible for low-quality knowledge to serve technical goals and their ultimate purposes, as in the development of a marketable drug whose characteristics are not fully understood.

The paradigm of the researchers combines with the other internal steering factors to produce (within the constraints of the external steering factors) an initial research program state $\langle H_0-T_0, I_0, P_0, Is_0, Pl_0 \rangle$ (Fig. 4.3).

Risks in applied research The situation here is similar to that in basic research. If the funders–controllers of the applied research have an ultimate purpose for the desired technique already in mind, they may carry out a preliminary risk analysis of the possible side effects of the intended application. Risks to the researchers and the local environment arising out of the research activity itself may be assessed by either the external interested agencies or the internal research administrators and personnel. The assessment of both types of risks and appropriate safety measures may be expedited by government regulations and public pressure. (Again witness the case of genetic engineering.)

Most applied research today is industrial R and D; in other words, it is industrialized research. As was pointed out earlier in this chapter, industrialized science is characterized by materialistic motives (profit, wages) and an alienating organization. Qualitative criteria tend to be superseded by quantitative criteria, and a narrow sectionalism and professionalism displace the traditional scientific paradigm of nonmaterialistic motives. To the degree that this is the case, scientific workers fail to concern themselves with the broader questions of real social utility and the long-run quality of the environment. This is bound to have the effect of increasing risk potentials and of decreasing the amount and the quality of risk assessment and of the appropriate responses to potential risks.

PRACTICAL APPLICATION PROGRAMS

A practical application program involves people, knowledge, equipment and technique, and a territory to be studied and modified (see Ravetz 1971, Krohn *et al.* 1978). A practical application program differs from an applied, or technical, research program in that its goal is not the application of knowledge to produce a specific technology, but rather the "ultimate purpose" of knowledge and technology in the transformation of some part of the world, be it the influx of a new product on the market or a restructuring of production.

Since the essential core of a practical application program is concerned with the application of knowledge and technique rather than with their development, our scheme of it will involve a praxiological sequence instead of an $\langle H, P, I, Pl \rangle$ sequence. On the other hand, our scheme of practical application programs will have much in common with those given for basic and applied research. The essential core of a practical application program involves a five-stage sequence: definition, information processing, decision planning, execution and control.

Definition of the program is a policy statement outlining the practical goal of the program. This may or may not include reference to the technology involved. A program for the development of nuclear power stations involves a certain type of technology from its inception, whereas a program for the reduction of alcoholism does not imply any particular technique.

The concrete problem of how to attain the goal is dealt with in the stage of "information processing." The goal and the knowledge and technology needed to attain it must be defined in greater detail. Information on the territory involved must be collected, especially the territory's susceptibility to various techniques and technologies. In many instances, the techniques and technologies required must be produced in applied technical-research programs. Studies of possible side effects may, and certainly should, occur at this stage of the program.

Information processing is followed by decisions as to the particularities of the goal to be effected and the mode of implementation (e.g. techniques to be used). The execution stage involves the actual application of technique and/or technology and the administration of the program "in the field." Execution, then, includes the putting together of an appropriate organization for the actual implementation and administration of the program. For instance, the execution of a large-scale birth-control program requires an organization for the distribution of information to the public and the operation of birth-control clinics. During the execution stage, technical problems may arise and necessitate some short-term applied technical research.

The administration of the program requires technical and organizational mechanisms for controlling the operations and effects of the programs. Feedbacks are used to monitor the progress of the program towards its stated goal (and subgoals). If progress is unduly slow, if road blocks or unexpected side effects occur, the control of the program may initiate modifications in the execution or administration of the program or even further back in the information-processing stage of the program.

Once again we can separate steering factors into external and internal types, although in actual practice there may be no clear dividing line. The main external steering factors are:

(a) The specific practical goal of the organization initiating the program, when the said organization is separate from the organization carrying out the program, as in a government-sponsored nuclear power program.
(b) The socioeconomic conditions and political circumstances responsible for the motives behind the program and any social need for the program. Here we have in mind such diverse circumstances as the profit motive in a competitive market economy, the existence of large-scale unemployment and social unrest, a need for cheap energy in an expansionist consumptive economy, and so forth.
(c) The funding of the program (when external to the program).
(d) The interests and policies of groups and institutions outside the organization carrying out the program, as with government agencies, consumer groups, environmentalist groups, etc.
(e) Secondary information, organization and instruments available from outside the program.
(f) Social ideology, which of course plays a rôle in all the above (e.g. ideological aspects of sociological studies of the poor used in formulating

social-welfare programs). Social ideology also influences the paradigm of the program.

(g) Paradigm of the program when its formulation and goal-specification occur outside the organization carrying out the program. The paradigm of the program is the conception of the social purpose of the practical goal of the program (e.g. a view of the supposed or actual social benefits to be incurred). The paradigm of the program is interwoven with social ideology, that is, social values and view of man.

In many instances some of the above may be internal steering factors, namely when the program is formulated, funded and carried out by the same organization (e.g. a corporation marketing a new product). In that case, the main internal steering factors are:

(a) The practical goal.
(b) Funding.
(c) Knowledge and instruments available from within the organization.
(d) Paradigm of the goal, which will influence the execution and evaluation of the program.
(e) Criteria used in the internal planning, processing and evaluation of the program (e.g. standards of administrative organization and efficiency).
(f) Paradigmatic influences within the organization. We have already mentioned the paradigm of the goal and its relation to social ideology. Paradigmatic influences are also at work in criteria (e.g. an implicit idea of administration, which involves a view of man and social relations, underlies explicit criteria of administrative organization and efficiency). What needs emphasizing here is the typical dual nature of the program paradigm.

The individuals and groups responsible for the formulation and overall administration and evaluation of the project hold to the project goal paradigm with its social ideals and long-term view. This can be the case even when the interests behind the project are self-serving and distinct from those of the beneficiaries of the program. For instance, a business corporation may decide to set up a worker health-insurance plan because it will reduce certain management—worker conflicts and increase the physical fitness of the workforce and hence perhaps also productivity. The public relations and policy statements of the corporation will, however, emphasize the benefit to the workers and the value of management—labor cooperation to the economy and nation as a whole.

In contrast to the project formulators and high-level administrators, the middle- and lower-level administrators and technicians have narrower administrative and technical goals to reach. Their working paradigm will tend to be more of a short-sighted bureaucratic technical paradigm in which the daily routine of the program and the project's social relations with its supposed beneficiaries are viewed in a formalistic and mechanistic manner. Immediate economic self-interests (as with sub-contractors to the program) and narrow sectional interests (as between different departments or sections within the program's organization) play a major rôle at this level of the program (Fig. 4.4).

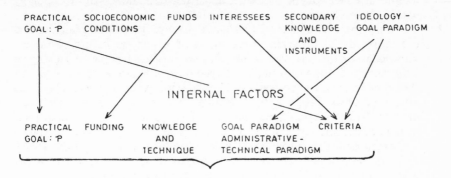

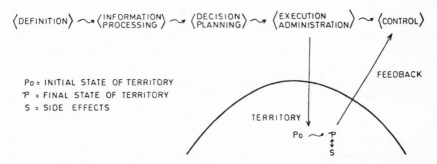

Figure 4.4 Steering factors in practical application programs (note that the execution stage may involve technical research programs).

Risks in practical application programs   In contrast to the localized risks of basic and applied research, the possible risks of practical application programs may involve large sections of the population and of the physical environment. This is so because the very nature of most practical application programs involves a socially and/or environmentally *extensive* application of a certain technique and technology. Another crucial difference between the risks generated in basic and applied research and those of practical application programs is the time duration involved: risks generated in the former types of programs tend to be immediate (e.g. laboratory risks) whereas those of the latter tend to be long term (e.g. dislocations of the economy or of ecological balances, the long-term risks to public health of certain chemicals or contaminants).

Practical application programs have a high risk potential. Some of the factors responsible for this are:

(a)   The extensive application of technique and technology to the social and physical worlds. The risks involved are great for the simple reason that current knowledge of the complexities of social and ecological dynamics is not sufficient to predict all possible or even highly significant short- or long-term effects of the introduction of new techniques and technology within those systems.

(b) The knowledge available to, and made use by, the overall planners and executors of the program tends to be of a general nature. Concrete knowledge of the territory to be affected is often lacking or lacking in sufficient detail for a thorough understanding of possible sides effects. On the other hand, those personnel who deal with the concrete details of the execution of the program tend to take a narrow bureaucratic technical view of their work and hence fail to actively seek out the potential risks of the designs and goals of the program. In short, the high-level planners and executors of the program may have too general and idealized a view and the lower-level executors too narrow and short-sighted a view for either group to anticipate the long-term risks of the program.

(c) Typically, the benefits of the program are obvious and short term, and the risks obscure and long term. The overall planners and executors of the program tend to be cognitively focused on the immediate benefits instead of the long-term risks (Björkman, Ch. 2).

(d) The "feedback loop" of practical application programs is quite long, that is, there is a large time lag between conception, execution and control. Negative side effects, especially longer term ones, may not manifest themselves until long after the execution stage is well under way. By then, the damage may already be done. The most common reason for the long feedback loop is the lack of a tentative, exploratory approach in the application of the new technique and technology. Instead, a few simplistic pilot studies of practicality and of any very obvious risks are done by persons who often have a vested interest in the program (e.g. company specialists and experts). This usually occurs in the information-processing stage, and the execution of the program then proceeds in an all-out manner.

Risk generation and assessment strategy in practical application programs A common way risks are generated and dealt with in practical application programs is the "post hoc" strategy: the program is executed, its results monitored and any side effects are dealt with in the control stage (Fig. 4.5). The most common response to negative side effects is what I will call the "ad hoc minimum action strategy": the control stage attributes the side effects to defects in the immediately preceding stage of the program and then, if necessary, proceeds backwards through the various stages of the program as adjustments at each stage fail to rectify the problem. In this way, as little of the program as possible is reworked.

For instance, a given program with a goal P effects a state T_p in the goal territory and with it a negative side effect S that is unacceptable to those involved in the program. If P is the desired goal state (P = P) then the control stage will, in this strategy, attribute S to errors in the execution stage (e.g. clumsy execution or poor public relations). If, on the other hand, P is not the desired goal state (P ≠ P) the side effect S is attributed to this fact. The failure to attain the desired goal state is then the problem requiring attention, and this failure will first require a check and reiteration of the execution stage.

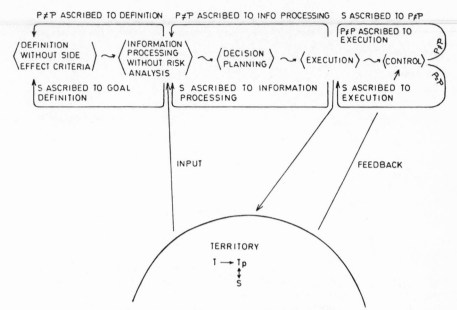

Figure 4.5 The "post hoc–ad hoc" strategy.

Failure to reduce or eliminate S (in the P = P case) or to reach the goal state (in the P ≠ P case) will result in a reiteration of the next major stage of the program, that of information processing and decision. If this reiteration fails, then the definition goal stage may be altered. If, in the P ≠ P case, control manages at some point to get P to match P and S still persists, then control proceeds as in the other P = P case, i.e. it starts with execution and works its way back as necessary.

An increasingly common form of risk strategy is the "technocratic fore-sighted" strategy (Fig. 4.6). In this case the definition stage includes a specifi-cation of an acceptable level of side effects S, and data pertaining to this are processed prior to decision and execution. If the negative side effects produced by the program exceed the preassigned limit, a minimum action strategy is used to deal with it.

In the technocratic strategy, the program is defined and controlled by a group, or groups, that is outside the territory to be transformed. The territory is treated as a passive recipient of the program's activities and technology. An alternative model is that of the populist strategy, in which the territory (in the case of a social program) or interested public groups play an active rôle in the conception of the program, of its goals and of the criteria to be used in con-trolling its execution. This strategy has the advantages of bringing a longer run socially purposeful commitment within the middle and lower levels of the program, so increasing the integration of overall general planning and con-crete information about the territory, and decreasing the length of the feed-back loops of the program's effects.

A more extreme form of the populist strategy is the "mass mobilization" strategy. In this case, the territory and/or interested public groups play an

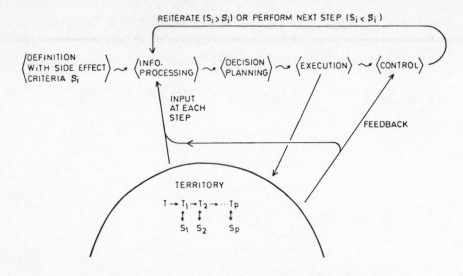

REITERATE $(S_i > S_i)$ OR PERFORM NEXT STEP $(S_i < S_i)$

$\left\langle\begin{array}{l}\text{DEFINITION}\\ \text{WITH SIDE EFFECT}\\ \text{CRITERIA } S_i\end{array}\right\rangle \sim \left\langle\begin{array}{l}\text{INFO.}\\ \text{PROCESSING}\end{array}\right\rangle \sim \left\langle\begin{array}{l}\text{DECISION}\\ \text{PLANNING}\end{array}\right\rangle \sim \langle\text{EXECUTION}\rangle \sim \langle\text{CONTROL}\rangle$

INPUT
AT EACH
STEP

FEEDBACK

TERRITORY

$T \rightarrow T_1 \rightarrow T_2 \rightarrow \cdots T_p$

$S_1 \quad S_2 \qquad S_p$

T_i = i-TH STATE OF THE TERRITORY BEING STEP-WISE MODIFIED BY THE PROGRAM
S_i = i-TH STATE OF SIDE EFFECTS PRODUCED IN THE TERRITORY BY THE
ACTION OF THE PROGRAM
S_i = MAXIMUM ACCEPTABLE LEVEL OF SIDE EFFECTS AT THE i-TH STEP
OF THE EXECUTION OF THE PROGRAM

Figure 4.6 The cautious foresighted strategy (technocratic form).

active rôle in all stages of the program. The mass mobilization strategy is found mostly in the more radical socialist countries (e.g. China, Cuba; Suttmeier 1977, Elzinga 1978).

The "cautious foresighted" strategy involves an initial risk analysis with specified levels of acceptable negative side effects and an incremental exploratory execution that effects a small change in the territory and studies it for possible side effects. The information-processing stage is kept in operation since the feedback of each exploratory step must be processed and the next execution step decided on the basis of that processing. The advantage of this strategy is that negative side effects may be discovered and the program appropriately adjusted before the side effects occur on an extensive scale. The cautious foresighted strategy may take a technocratic, populist or mass mobilization form. Depending on the cultural and socioeconomic context, and on the technical difficulty of the program, it would appear that the cautious foresighted strategy in one form or another offers the most cautious and knowledgeable conditions for risk assessment and the control of risks.

In industrialized science today, basic and applied research are increasingly tied to practical application programs. "Cautious foresighted" risk strategies should then be adapted to the whole research and development complex. Ultimately though, modern industrialized society must deal with the problem of values and motivations. This may require nothing less than a restructuring of social relations in the work place and in research systems.

References

Bunge, M. 1967. *Scientific research*, vols 1 and 2. Berlin: Springer-Verlag.

Elzinga, A. 1978. *Red and expert*. Report No. 35, parts I–III, Göteborg, Sweden: Institute for Theory of Science.

Greenberg, D. 1969. *The politics of pure science*. Harmondsworth: Penguin.

Kaplan, N. (ed.) 1965. *Science and society*. Chicago: Rand McNally.

Krohn, W., E. T. Layton, Jr. and P. Weingart (eds) 1978. *The dynamics of science and technology*. Holland: D. Reidel.

Mendelsohn, E., P. Weingart and R. D. Whitly (eds) 1977. *The social production of scientific knowledge*. Holland: D. Reidel.

Ravetz, J. R. 1971. *Scientific knowledge and its social problems*. Oxford: Clarendon Press.

Rose, H. and S. Rose (eds) 1969. *Science and society*. London: Allen Lane.

Rose, H and S. Rose (eds) 1976. *The political economy of science*. London: Macmillan.

Suttmeier, R. P. 1977. *Science policy and societal changes in China*. London: Lexington Books.

Tornebohm, H. 1973. *Perspectives on inquiring systems*. Report No. 53. Göteborg, Sweden: Institute for Theory of Science.

5 The study of risk in social systems: an anthropological perspective

KAJSA EKHOLM FRIEDMAN

Introduction: the social scientific study of risk

The study of social "risk" can best be understood in terms of the couple risk/catastrophe. The latter refers to the time-dependent aspect of social development seen from an "as if" perspective. Risk is thus catastrophe in its latent form. Risk research stands in opposition to both fatalism and voluntarism insofar as it is predicated upon the possibility of predicting future catastrophes in order to plan around or against them.

Anthropology's contribution to this kind of research is to lay bare the kinds of risk that have emerged and emerge in social evolution. The relation between risk and catastrophe can be visualized as shown in Fig. 5.1.

This diagram presents the field of analysis of social risk in terms of two components. Social catastrophe, which we take to refer to structural disturbances of critical proportions, cannot be understood within the bounds of a given society and its peculiar development. As development is a process that occurs at a global level, any analysis must include two kinds of totalities, *the local society* and *the larger system* in which the latter is integrated.

The study of the future can only be meaningful on the assumption that social change is a lawful process whose properties can be known. This lawfulness, however, is largely due to the fact that social evolution is blind and beyond the grasp of consciousness. Man has never understood, or had control over, the conditions of his social existence. He has thus been the tool rather than the subject and producer of history. It is, in fact, this self-victimization that makes a social science possible. But insofar as the latter can, in its turn, produce knowledge that can be effectively employed in the continual reconstruction of social relations, we may ultimately be able to escape the "laws" of history.

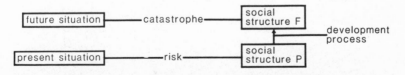

Figure 5.1 The relation between risk and catastrophe.

The study of the future and a general social science

The future cannot be a self-contained object of research quite simply because it does not exist. There is no empirical basis for futurology other than in the understanding of the past and the present. The future can only be made comprehensible as part of a general social science, one which has a totalistic perspective that is only barely emerging today. Our basic assumption is that social reality does not consist of autonomous bits and pieces but forms an inclusive totality which today is represented by the world system and which can, I think, be traced back, through smaller "global" systems, to the very origins of "civilization." A general social science has as its field the development of global systems over time, as well as pre-civilized systems that have traditionally been the province of anthropology and archeology. This field straddles a number of present academic divisions whose isolation can only be a hindrance to the kind of research necessary in such an approach. A general social science, in overcoming such divisions, would, I think, enable us to arrive at a clearer perspective of our own present and future (Fig. 5.2).

The results of futurological research have not been exactly impressive. Constructions of the future have usually been so vague that they cannot be proved to be false. Where they have been more precise, they have often been wrong. One of the most significant kinds of error can be found in Mit's I. Adelman's forecast in 1969 that the price of crude oil would continue to fall throughout the 1970s and that Middle Eastern countries would never be able to overcome their internal conflicts in order to arrive at a common policy. We need not comment upon this painfully typical misjudgement in order to see that there are fundamental problems with the kinds of projections made. The critical weakness of most futurological research is that it consists essentially of projecting current trends into the future without providing any analysis of the mechanisms that might generate them. Without an adequate theory of the dynamics of the present social system we are as likely as not to make projections that are false.

In order to predict the trajectory of a social structure we need a precise description or model of the structure at time p and at time f in the future as well as a model of the developmental process connecting the two structures. It might appear that, since we are dealing with one and the same society, the mechanisms of change ought to be endogenous. We shall be suggesting that

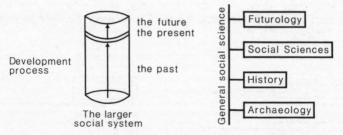

Figure 5.2 The relation between the social totality in time/space and academic fragmentation.

this is not the case; that societies participate in larger systems of reproduction which largely determine both their conditions of existence and the direction and form of their development. In order to grasp the nature of global processes, we need models for both "society," the politically bounded unit, and for the global system.

SOCIETY

There are already numerous models of society as a totality. Typical for social anthropology is the classic structural functionalist model dividing social reality into ecology, economy, social structure and ideology or religion. Historical materialism maintains similar categories to cultural materialism. Structural functionalism merely contends that the parts form an integrated system, whereas materialism tends to envisage all levels as functions, in one sense or another, of the economy or forces of production. Some marxist models also include the importance of internal contradictions as the motor of development, but for most of them, contradictions are mere dysfunctionalities caused by the development of the forces of production. Although the materialist model is, I think, entirely wrong due to its focus on the individual society as a sufficient unit of explanation, there are clearly aspects of both this model and the more general structural functionalist approach that can be redeployed. It is necessary in the construction of models of society to grasp the interrelatedness of processes, from the socialization of individuals to the interaction of economy and state (where such categories exist) in terms of social reproduction. In such a framework, society is understood as open to a larger process and its internal structure is constituted by relations among institutions as well as among the human-mediated processes of construction and destruction of institutions.

GLOBAL SYSTEMS

Totalistic models of global politicoeconomic systems have been emerging in a number of fields including anthropology and archeology (Ekholm 1976, 1980, Friedman 1976, 1978, Ekholm & Friedman 1979, 1980, Kohl 1978), economic history (Braudel 1973, 1977, Wallerstein 1974, 1980, Lombard 1975), and economics (Frank 1978, Busch 1974, Schoeller 1976, Fröbel et al. 1977). Even within system theory there has been work on a formal model of contradictory global systems (Barel 1969).

From the emergence of the earliest civilizations (i.e. Mesopotamia 3000 BC) we find ample evidence of larger economic systems (Ekholm & Friedman 1979, Kohl 1978). In fact it can be argued that civilization is largely coterminus with the emergence of center/periphery structures in which highly developed polities producing manufactured goods on a mass scale exchange with relatively underdeveloped zones that produce largely raw materials. The perseverance of such regional inequalities throughout civilized history is rooted in the nature of development itself. The latter has never been based on exclusively local resources, but upon what might be called *a supralocal environment*. Civilization is a machine for the transformation of raw materials from a large region into finished products at one location within that region. The definition of the center is thus simultaneously the definition of an underdeveloped periphery.

The essential characteristic of social evolution has been the discontinuous shifting of centers of development from one geographical area to another. There are always center/periphery relations, but they have never been geographically stable. Areas that have experienced high culture have also had their dark ages and have been peripheries to other centers (Fig. 5.3).

Thus social evolution can be understood in terms of two essential aspects, a general growth in scale and complexity as a continuous process, and a local discontinuity that takes the form of geographically shifting "rises and falls". Regional discontinuity results from the loss of control by centers over their supralocal resource base. In order to maintain such control, centers of civilization need to maintain a monopoly over industrial production in the larger system. The centralized conversion of a region's raw materials into re-exportable finished goods is only possible if the periphery has no other access to such manufactures. In spite of the monopoly basis of this fundamentally unequal redistributive system, there has always been a tendency to a decentralization of manufacturing in the long run. In his description of the Roman Empire, Walbank (1969, p. 50) uses the very words "decentralization of industrial production" to the provinces in his analysis of the undermining of the power of Rome. Decentralization need not be the direct result of the export of capital or of real production. The economic expansion of Western Europe after AD 900 consisted in setting up the same types of industries as could be found in the dominant Arab centers of the period, i.e. textiles, glass and paper. The Middle Eastern connection is evident here, and the European export to the same markets as those once monopolized by the Arabs seems clearly related to the contraction that overcomes the Middle East in the 1100s. Although the Arabs played a rôle in this decentralization, especially in the Mediterranean and Spain, credit is due to the Europeans themselves.

The loss of monopoly over industrial production implies:

(a) loss of central position;
(b) which leads to loss of supralocal environment;
(c) which leads to a decline in production in the center;
(d) which leads to a process of underdevelopment and decline in living standard.

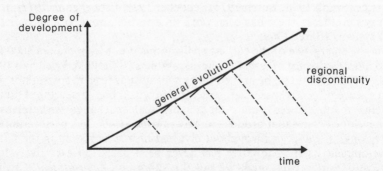

Figure 5.3 Two aspects of development: general evolution versus local discontinuity.

The decentralization of production in the larger system is, then, equivalent to the decline of the center. The latter takes the form of a series of crises. First there is marked increase in the level of competition in the system as a whole, a competition wherein the center is at a great disadvantage due to its high costs of production. This is accompanied and followed by a series of social crises, class and other conflicts among social groups, and, ultimately, that radical transformation of society that has sometimes been described as the advent of the dark ages.

THE LEFT AND THE FUTURE

The Left critique of futurological research is founded on the association of state planning in capitalism with an attempt to adapt national societal structures to the needs of capital in crisis. As such, it can be no more than an ideological or political exercise in social control rather than a real contribution to social problem solving. In a recent work (Dencik & Dencik 1976) such criticisms are combined with a blind faith in the natural evolution of capitalism to socialism. "How can the route be altered when the train is already in motion and we are on it" (Dencik & Dencik 1976, p. 297).

For historical materialists and orthodox marxist economists there is no need to research the possibilities of the future since it is given by definition. No change is necessary, we need only wait for the socialist millenium which must necessarily arise from the ashes of the present capitalist world crisis. If any action is necessary, it is that which might hasten the crisis and the final transformation. The ideological basis of this kind of analysis is that social development is essentially a national phenomenon and well within the potential control of the nation state, and that socialism is the necessary outcome of capitalist decline. Because the larger system is not taken into consideration, the possibility of economic devolution and misery is not even included within the realm of discourse.

When it is realized that the present crisis of the West is not simply another depression, or a contradiction of capital accumulation within each Western nation, but the expression of a shift of capital accumulation out of the West as a whole and a decentralization of world accumulation, then the whole question of the development of socialism is upstaged by the impending threat of poverty.

It is often assumed that the state is somehow identical with the interests of capital, especially in "late capitalism." Although this may sometimes be the case in terms of strategic decisions, it is absurd to suggest that the nation state as an institution exists in a harmonic relation to capital. The multinationalization of capital is, as we have suggested, the essential process behind the present crisis of the state in the West. The reproduction of capital is, in fact, secured by its nonidentity with the state, i.e. its possibility of free mobility in the world. State-controlled forms of accumulation, as in state capitalism or Soviet-type economies, are only successful to the extent that they too maintain their position in the world market. The nationalization of capitalist industries in periods of crisis is not, in our analysis, a progressive step. Capital moves out because it cannot survive at home. Its nationalization only proves the point.

Structural crises and economic regression

When we speak of expansion and contraction, we refer to economic phenomena. While some kinds of societies are so placed in larger systems that they have been able to reproduce themselves and expand on the basis of trade profits alone (i.e. the medieval Italian cities), their very existence has depended upon the fact that most societies base their development on the expansion of production. Historical materialism is certainly correct in insisting that production is the basis of the entire social formation. But this is only half of the story. We must also ask what it is that determines the economic base. At least since the emergence of civilization, it is safely said that the productive base of society is a great deal more fragile than in primitive conditions. History is full of examples where the economic base of society has simply vanished. The reason for this is that the reproduction of production depends upon factors beyond the direct control of society, i.e. upon supralocal exchange. Sweden as a sub-unit of the world system is above all an import–export node whose continued existence depends upon the maintenance of crucial ratios of exchange.

Production and trade are equally necessary parts of the same structure, although production is local whereas trade is supralocal. However, international exchange is the weak link in the structure insofar as its stability, which is not a simple effect of production, determines the conditions of functioning of the producing society. This is related to the fact that economic reproduction is intimately dependent upon the combination of export production and a supralocal resource base. Sweden exports approximately 40% of its industrial output. It would thus appear to be more dependent on the world market than countries such as the USA or the USSR. This quantitative difference does not change the structural necessity of industrial export for economic development. Production for the home market is structurally secondary to the export sector. This might explain why decline in external trade cannot be meaningfully offset by expanding home markets. Keynesian policies only seem to function in periods when external markets are expanding. The evidence is clear for Europe.

INDUSTRIAL PRODUCTION IN SWEDEN

After World War II, Western Europe experienced a rapid economic growth, largely due to the massive import of American capital and the expansion of the world market. For the first two decades it was truly a seller's market (Norgren & Norgren 1970, p. 12). From the beginning of the 1960s, however, this expansion slowed, leading to increasing competition within the Organization for Economic Cooperation and Development (OECD). In order to increase competitiveness, the Swedish government undertook a program of structural rationalization, the reduction in the number and increase in the size of enterprises and their geographical concentration to a few locations, resulting in widespread demographic and social dislocation. This reorganization did not, however, overcome the fundamental problems of higher costs, and from 1975 production began to decline (Table 5.1).

In 1976, factories began to close down at an alarming rate and our major

Table 5.1 Sweden's volume of production 1969–75 (index 1968 = 100) (*Statistical Yearbook* 1976, p. 140).

Year	1969	1970	1971	1972	1973	1974	1975
Production	107	114	115	118	127	134	131

export industries ran into great difficulties. Rising relative costs of production combined with technological changes that lowered the necessary qualifications of labor (e.g. in special steel) are the main factors that shook the entire Western world. An essential element in the decline of production in Sweden is the export of capital. In a report from 1976, the Swedish LO (Confederation of Trade Unions) stated that Swedish foreign investments did not lead to increasing demand in Sweden since foreign branches tended to buy from non-Swedish firms rather than from the mother company. The report also showed that although Swedish direct foreign investment had increased by a factor of five in the past 15 years, foreign investment in Sweden had all but stagnated (LO-Kongressen 1976, p. 131) (Fig. 5.4).

The statistics from 1976 demonstrate a clear continuation of the above trends. Foreign investment in Sweden declined by 95 million kr. in current prices and the export of capital soared to new heights. This trend is quite normal: if Swedish capital moves out to avoid rising costs there is no reason why foreign capital should take its place in this increasingly disadvantageous position. There is a general tendency for capital that produces world market goods to move to areas of low costs. But there is also a tendency to set up production in areas, especially within the West, where increasing competition has made

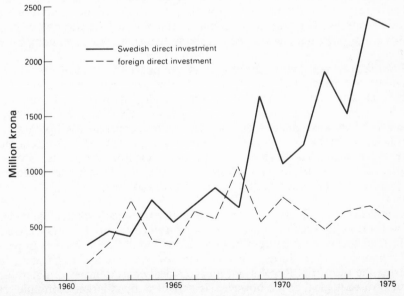

Figure 5.4 Swedish direct foreign investment and foreign investment in Sweden (from LO-Kongressen 1976, p. 132).

it necessary to protect former export markets. This is also a cost-reducing mechanism that accounts for the high level of direct investment in the USA, West Germany, England and Denmark.

As the deindustrialization of Sweden continues, the state loses income at the same time as costs are increasing, placing a heavy burden on the welfare system. Unemployment will certainly become a problem. Conflicts between classes and between ethnic groups will be exacerbated. Alcoholism, drugs and criminality will all be on the rise. The stability of the social order will be placed in serious jeopardy. Social catastrophe is only just around the corner from the economic miracle.

THE GENERAL PATTERN OF ECONOMIC REGRESSION

To get some idea of the direction of economic regression today we can look to similar processes in earlier periods of history.

Deindustrialization This is the beginning of the end. It is, as we have said, not a local process, but a local expression of the shift of centers of accumulation. It results from successful competition from newly rising industrial centers whose costs of production are significantly lower, and which, historically, have often been located in former peripheral zones. The high costs of production in the center are themselves mere expressions of development as such. They reflect high levels of consumption, a differentiation of activities in a direction leading to a high ratio of nonproducers to producers, a great deal of money in circulation relative to real production, etc. The decline of industrial production in the Middle East in the period 1000 through the 1100s is largely due to increasing competition from Western Europe which had, until that period, been a raw material and slave exporting periphery of the Arab-dominated world economy. The continuing decline of the Middle East was not, of course, a smooth process but led to a crisis in the system as a whole, including Europe.

Technological regression Insofar as developed technological processes depend on the presence of a supralocal resource base, the disappearance of the latter leads to real regression in the former. One of the earliest examples of such a process occurs in the Old World crisis of 2300–2200 BC when bronze vanished and was replaced by cold-hammered copper in Mesopotamia, the result of the breakdown in the tin trade. The more advanced the technology, the more dependent it tends to be upon external resources. Even the agricultural base of today's Western societies has become technologically dependent on its center position in the world economy.

Ecological crisis Economic crisis is usually associated with ecological crisis. This is primarily because it becomes simply too costly to offset the destructive effects of technological intensification, a possibility that still exists in periods of expansion. England was able to change from wood to coal as an energy base during the Industrial Revolution, an ecological crisis that never materialized. Our own ecological crisis, however, is part of a much larger economic crisis. The ecological destruction of Southern Mesopotamia at the end of the third millenium BC was largely the result of salinization caused by intensive irrigation. It is sometimes implied that this salinization was the major cause of the Mesopotamian crisis of about 2300 BC. We would suggest, however, that it was the effect of an overintensified and overstrained economy. Ecological crises can only be overcome in expansive economic conditions.

Demographic crisis   When the economy crumbles, the former balance between population and resources is suddenly disturbed. Overpopulation is not an absolute phenomenon but can only be understood as a relation to a systemically determined economic base. It is more the product of declining resources than of increasing population. Carrying capacity is a socially organized threshold and not a simple technoecological phenomenon. The cannibalism reported from many areas of the so-called primitive world by early travelers is to a large extent the result of economic collapse following in the footsteps of European expansion. Where the social organizational basis of production disintegrates as it did for large parts of Africa and the Americas, decline is often violent. If such relatively small-scale systems collapsed with such bloodshed, we can only speculate on the catastrophic effects of a declining high civilization such as our own.

Social relations   A traditional explanation for the fall of civilization is the so-called barbarian invasion. Closer analysis, however, usually reveals that civilizations are perfectly capable of self-destruction without outside help. In fact, many so-called invasions are no more than the apparent form of regional conflicts within the same system (often between hegemonic centers and their former clients or even peripheries). Imperial structures are prone to dissolution when the financial means of their maintenance fades. The result is a feudalization or fragmentation of the former power structure, a process all too familiar from the decline of the Roman Empire. The self-contradictory structure of the system becomes clear in periods of crisis. Warfare between central states is accompanied and followed by internal war between classes, estates and/or other opposed groups. Even inter-individual relations are placed in jeopardy. Societies are not mere victims of crises in larger systems. They seem rather to take the latter as cues to begin dismembering themselves.

Science and ideology   It is to be expected that economic regression will effect a general cultural disintegration, especially as the latter takes the form of institutional organizations that have a certain cost of maintenance. Scientific research tends to become too expensive to maintain and general standards decline. There are many historical examples of the emigration of the technical and cultural core of a society to areas where conditions of existence are better. In the period of the decline of classical Athens and the rise of the Hellenistic states, there is an exodus of large numbers of handicraft masters and intellectuals to the more prosperous cities of the Orient. Today, there is a tendency for qualified individuals in semi-peripheral developing areas to receive increasing portions of outflowing capital. As the head of a leading Swedish chemical company remarked with respect to recent plans to establish a research institute in India, "an Indian researcher costs a fifth of a Swedish researcher" (Dagens Industri February 17, 1977). Insofar as cultural organization as well as scientific research is reproduced by the economy, it too disappears in periods of decline.

There is not only a decline of scientific activity but a general disintegration of the organization of knowledge. Literacy disappears, the means of recording is often lost, antirational cults may emerge that invoke supernatural forces in an attempt to understand and control a reality that has become uncontrollable.

The modern global system

The center/periphery structure of the world system today is similar to previous periods, but it is very much larger in scale. The center is divided into a "private" capitalist Western block including the USA, Japan and Western Europe, and a state capitalist or "socialist" Eastern block including the Soviet Union and Eastern Europe (excluding Yugoslavia and perhaps Poland which has been peripheralized in the last decade). Each block has its own periphery with which it exchanges manufactures for raw materials and where the arms trade has been and is the leading sector (Fig. 5.5).

China has had a special position in this system insofar as it remained, for a number of years, closed to the rest of the world economy in its attempt to develop itself on the basis of its own resources. This closure, of course, was a political act that occurred after over a century of peripheralization within the Western-dominated world economy, and it has now ended abruptly after the replacement of the Maoist regime. Although at present a periphery of sorts, it contains a whole world economy within itself and has the potential to rise to center status.

The above representation of the system is inaccurate insofar as it is static and does not contain the mechanisms causing crisis, shifts in power, and structural tranformation. Its usefulness lies only in the simultaneous presentation of a number of fundamental relations within one global structure. Three basic kinds of relations are expressed here:

(a) relations within the West, between Western Europe, Japan and USA;
(b) relations between West and East, between the two competing blocks in the center;
(c) relations between center and periphery.

Figure 5.5 General model for the modern global system.

It is in the examination of these relations that changes in position can be detected. Our central hypothesis is that the West is presently losing its center position and that this is due to a decentralization of industrial production in the system as a whole beyond limits compatible with the maintenance of a center/periphery structure. The processes involved here deal a severe blow to dependency theories of imperialism that exclude decentralization by definition. Here, after all, we have a developing situation in which it is no longer clear that the center is still the center and the periphery still peripheral.

At the same time as industrial development has accelerated in certain parts of the Third World, the West has been plagued by a growing economic crisis, one that began to take on serious proportions at the end of the 1960s. Its most obvious expression has been a contraction in the industrial sector, a phenomenon noticed by both marxists and nonmarxists (Gamble & Walton 1976, p. 6):

"The classic definition of an economic crisis under capitalism is an interruption to production and to the process of growth. This happened in 1974 — the first time since 1945 that economic activity declined in all parts of the capitalist economy simultaneously. A period of generalized recession began, which was expected to last until the end of 1975."

This decline, however, did not reverse itself at the end of 1975, nor in 1976, and it does not appear that an upswing is imminent today. The immediate cause of the crisis, of course, is not a decline in production, but a contraction in markets for final consumption. Increasing unemployment follows from declining production, whether disguised or not. Inflation is another symptom, increasing from low levels in the 1950s and 1960s to an average of over 10% in the 1970s. In the UK, it rose to 19% in 1974 and 27% in 1975. Finally, there has been a general decrease in real income and a liquidity squeeze that has led to increasing use of credit in a situation that could only provoke a catastrophically high level of debt, in consumer, producer and state spheres. The result is the economic crisis of the state as well as of the individual. The working-class reaction to crisis, via strikes and higher wages has been totally offset by the general inflation.

The wave of USA investment in low-wage zones came in the period between 1958 and 1967. It began with simpler forms of industry: shoes, textiles, leather goods and electronic assembly. The products were re-exported to the USA where they outcompeted home production. In Lynn, Massachusetts, for example, the number of shoe factories was reduced from 36 to 12 (Barnet & Miller 1975, p. 157). There is a vicious circle that leads from the export of industrial capital to the decline of home production (via cheaper imports) to a demand for increasingly cheaper imports when incomes decline (Roberts 1975, p. 94).

"As inflation racked the United States in the late 1960's, billions of dollars worth of foreign goods poured into the American market; higher-priced U.S. goods found it increasingly difficult to meet competition in foreign markets, the inflated dollar grew weaker and weaker, periodically upsetting the international monetary system."

The first wave of foreign direct investment so weakened the central economies that it created the conditions for the massive outpouring of more advanced productive capital in the 1970s. Rapid technological developments, themselves the outcome of increasing competition, are instrumental here. Forms of production, such as special steel, that formerly required highly skilled labor can now be organized with unskilled labor (and computer technology) in more backward areas. Industrial capital finds itself forced to move to cheaper areas in order to survive. The result is a deindustrialization of important sectors of the Western economy.

DECENTRALIZATION OF INDUSTRIAL PRODUCTION: GENERALITIES

Industrial decentralization is nothing new in the history of capitalism. In 1820, the UK stood for approximately 50% of the world's industrial production. Following this, production decentralized rapidly, largely as a result of English investment in Europe, Russia and the USA. Swedish industrial development in the 19th century is largely a product of British investment. A principal reason for large-scale export of capital is the emergence of profit gradient linking a rich and increasingly expensive center to poorer and cheaper peripheral areas. By 1870, the British share of world production had fallen somewhat to a still sizeable 32%, but now the USA and Germany had become major competitors. This early decentralization of industrial accumulation led to the first of industrial competitions, the elaboration of colonial empire and the major confrontation of World War I.

By the end of World War II, the USA had largely taken over the position occupied by Britain in the 19th century. The emergent USA hegemony was very much predicated on the destruction of large parts of both European and Japanese industry. A new wave of decentralization began immediately. By 1950, USA investment abroad had risen to 1.7 billion dollars. In 1959 it stood at 5.3 billion and in 1969 it was as high as 21.6 billion. There was a marked economic growth in this period, especially in Europe and Japan. The USA was much weaker, experiencing a number of recessions (Table 5.2).

From 1899 to 1957 there was a general decentralization of production in the world. This can be expressed (Table 5.3), in the comparative percentages of

Table 5.2 Average annual growth of gross national product (GNP), 1950–73 (from World Tables, 1976, p. 398).

| Country | GNP | | | |
	1950–60	1960–65	1965–70	1965–73
USA	3.3	4.9	3.5	3.5
Belgium	3.0	5.2	4.9	5.0
France	4.4	5.9	5.8	5.8
Holland	4.5	5.1	6.0	5.6
Italy	6.1	5.1	6.0	4.9
England	2.8	3.3	2.5	2.5
Sweden	3.4	5.1	3.9	3.1
Switzerland	4.4	5.1	3.6	4.0
West Germany	7.9	5.0	4.8	4.6
Japan	8.7	10.2	12.4	10.8

Table 5.3   Share of the world export market for industrial manufacturers (*1950 and 1967 values for Germany refer to West Germany only). In 1937, the West German share was approximately 16.5%) (from Magdoff 1974, p. 283).

Country	Share of world export market (%)					
	1899	1913	1929	1937	1950	1967
USA	11.7	13.0	20.4	19.2	26.6	20.6
UK	33.2	30.2	22.4	20.9	24.6	11.9
Germany	22.4	26.6	20.5	21.8	7.0*	19.7*
France	14.4	12.1	10.9	5.8	9.6	8.5
Italy	3.6	3.3	3.7	3.5	3.6	7.0
Japan	1.5	2.3	3.9	6.9	3.4	9.9
others	13.2	12.5	18.2	21.9	25.2	22.4
totals	100.0	100.0	100.0	100.0	100.0	100.0

the world market for industrial manufactures. In 1899, Great Britain controlled 33% of the world market, Germany 22% and France 14%. By 1967, export production was significantly redistributed. The above three countries' share of the market has fallen from 69% to 39%, i.e. a 30% decline. The USA now had 20%, Italy 7% and Japan 10%. The category "others" had increased its share from 13% to 22%. There were also some important shifts in ranking. The USA increased its share until 1950 but then began to decline. For both Britain and France there was a continual decline. Between 1950 and 1970 West Germany, Italy and Japan made the most headway on the world market.

It appears that at first the decentralization of production was limitless and unproblematic, but this, of course, could only continue so long as the capacity of the market increased. After 1960, the limits of expansion began to make themselves felt. Competition increased at the same time as capital was exported at an accelerating rate. Although more regions of the world entered the supply side, there was a decrease in the number of firms in the center's industry and a centralization of the capital that remained.

There are three main types of foreign direct investment:

(a)   in raw material production;
(b)   to protect former export markets in conditions of increasing competition;
(c)   in areas with lower production costs for industry.

The first type of investment corresponds to the classical form of imperialist structure and need not interest us here. The second type has increased dramatically since the 1960s and is largely a response to decentralization itself (the third type), especially within the center where the major consumer markets are located. The third type of investment is the fundamental mechanism behind industrial decentralization, since it lays the foundation of the export of direct investment from the center as a whole.

THE MOVEMENT OF INDUSTRIAL PRODUCTION FROM CENTER TO PERIPHERY

Until quite recently, dependency theory reigned supreme. Underdevelopment was accounted for in terms of the bond between periphery and center. It was, and is still, assumed by many that the development of the Third World depends on breaking the link to the West, and that if this does not occur the only result can be increasing polarization between the poor and rich nations. Third World ideologists, representatives of emerging upper classes, have tended to make dependency theory into a new dogma geared to the forced transfer of wealth from the West to the rest (the New Economic Order). It is ironic that this development should occur just in a period when the dependency model is being falsified by the expansion of industry in the periphery (Friedman 1978). As far back as 1973, Warren analyzed what appeared to be a reversal of the underdevelopment trend (Warren 1973). He showed that while there has been a slow increase in the share of Latin America, Asia and Africa in world industrial production since 1937 (from one-ninth to one-seventh of that of the West), industrial growth in the Third World began to accelerate in the 1950s. While, for example, USA growth from 1955–7 averaged only 2% a year, Asia had an annual growth of 16%. Throughout the 1950s, in fact, Asia was by far the fastest growing economic region (Table 5.4).

From 1951 to 1969 the distribution of industrial expansion in the periphery was not, of course, an even one. It was limited to a number of countries in Asia and Latin America with average annual growth rates for industrial production for 1951–69 as follows (Warren 1973): Brazil, 7.8; Iran, 11.2; South Korea, 16.9; Singapore, 14.8; Thailand, 8.7; Taiwan, 14.8; Venezuela, 10.5.

Industrial production as a share of total production has also increased significantly, from 14.5% in 1950–4 to 17.9% in 1960–4. The latter figure is almost two-thirds that of the developed capitalist world (31.3%), an indication of the degree to which the Third World has developed an industrially based economy. It has also been shown that industrial export has grown faster in the periphery than in the center in the 1960s; 14.3% against 10.8%. The export of machinery and transport equipment has grown by nearly 20% (Adám 1975, p. 99). This development indicates that there is indeed a decentralization of world industrial production, one that must be included in any model of the world economy that hopes to go beyond the simple structural description of a particular historical period.

Table 5.4 Average annual growth of industrial production 1937–59 (from Warren 1973).

Country	Average annual growth			
	1937–50	1950–55	1955–57	1937–57
North America	5.2	4.5	1.9	4.7
Western Europe	1.7	7.1	4.9	3.3
Oceania	4.3	5.2	4.9	4.6
Latin America	5.2	5.3	5.6	5.3
Asia	−0.6	12.4	16.0	4.1
total	3.6	5.7	3.9	4.2

MECHANISMS AND PHASES IN THIRD WORLD INDUSTRIALIZATION

At the end of World War II, the USA was the world's dominant industrial nation. It had, however, two major competitors in the world arena; a weakened

Europe and the USSR. From the end of the 1940s the USA attempted to take over large portions of the former colonialized zones. It was also necessary to contend with the then expanding politicoeconomic power of the USSR. Large sums of money in the form of aid found their way to selected areas. Gifts of arms were also a crucial method of gaining clients throughout the world. In the case of Iran, for example, where the USA outmanoeuvered the UK for control and where Soviet troops were never far away, large sums of American money began to flow into the country from 1949. Iran turned into a powerful military machine that, by the 1970s, with the emergence of OPEC, was undergoing a rapid industrialization.

Aside from the flow of money and arms, the usual import of cheap raw materials was maintained in this period. The major form of new industries were those aimed at local consumer markets. From the 1960s onwards, the pattern changed. Now industrial production exported to the periphery was dependent on Western mass markets. It began first with the export of simpler forms of technology and then was supplemented by the movement of more advanced production. The reason for these changes can be found in the increasing competition in the center, which was itself a result of the decentralization that occurred there. Since it was the UK and the USA that were the least competitive in terms of home production, these two countries were the major exporters of capital to low wage zones (Table 5.5).

The export of capital was accompanied by, and expressive of, stagnation at home. The first recipients were small countries like South Korea, Hong Kong and Taiwan, all under close Western supervision. Later, larger more independent lands like India and Brazil became important investment areas. Adám (1975, p. 98) has argued quite forcefully that technology has developed in such a way that "almost anything can be produced in any country" resulting in a tendency to a global reorganization of production that is apparently self-reinforcing. While Adám interprets this as a qualitatively new phenomenon we would argue that it is merely an expression of a general shift in world accumulation. The driving force here is the vicious circle leading from increasing multinationalization to stagnation in the center to accelerating multinationalization. A decade ago it could be argued that the center could still maintain a monopoly over advanced sectors of production. This was, and still is, seen by some as a basic characteristic of continuing imperialism. All that is changing rapidly today. It has been contended for some years that "modern

Table 5.5 Expansion of sales (%) 1957–65 accounted for by manufacturing firms (from Rowthorn 1971, Table 22).

Country	Exports	Overseas production	Overseas sales
USA	2	13	15
UK	12	20	32
France	6	1	7
Germany	14	2	16
Italy	24	5	30
Netherlands	27	17	43
Canada	33	13	46
Japan	17	2	20

technology in some industries is such that relatively unskilled labor can be combined with fairly sophisticated equipment" (USA Tariff Commission 1973, p. 118). Today, large sectors of the West's mass consumption industries are moving out; textiles, clothing, electronics and automobiles. The age of the private multinational giant is not merely a further evolution of capitalist organization, but part of a major decentering of the World economy. The tendency is strong enough to affect even state-owned industries. Sveteco, the Swedish state-owned textile industry, decided in 1977 to move production to South Korea (Aftonbladet April 20, 1977) in order to escape the high Swedish wage level. A state in economic crisis because of the decline in national production must ultimately be forced to act as a private capitalist.

THE CHARACTER AND CONSEQUENCES OF THIRD WORLD INDUSTRIALIZATION

That the West shall continue to grow richer while the Third World sinks deeper into the depths of poverty is a fundamental assumption of standard imperialism theory. Amin (1974), for example, distinguishes between capitalism in the center, which developed internally, and capitalism in the periphery, which is merely an externally implanted appendage to the center's "self-centered" economy. We have indicated that this is an ideological representation in which both capitalism and imperialism are essentially Western phenomena, so that the expulsion of Europeans and Americans, and their replacement by a local élite should solve the problem of underdevelopment. Such a model of reality is more than coincidentally suited to the emerging élites themselves.

The classical model is also absolutely static since the center/periphery structure is included within the very definition of capitalism. The only development in this approach is increasing polarization. Although authors such as Amin (1974) and Palloix (1975) have recognized that there has been industrial development in some parts of the periphery, they can only interpret this as an expression of increasing exploitation by the West. For Palloix (1975), what is, in fact, a massive export of productive capital, appears as a means for the center of ridding itself of traditional (backward technological) industries while maintaining a monopoly over the most advanced sectors. But as we indicated earlier, this is no longer the case. Secondly, it seems to have gone unnoticed that the so-called traditional industries are, in fact, the major mass-consumption suppliers. The control over advanced nuclear technology is insignificant economically when compared to the textile or automobile industries.

Finally, the significance of industrialization in the Third World is minimized because it is connected to the world instead of the national market. As the growth is not based on internal consumption, it is not considered to be real capitalist growth. Thus, it has been suggested that Brazil's mass consumption is restricted to only 2.5% of the population (Annerstedt & Gustafsson 1976, p. 114) and that while the élite (1% of the population) saw a 112% increase in per capita income in the 1960s, the lower half of the population saw an increase of only 7.5%. But to use facts to argue against the existence of industrial development by comparing it with the internal mass markets of today's West is absurd. The industrialization of Britain was not based on internal mass consumption. On the contrary, it was more dependent on a single leading export sector, the textile industry, whose markets were for the most part not only outside of Britain, but outside of Europe. The industrial revolution was systemically linked to the mass poverty of a growing semi-employed proletariat.

The general pattern to be found in industrializing areas of the Third World is one that combines an almost exclusive export orientation with mass underconsumption. The latter is not a sign of weakness, but the basis for the attraction of capital. The Soviet Union and Eastern Europe, while maintaining significantly higher standards of social security, have a similarly low level of internal consumption. In both cases, low consumption is equivalent to cheaper costs of production, something which has proved to be an important competitive advantage in the world market, both for the sale of goods and the attraction of capital.

The increasing industrialization of the Third World, via multinational production or other forms of capital export does not imply a simple shift in center. On the contrary, the movement is contradictory in its essence, and tends towards a general crisis of overproduction on a world scale. The process can be summarized as follows:

(a) A general contraction in the size of the center's export market is effected by the earliest type of capital export which takes the form of import substitution industries. This begins with simple consumption goods such as cloth, shoes, soap, cooking oils, etc. and advances to more sophisticated goods.

(b) The differentiation of costs of production in the world market is the basis for the general increase of multinational production. High profits and rates of investment in low-cost zones results in a combined increase of multinational and decrease in national production for the center. The former increase is greater than the latter decrease, of course, given the advantages of low-cost production. As a result, there is a rapid increase in the number of producing areas and total products on the market. But, since the basis of this expansion is low wages, it remains largely dependent upon the Western market. But the latter is either stagnating or contracting due to the lack of investment and industrial decline in significant sectors. The reality of this situation is only forestalled by the generation of great amounts of credit and fictitious capital which add fuel to the fire in the long run.

(c) Increasing production in the periphery (some members of which are now classified as semi-peripheral) and a stagnating Western market, lead to even more competition, especially in the West which is at the greatest disadvantage. This is abetted by growing tendencies in the Third World for the emergence of new market connections, a further contraction of the center's export possibilities. The result is a further increase in the export of industrial capital and an amplification of the whole contradictory process.

Thus, the acceleration of multinational production, of the decentralization of production in general, accelerates the growing contradiction between total supply and total buying power. Underconsumption, the basis of lower costs, increases the competitiveness of the individual firm, but it undermines the expansion of the market. An eventual crisis of the Western economy, then, will drag its periphery along with it.

NOTE ON THE OIL CRISIS

In terms of the perspective presented here, the oil crisis does not appear as a mere random event that suddenly changed the conditions of operation of the world economy. Rather, it is one of the essential discontinuities or "catastrophes" in the continuous process of decentralization of capital accumulation. First, the initial price rises on crude oil began before the activities of OPEC in 1973 and it is known that the big oil multinationals had a major rôle in subsequent developments. However, it is also clear that there has been a gradual shift of control away from the oil companies who owned 90% of the Middle East's production at the start and now own only 20%. The emergent politicoeconomic power of OPEC is itself an indication of the loss of control by the central powers over their economic conditions of reproduction (Crotty & Boddy 1975, p. 86):

> "Even in the case of the oil prices, the declining world power of the United States has played a role. As long as this country enjoyed a virtual monopoly on economic, political and military power, it could depend on a supply of cheap raw materials. Because of our weakened international position, however, it was impossible to prevent the oil-producing countries from quadrupling the price of crude oil in the fall of 1973."

The rising cost of energy (as well as other raw materials, also increasingly controlled by Third World alliances) has certainly amplified the world crisis, with Europe and Japan being the worst hit. Enormous national debts have appeared in the West (note, though, that the USA already had such a debt before the oil crisis). Trade balances have been strained to the limits. Bankruptcies have multiplied. Financial markets have become increasingly unstable, and we have been dangerously close to crisis/collapse several times (*Business Week* December 12, 1974). This has all been accompanied by an equivalent accumulation of capital in OPEC countries and in some cases to a rapid industrialization. It has also speeded up the realignment of political power and influence (e.g. in the UN) to the detriment of the West. The oil crisis and the rise of the Middle East as a semi-periphery with claims to central status is an expression of the decline of the western-based world economy with all the dislocations that it implies, as well as the potentiality for new centers of world accumulation.

THE EAST BLOCK AND THE FUTURE OF THE WORLD ECONOMY

While the Middle East does not seem a likely candidate for the shift in world accumulation, and while the Eastern Asian industrial development also appears fatally dependent on Japan and the West for markets and capital, the Soviet/Eastern European area does, I think, appear to have possibilities for assuming hegemonic status after the West. Structurally, the East Block is not dependent on the West to the same extent as the present Third World. While they do export raw materials and import industrial manufactures in their relation to the West, they also have their own periphery which they have removed from Western control and which has been expanding since the end of World War II. There is, further, a developed trade in manufacturing and raw materials within the Block itself that has remained relatively isolated from the Western economic network (except, of course, Yugoslavia). The low cost of labor, the disciplined workforce, the lack of speculation and fictitious capital in a state-controlled structure of accumulation, all makes for highly competitive production. In spite of technological problems in certain crucial areas and bureaucratic bottlenecks, the real profit on "capital" is high. Centralized state accumulation is an efficient contender in the world market.

It is often assumed that the East Block is essentially a periphery of the West and not an interesting economic challenge to its dominance. In support of this, it is pointed out that the East Block is dependent on the West for almost all of its advanced technology. On the surface, this might appear similar to the recent relation between the West and industrializing areas of the Third World, but on closer examination there are important differences. The capital import to the East Block is essentially a question of building heavy industry and not merely a decentralization of production for western mass consumption. Entire factories are imported in connection with activities such as the industrialization of Siberia. The industrial investments reach very large proportions even by Western standards. Thus, a French–Soviet joint venture in aluminium production "will be the largest aluminium complex in the world, to cost $1,700 m., with an annual production capacity of 500,000 tons" (Wilczynski 1976, p. 91). And a petrochemical venture with Occidental Petroleum, "involving investment of $20,000 m., is the biggest non-intergovernmental deal concluded in history" (Wilczynski 1976, p. 94). While the Eastern Block export of manufacture goods to the West was only 42% of the total as compared with 72% export in the opposite direction in 1973 (Wilczynski 1976, p. 99), they are as, or more, advanced in several important branches of industry, "particularly in metal-working machinery, metallurgical equipment, electric generators...oil drilling gear, communications equipment, welding apparatus, shipbuilding, certain types of aircraft and helicopters and nuclear equipment and fuels. These countries have become exporters of sophisticated items not only to less-developed areas but also to the industrialized West" (Wilczynski 1976, p. 61).

It is, of course, true that the East Block is tremendously indebted to the West. It is also true that the debts may never be payed off (who would collect them?). What we have here is a growing industrial power, which is also, perhaps, the world's strongest military power, its number one weapon exporter and the only sector of the world system that is expanding in both the political and economic sense. The fact that they import a lot of industrial capital may be an indication of their rise to hegemony rather than their dependency.

Conclusion

We have argued in the very limited space of this chapter, that there are fundamental similarities between processes involved in today's world crisis and those of previous declines of civilizations. In order to be able to think about the possibilities of intervention in a period of crisis, it is necessary to understand the structure and dynamics of the system in which it occurs. It is on this basis that we have criticized traditional econometric futurology for its lack of theory and historical materialism (as well as macroeconomics in general) for its misunderstanding of the fluid and shifting nature of world accumulation over time. A precise model of the system would, of course, be needed if one were to try to come to grips with phenomena as apparently distant from one another as Third World industrialization and the increasing social malaise, drug addiction, alcoholism and criminality in the West. We can do no more than suggest some of the characters of a longer-term research project. If, however, the present capitalist world system is no more than a subset or variant of a more general global system, a larger and more technologically explosive one, then our ultimate strategy must be elaborated with respect to the whole history of civilization on earth and not merely to the present. What has to be changed is the entire catastrophe-generating nature of human "civilized" systems. To avoid this ultimate problem is to run the perhaps terminal risk of repeating ourselves just one more fatal time.

Explanatory note

This article is a summary of a longer work (Ekholm 1977) written for the Swedish project on the generation of risk in a social perspective. As such, it is based on statistical material gathered not later than 1976. The only more recent items added in the English translation are bibliographic references that are relevant to the general arguments of the article.

References

Adám, G. 1975. Multinational corporations and world-wide sourcing. In *International firms and modern imperialism*, H. Radice (ed.). Harmondsworth: Penguin.

Amin, S. 1974. *Den globala kapitalackumulationen*. Uddevalla: Zenit, Rabén & Sjogren.

Annerstedt, J. and R. Gustavsson 1976. Mot en ny internationell ekonomisk arbetsfördelning? In *Om kapitalets internationalisering*, K. Lindkvist (ed.). Nordiska Sommaruniversitetets skriftserie nr 10, Lund.

Barel, Y. 1969. *La reproduction sociale*. Paris: Anthropos.

Barnet, R. J. and R. Miller 1975. The negative effects of multinational corporations. In *The economic crises reader*, D. Mermelstein (ed.). New York: Vintage Books.

Brandel, F. 1973. *The Mediterranean and the Mediteranean world in the age of Philip II, Vol. 2*. New York: Harper & Row.

Brandel, F. 1977. *Afterthoughts on material civilization and capitalism*. Baltimore: Johns Hopkins University Press.

Busch, K. 1974. *Die Multinationalen Konzerne*. Zur Analyse der Weltmarktbewegung des Kapitals. Frankfurt: Suhrkamp.

Crotty, J. and R. Boddy 1975. Who will plan the planned economy? In *The economic crises reader*, D. Mermelstein (ed.). New York: Vintage Books.

Dencik, L. and P. Dencik 1976. Samhallsutveckling och statlig planering under senkapitalismen. In *Planeringens granser*, Björkman, Dencik, Sandberg, Svensson & Wangborg (eds). Lund: Forum.

Ekholm, K. 1976. Om Studiet av det Globala Systemets Dynamik. *Antropol. Stud.* **20.**
Ekholm, K. 1977. Om studiet av risker i samhället och av hur risker kan avvärjas. Projektet Riskgenerering och riskbedomning i ett samhälleligt perspektiv. Samarbetskommittén for långsiktsmotiverad forskning.
Ekholm, K. 1980. On the limitations of civilization: the structure and dynamics of global systems. *Dialec. Anthropol.* **5.**
Ekholm, K. and K. Friedman 1979. "Capital" imperialism and exploitation in ancient world systems. In *Power and propaganda: a symposium on ancient empires*, Larsen (ed.). Copenhagen.
Ekholm, K. and K. Friedman 1980. Towards a global anthropology. In *History and underdevelopment*, Blussé, Wesseling and Winius (eds). Leyden: Nijheff.

Frank, A. G. 1978. *World accumulation, 1492–1789.* New York: Macmillan.
Friedman, J. 1976. Marxist theory and systems of total reproduction. *Critique Anthropol.* **7.**
Friedman, J. 1978. Crises in theory and transformations of the world economy. *Review* **II,** 2.
Fröbel, F., J. Heinrichs and O. Kreye 1977. *Die neue internationale arbeitsteilung.* Hamburg: Rowolt.

Gamble, A. and P. Walton 1976. *Capitalism in crisis.* London: The Macmillan Press.

Kohl, P. 1978. The balance of trade in Southwestern Asia in the mid-third millenium BC. *Curr. Anthropol.* **19,** 3.

LO-Kongressen 1976. *Fackföreningsrörelsen och de multinationella företagen*: rapport till LO-Kongressen 1976. Lund: Bokförlaget Prisma.
Lombard, M. 1975. *The golden age of Islam.* Amsterdam: North Holland.

Magdoff, H. 1974. Moderna drag i imperialismen. In *Utvecklingsekonomi I: underutvecklingens mekanismer*, M. Lundahl and B. Södersten (eds). Malmö: Aldus.

Norgren, M. and C. Norgren 1970. *Svensk industri: Struktur och omvandling.* Ystad: Rabén & Sjögren.

Palloix, C. 1975. *L'Économie mondiale capitaliste et les firmes multinationales.* Paris: Maspero.

Roberts, D. 1975. The ripening conditions for world-wide depression. In *The economic crises reader*, D. Mermelstein (ed.). New York: Vintage Books.
Rowthorn, R. 1971. *International big business 1957–67.* London: Cambridge.

Schoeller, W. 1976. *Weltmarkt und Reproduktion des Kapitals.* Frankfurt: E.V.A.
SOU 1975. *Internationella koncerner i industriländer: samhällsekonomiska aspekter – betänkande av koncentrationsutredningen.* SOU 1975: 50. Liber Göteborg.

US Tariff Commission 1973. *Implications of multinational firms for world trade and investment and for US trade and labor.* Report to the Committee on Finance of the US Senate. Washington: US Government Printing Office.

Walbank, F. W. 1969. *The awful revolution.* Liverpool: Liverpool University Press.
Wallerstein, I. 1974. *The modern world system, vol. I.* New York: Academic Press.
Wallerstein, I. 1980. *The modern world system, vol. II.* New York: Academic Press.
Warren, B. 1973. Imperialism and capitalist industrialization. *New Left Review* **81.**
Wilczynski, J. 1976. *The multinationals and East–West relations.* London: Macmillan.

6 *Psychological aspects of values and risks*

ANNA-CHRISTINA BLOMKVIST

Introduction

Much of human behavior may be viewed as a succession of choices where the choice creates new alternatives. This makes evaluation a continuous process. Generally we evaluate and choose without noticing, but sometimes the feelings of uncertainty about what really is the best choice turn out to be more insistent. We then have to scrutinize goals and values.

This chapter deals with psychological views of values; values ordering alternatives on a scale from good to bad and also forming our goals and thus guiding our behavior. The values are partly discussed here in the context of risk. The standpoint toward risk taken is that risk is the possible loss of something of value, and anticipated perhaps-cost or a perhaps-loss of benefit. What one does not value, one cannot risk.

Perceived risk generally causes avoidance, but all risks are not perceived. If something that will be needed later on is not valued today, nobody will care whether we are destroying it now, so parallel to avoidance of risk there is an urge for knowledge about what values there are, or should be. It is therefore essential to know about values and how values are learned, how they change and how they relate to needs and social harmony, if the diversities of the risk debate are to be understood and risk avoidance effective.

Presentation of concepts

The presentation of value and concepts relevant to its context in this section is but one possible explication. This is because value-relevant concepts are usually not satisfactorily defined, neither in the social sciences nor in philosophy. Needs, desires, values, order of values, attributes, motives, morals, goals, preferences and perspectives will be briefly described here according to the author's choice of their meaning.

Consider needs first. There are individual needs, just as there are individual desires and values, but the three words are not interchangeable. Needs are best described as objectively definable conditions necessary for the physical survival of the organism. Needs are not always recognized, and the conditions needed are not always valued.

Desires, on the other hand, or wishes, wants and longings, are highly individual and often private. They reflect psychological states which are related to learned or innate requirements of the organism. Desires result from inclinations looking for a focal point. Uneasiness developing into a wish for exercise or sedatives, hunger forming into a desire for a piece of bread and butter, or loneliness leading to longing for company, are all desires reflecting states of the organism.

Values, thirdly, are more or less complex judgments about the benefit or disadvantage of something to us, guiding us to approach or withdraw. The judgments might be momentary and cursory, as values brought to mind in a discussion of whose turn it is to make the coffee. The values used in such a situation might be forgotten when the arguing is over. When we choose friends or a job – or the number of nuclear power plants – we want to know about features of more permanent value to us. It seems natural to assume that a cursory inference is more susceptible to influence from acute desires than an elaborate judgment, and that values thus have rather different generalities dependent upon the situation and one's scope of judgment.

Described and differentiated in this way, needs, desires and values order themselves according to degrees of freedom. Needs are absolute, desires can be molded, and values are rather arbitrary. All three concepts also range from a concrete or physical level to a more abstract or cognitive one.

It must be possible to order values in hierarchies so we can find out what is best and work toward single goals. The ordering of values is sometimes called order of preference, but order of preference might as well be an ordering of strength of desires. The societal ordering of values is mirrored by morals, and in more limited situations by norms. Morals and norms do not explicitly state the values they emphasize, but specify the appropriate behavior which favors the values according to the approved order. A moral rule stating that you shall not steal, preserves the value of private property, but does not say so outright; it only prescribes how to behave.

If one aims at an object but stops to evaluate it more carefully, there usually turn out to be several attributes of the object, such as firmness, tint, capacity and sentimental values, which are then evaluated and joined to form a result-ant (composite) value. Finding all relevant attributes is a problem in itself, and today decision aids put great emphasis on finding the relevant attributes of the goals to choose amongst.

A cautious evaluation also has to take the perspective into account. The perspective might be the individual's own or that of his family and colleagues, or the nation. There is also a time perspective, discussed in detail by Björkman (Ch. 2). In particular, evaluations of social programs demand careful choice of time perspective, and such a choice should be classified as a political position. Evaluations from a nationwide perspective often also require a long-term perspective. Individual perspectives are generally, though not always, short-term ones.

Value is often identified with human or social value. When value was described above as a more or less complex judgment of only the advantages and disadvantages of a course of action, the concept of value was made broader than is generally the case. This may be compensated for by the concept of perspective. Dependent on the degree to which the value judgments consider the social context, there are social perspectives and nonsocial perspectives; the former implying what is usually called moral, human, or social values.

When we take different social perspectives in different social situations, we are said to take on rôles that are reflected in formal – or normative – patterns of social behavior, such as the rôle of the teacher, customer, or post office clerk. When acting from these different perspectives, we rely on different orders of values. What risks to consider is a decision that is also dependent on what perspective or what rôle was taken and what attributes were attended to.

The following two sections discuss functions of values and some relations between the concepts mentioned. This is to shed light not only on values, but also on values as determinants of personalities and societies.

The functions of the individual's values and moral development

Schopenhauer stressed that the intellect has evolved not to analyze and understand the environment, but to orient us in it. The same consequence, as to the relation between the intellect and the environment, can be drawn from pragmatism. According to pragmatism the most advantageous insight about the world, from the individual's point of view, is given the same status as the finding of truth by earlier philosophers. What is more advantageous to our intellect than the knowledge that something is to our benefit or disadvantage?

The presumption that the capacity of the intellect is adjusted toward orientation rather than analysis gets some support from a recent article by Zajonc (1980). In a review in favor of the hypothesis of affective reaction being prior to cognitive analysis of stimuli, Zajonc described fairly immediate evaluations of presented stimuli. He noted that liking judgments or aesthetic judgments were prior even to recognition. Experts on brain functions seem to be tending to the same point of view (Kinsbourne 1981).

Also in line with the thoughts presented above is Kelvin's (1969) position. He argued that one cannot cope with the environment if it is not reasonably orderly and predictable, and that the main way to keep the environment (seemingly) orderly is through values by which things are judged to be more or less for and against us. Evaluation is thus seen as a fundamental process, and Kelvin stressed the necessity of evaluation so much that he called animals' instincts genetic programs that order values for the animals.

A characterization of values as guidelines for choices can be defended in quite different ways, too. Rescher (1969) pointed to the custom of the behavioral sciences of construing values as that which influences individuals or groups when they choose among possible acts or obtainable goals. He himself called the value "a slogan" and seemed to put the emphasis on the justification of chosen acts. Investigations on Festinger's (1957) theory of cognitive dissonance have also drawn attention to unresolved value conflicts which exist after the decision is made.

Human values are not ordered by instincts and most of the ordering of our values is probably learned and taught by rules, i.e. morals and norms. The ability to understand the arbitrariness of the value system is not necessary for the acquisition of behavior supporting the system reasonably well. The "insight" of the arbitrariness of values may, of course, even be detrimental to their acquisition and application. It has also been suggested that arbitrariness could be misunderstood to imply that there are no moral limitations on action.

The gradual assimilation of the implicitly taught values, the "moral development", is a subject for research in psychology. The development is described as passing different stages parallel to mental growth and the growing knowledge about the self as an object. Classification into stages refers to manner of argumentation, and not to outcome of decisions. In their most elaborated stage, morals are conceived by the individual as principles abstract and flexible enough to suit all imaginable situations but only a minority is assumed to reach that particular developmental level.

Peck and Havighurst (1960) named five stages of moral development or types: amoral, expedient, conforming, irrational-conscientious (starting to feel personal guilt, but not yet aware of the man-made quality of values), and the rational-altruistic type. The sequence is similar to Kohlberg's stages illustrated in Fig. 6.1.

Investigations on what portions of a population reach each stage of moral development have found cultural differences as well as sex differences. More men in the industrial states master moral reasoning on a principal level than do women or people elsewhere (e.g. Haan 1977). It has also been shown that moral reasoning may decline after school is finished. Kohlberg (cited by Muson 1979) recently denied to have claimed that the stages were reached once and for all, and also seemed hesitant to regard the order of stages as reflecting an order of development. One cause for deficits of consistency or reliability of measurement may be that moral reasoning applies to such a wide range of situations. Attempts to find a scale of moral levels are likely to fail because they assume too much consistency and invariance. In particular, it may be that one has to adjust one's level of reasoning to that of the people around.

At higher stages of moral reasoning, there is greater resistance to the pressure to conform. Moral thought is thus more autonomous at higher stages, but not moral action (Blasi 1980, Dreman 1976). The evidence from experiments is also clearly in favor of the hypothesis that individuals at higher moral levels tend to be more honest and more altruistic in their reasoning.

In a moral debate the main differences between standpoints probably originate from differences of perspective, and the possibility to make oneself heard might be a matter of ability to adjust the perspective and level of reasoning. To manage argumentation on a high moral level promotes confidence, we believe, and the more abstract the argumentation one accomplishes, the easier it should be to seem to be consequential and thus also autonomous. On the other hand, such an accomplishment by no means guarantees that the arguments are accepted, even if it does, for the moment, silence less verbally skilful opponents.

The suggestion of moral development as parallel to the knowledge of the self implies a further function of the individuals' values. A preference for X not only means that X is better, but that the individual knowingly or unknowingly chooses his or her own self: to choose X is to choose the rôle of the individual who chooses X. The importance of such rôle-taking consequences of stating a preference probably varies considerably, depending on the type of choice objects under consideration. Further, there is a *demand* for individual consistency. Tversky (1969) noted in a study on choice that the will to be consistent was strong enough to make subjects change preference judgments.

Figure 6.1 Kohlberg (cited in Brown & Herrnstein 1975) suggested six stages of morality organized in three levels of two stages each: preconventional level (obedience orientation stage), conventional level (approval orientation stage and law and order orientation stage) and postconventional, autonomous level (social contract orientation stage and universal ethical principle orientation stage). His stages are exemplified by dilemmas concerning more serious matters than mintcakes, but the developmental change in cognitive structuring resembles the development illustrated above, in our opinion.

People usually adjust their views of beliefs and values so as to de-emphasize inconsistencies (Sjöberg 1982, Sjöberg & Biel 1983). Politicians seem often to be sensitive to accusations of inconsistency, particularly of the simple type that a change of mind has been made over time. It is, apparently, implicitly held that it is somehow a sign of weakness or dishonesty to change one's mind about anything.

The function of values in society

The most unpredictable figure a human being can face is another human being. As we cannot cope well with a capricious world but have to make our environment reasonably orderly and predictable, and values are a primary instrument for promoting social order, social coping is probably more determined by value systems than any other coping. For the coping to work out, social values also have to establish mutual trust.

Social values are communicable, for example, as "slogans", dictates or rules. They are also debatable, whereas needs are not. If somebody needs water, it will not help to try to talk him out of it. No amount of discussion will change the need. But values can be discussed, and social values have to be. In the context of a community, values prescribe the goals of the community and the relations between its members, and have to be agreed upon. It is one of the tasks for the social order embracing many individuals to find means to unify values from different perspectives. The social sciences have mainly described how (unifying) values are learned through social interaction, and how values unify groups and also separate them from each other.

Normative analyses of values have led to various approaches for aggregating values over individuals. Aggregation of values demands that values be measurable at least at the level of rank order measurement. Aggregation, however, is not always the solution to which values are best or most realistic, or even to which values are most wanted in a community, though the values resulting from an aggregation should mirror the most widespread individual preferences. They might not be the most wanted in a community since values are not always reciprocal ("mutual"). If so, one does not want others to prefer the same value order for their own sake as one does for oneself: one might not risk one's hands or eyes to save another person's life, but wishes that others take such risks to save one's own life. One might think it better to save one's own fortune abroad than to share devaluation loss with the rest of the fellow citizens. Such choices are not accepted by society as a whole; even if everybody preferred the egoistic choices just mentioned, they might also strongly agree that such choices should not be permitted by law. The same individual then has made different orderings of values when taking two different perspectives. Sometimes the perspective of a society as a whole has to be taken into account to favor society, and sometimes private perspectives have to be favored to stimulate individual development.

By communicating values to each other, people in a society try to make desires and values converge. Such convergence is necessary for values to have rewarding power (Brown & Herrnstein 1975), otherwise conflicts are likely. For the maintenance of life and societies, desires and values also have to be realistic in the sense that they should promote need fulfillment (see Fig. 6.2). But the environment changes, and the means for satisfying needs have to change too. Values are the tool for molding of desires, and social values should, to work well, modify desires in accordance with new conditions without splitting up the private and the social perspectives or impairing trust.

In the close social context, a value judgment immediately affects a judged person or someone sharing a judged thing with the judge, and thus also may elicit countereffects. One might say that value judgments in such cases are

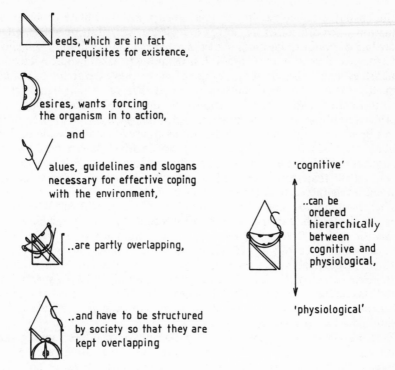

Figure 6.2 A schematic representation of relations between needs, desires and values.

performative utterances, they are more than slogans or contributions to a debate; they are like acts. This is one dynamic property of values that awakens many perspectives on the telling of values (also to canvassers), and thus to the values told. It may be urgent to display some values and to hide others, and it may be threatening to reveal one's opinion about something one has not decided on yet. In a social context, values are tactical, although when they reflect virtues in a community such as honesty (to be described next) they obstruct tactics.

The contents of values

It was said in the beginning of the section presenting concepts that the concepts are usually not satisfactorily defined. The psychological literature has mainly been concerned with phenomena that are believed to be effects of values, such as attitudes or public opinion fluctuations, and has also dealt with moral reasoning and development, choice strategies and methodology. When introducing such studies, the emphasis has been on operation of the concepts and actual contents. However, various framings of objectively defined options alter the preferences among options (Tversky & Kahneman 1981). The framings are about as meaningful to the judgers as the hypothetical outcomes constructed by the researchers. Also, there is considerable empirical evidence on the cognitive difficulties judges face when trying to isolate problems for evaluation, such difficulties as lack of knowledge, sensed incoherence, effects of labeling of options, questioning of the relevance, misattribution and choice of perspective (Fischhoff *et al.* 1980). It is tempting to ask if people hold values (establish evaluative beliefs about things) or merely have the ability to evaluate momently for acts. A reasonable suspicion is that value judgments seldom apply to isolated matters but to imagined or anticipated situations and rôles, and thus a doubt arises on the possibility of finding objective ways to distinguish stimuli for evaluation. When the situations are obvious, unequivocal and familiar, the evaluative beliefs, of course, are relatively well established and acts are habitual. What is problematic about contents of values is how to apply values, rather than what we hold in esteem "in theory." On some very common levels there are common contents of values.

What, then, are the most general "shoulds" of the individual? What do we regard as virtue? The cardinal virtues, axioms thought to form the basis of all morals, in ancient Greece and Rome were the "human virtues" of wisdom, courage, temperance and justice. Catholicism traditionally gives prominence to three theological virtues; faith, hope and charity, and, in addition, Catholicism adopted the four human virtues. Catholicism also specifies the mortal sins as the opposites of good values. It should be noted that religions and ideologies *order* values; they dictate what to hold in particularly high esteem and what to sacrifice.

Frankena (1963) stated that several philosophers of ethics, among them Schopenhauer, took generosity and justice for cardinal virtues, as did Frankena. Such virtues should not be carried out in appearance only. It is implicit that the generous adult has the best wishes for the recipient (Krebs 1970). Furthermore, according to Frankena (1963), adult morality is supposed to be concerned not with superficial rules but with the cultivation of dispositions or traits. Thus, the virtue of "honesty" or "trustworthiness" is understood as a prerequisite for a morality in accordance with the virtues. Frankena also favored a second-order virtue; the disposition of thinking clearly.

Hedonistic ideas or pleasure principles have often been claimed to form fundamental values from which other values can be deduced. Among less carnal ideas about such uttermost principles are to be found Aristotle's idea of superior performance, Augustine's and Aquinas' communication with God, Spinoza's knowledge, Bradley's self-realization and Nietsche's power. Composite goals commonly mentioned in philosophy, giving no priority to any single element, include pleasure together with knowledge, esthetic experiences, truth, virtuousness, harmony, love, friendship, freedom and self-fulfillment. Composite goal descriptions are also most common among contemporary psychologists and they get even more complex by the addition of new goals such as curiosity and change.

On a less individual and more social level, three basic moral principles should be mentioned: *the principle of justice* (individuals comparable on morally relevant dimensions should be treated alike), *the principle of utility* (one should act to create the greatest possible advantage of good over evil), and *the principle of freedom* (one should not infringe upon or interfere with the freedom of others) (see e.g. Hermerén 1973).

The debate on justice is generally conducted in terms of egalitarianism. The most pronounced antagonisms between Swedish groups feeling unequal are, according to Allardt (1975), those between: (a) capital owners and workers, (b) rich and poor, and (c) politicians and the people. Nordenstam (1972) claimed that there had been no equalization in Sweden since 1945 on any single dimension such as political power, capital, income, education, and housing standards, compared with the revolving equalization in Sweden between World Wars I and II. Any perceived equalization might well have been a fallacy brought forth by the increase in general income.

Equality between the sexes is an everlasting problem aggravated by the fact that the sexes are partly defined through the unfair sex rôles. It is appropriate for women to be unpretentious, impotent and dependent, and appropriate for men to make their way. Other lasting problems are the difficulties in comparing different kinds of crimes. The maximum penalties for murder or thefts are much higher than for economical crimes in Sweden, and probably in most other countries too. But economic crimes may be rather extensive and can have severe consequences for those defrauded. Over the past years, the budget proposals from the Swedish Ministry of Justice have emphasized measures against fraud since these crimes undermine trust of enterprises and financial authorities, so a change of values may be on the way.

The utility principle implies striving for the best; good is not good enough. Further, the value of action is evaluated according to its consequences. Good will and honesty come second in applied utilitarianism. Utilitarianism promotes the greatest possible balance of good over evil, however it is distributed among people. Justice and freedom refer to the distribution of goods.

Decisions concern the future. We have to plant so-and-so many trees now so there will be a forest in the year 2015. When will a mine opened now start to pay its way, how long will it be profitable and how much has to be set aside every year to pay for restoring nature afterwards? For how long should containers for nuclear waste be planned to last? The first questions could be answered on the basis of previous experience. The last cannot be answered nearly as well, but is an example of how a time perspective of utility sometimes has to be chosen without any knowledge of the best length of time, especially as we cannot know the opinion of the generations to come.

Some goods are incompatible, i.e. they cannot be obtained simultaneously. Employment versus conservation, and maintenance of the existing public sector versus reduction of progressive income taxes, are just two examples of current interest. Controversies between central and local authorities or local populations concerning where to deposit radioactive waste, where to build plants for chemical destruction, and dams for water power, reflect attempts to fulfill utilitarian goals, but with insufficiently thought-out perspectives. Who are the beneficiaries and who should bear the costs? How should conflicts be resolved?

The principle of freedom introduces even more controversies between beneficiaries. Subjects of discussion are family integrity versus child and/or wife beating, individual integrity versus expansion of stored data files, and the fact that individual freedom to self-destruction limits the individual freedom later on. Freedom to choose to drink alcohol, smoke, vote for an undemocratic party, gamble with unlimited stakes, etc. generates many risks.

It is a common standpoint that the individual gains freedom if those limiting choices are restricted. Today society is taking an increasingly negative attitude towards drug abuse after a period of "liberal" leniency.

Earlier subjects in the discussion of freedom have been possibilities of choosing one's education, job, housing, old-age pension insurance, etc. In the late 1950s, it was argued that as some people were more easily tempted to waste money than others, pension contributions ought to be obligatory.

Integrity is emphasized in the discussion of freedom today, probably partly because of the increase in the business of information. A Swedish evening paper (*Aftonbladet*, December 27 1980) wrote that there were 32 000 official registers of people in Sweden. (Everybody has the legal right to see his or her entries, but 32 000 letters with that inquiry would cost about $16 000.) Businesses buy excerpts with names and addresses of, say, all mothers earning at least $12 000 a year with a child younger than two years of age, or of every owner of a car more than seven years old. Most debate, though, concerns combinations of registers, since such information is wanted by authorities to track down dishonest citizens.

It should be noted that the three value principles, the principle of equality, the principle of utility and the principle of freedom do not imply the presence of each other. The concepts are independent. Those who hold freedom to be the highest principle do not have to do so because it would be advantageous to utility or justice. They may choose freedom first. Neither is equality justified by utility. Those who hold equality to be the prime value, do so because equality means more to them than the maximization of goods. And, as already stated above, utilitarianism promotes utility, regardless of its distribution.

Research on risk perception and comparison of risks has tried to identify underlying dimensions of evaluation, with the aim to understand and predict risk judgments (e.g. Fischhoff *et al.* 1978, Golant & Burton 1969, Otway & Fishbein 1976, Slovic *et al.* 1979, Starr 1969, Swaton *et al.* 1976). Risk dimensions often attended to – either examined or causing the research – are listed below with the unwanted rôle underlined:

voluntary	— involuntary exposure
not fatal	— fatal
familiar	— unfamiliar
common	— dreadful
natural	— man-made hazard
knowingly	— unknowingly exposed
known	— unknown to science
controlled by skill	— uncontrollable
active	— passive victim
simple	— advanced technology
old	— new

Some of the terms overlap, such as new, unfamiliar and advanced technology. Advanced technology further seemed to be uncontrollable, man-made and causing damage to passive victims.

As this kind of research, and thus the kind of structure, is fairly modern, it is hard to judge its generality. It does pertain to the Western culture of today, but maybe also to yesterday's mankind. It can be seen in comparison with the social and human values just described that the dimensions do not describe values, except for the implicitly depressed "freedom" (neither negative values), but conditions that will amplify values. For instance, if a bad thing is introduced under circumstances beyond one's control, it appears even worse.

Value changes

The three value principles, justice, utility and freedom were selected because they have been relatively stable and are recognized as societal good values, as the first-mentioned cardinal virtues or recognized good human values. Threats to these values are grave risks, especially the human values themselves but they are not often explicitly debated. The threats to them are implicit in reports and in questions about whom is to blame for accidents or offenses. They are simply taken for granted. It is values undergoing change that are explicitly debated.

Quality of life inquiries probably bring forth changing, or not yet established, debatable social values, but also more specific values of little general interest. If people are asked about their private opinion and do not have to defend it in socially appropriate terms, they are free to mention values that are quite private, or values they have recently learned about in the media or in peer groups. In a Swedish study on quality-of-life attributes, Edvardsson and Vegelius (1976) got answers such as (the negatively valued instances of) over-production of luxuries, lung cancer, noise, commuting time, radioactivity, and changes in the flora, the fauna and the atmosphere. The instances seem to belong to new risks of advanced technology, and the values that are changing are probably the downgraded utility of technology, and the upgraded utility of health. On subjective dimensions, people wanted to be free from risk and anxiety, and wanted equality, self-fulfillment and friendship. These examples resemble more stable values. Expressions of disgust at maltreatment of animals in experiments and at zoos and chicken farms were also seen. Disgust at cruelty toward animals has been very pronounced in other studies (Cason 1930, Gallup 1976). ("Animal welfare" does not appear among established virtues, probably because it does not go along with Christian values, so one feels disgust rather than indignation at maltreatment.) Another study of quality of life names health and longevity, along with comfort, work, love, novelty, freedom of choice, freedom from worries and risk taking (Holmberg 1971); again not very new subjective values.

Rescher (1969) has noted the upward permutation of values markedly threatened or badly needed. The permutation of values when society is under some kind of change or "stress" is essential to note for anybody who is interested in understanding the risk controversy. Causes for the permutations are to be found either in anticipated changes or, more probably, at least in the present author's opinion, in environmental changes that have already occurred. First the financial strength of advanced technology was distrusted (it promised too much?), then criticism of that technology started; criticism that was equally well-founded all the time. First there was less need for the family as a financial unit, then the liberation of women was inevitable. First, parents received pension benefits and were less dependent on their offspring, then they could be heard saying: "We do not care whether our son wants to be a nobody if only it makes him happy." New values are like prognoses; they are extrapolations of a sensed change.

In these days of economic stagnation, sensitive intellectuals turn inwards to explore new areas and find new possibilities for individual growth and freedom. Maybe religiousness will increase; there is some influx of exotic confessions in Sweden and some people even turn to the occult.

It was stated earlier that people differ in their level of moral reasoning. Some people are more autonomous, more aware of the arbitrariness of values, so they are more inclined toward moral reasoning leading to or defending new values, and they can choose. Do value changes demand either intellectual advocates or affiliation with groups where members support each other? New values lie smoldering for a long time till the flames burst forth in igniting slogans. An exception seems to be status values connected with new possible activities. Despite a threatening controversy between automation and employment, micro-electronics (such as tools for calculation and for measurement of size and temperature) seems to have status value among workers and, despite criticism of advanced technology, video equipment and other electronic entertainment aids in the home seem to have status value, especially among younger people.

Value-probability interaction

Values are dependent on frequency, and so on probability or relevance. From where does a rarity get its value as a collector's item? Not only from the extraordinarily excellent handicraft but also from a once wrongly adjusted printing press for stamps or bank notes. The assumption of independence of values and probabilities often made in studies on value measurements and decision aids has to be taken cautiously.

Some vital event that is not certain to happen occupies us with feelings of uncertainty or excitement. Some people avoid uncertainty, and others want to gamble. The interest in lotteries probably shows that uncertainty has a value; it is exciting. But to feel very dependent (e.g. on a loved person) may become unpleasant through uncertainty of reciprocation. Optimism, a tendency to expect the best possible outcome or a disposition to hope for the best, also points to interaction between probability and value, but in the other direction; a value-influenced probability estimate.

Tversky and Kahneman (1973) showed that incidents that were specially attended to received overestimated frequency judgments. It is also suggested that we pay more attention to news the more relevant it is to our own situation and cultural group (Prakke, cited in Hadenius & Weibull 1970). The frequency of threats to us then depends on how we characterize our own group. To identify with a broad category should then be more terrifying; lots of awful things could happen to us. Skilled people are better off. They are unique and almost nothing happens to them. Car drivers believe themselves to be skilled people. Between 70 and 90 percent of car drivers in a sample believed themselves to be better than the median driver in their group (Näätänen &

Summala 1975, Svenson 1981). It was first shown by Cohen (1960) that belief
in skill has a significant effect on risk judgment.

Next to frequency of events, their variance seems to play an essential part
in our perception of value, most notably in the context of loss of value, i.e.
risks. The sun goes down and the evening appears dark and cold. But that is
not disastrous. Tide, winter and ageing come, and they are generally not
perceived as being catastrophes. Their frequency is too regular and they come
too often. Some people even get adapted to typhoons and floods when these
recur yearly (Velimirovic 1975).

The kind of disasters called catastrophes are mostly sudden and widespread
and it is implicit in the concept of catastrophe that the victims cannot handle
the situation. High variance then contributes to the catastrophe. Accidents
with high variance are accidents involving passenger trains and aeroplanes,
ferry boats, volcanic eruptions, earthquakes, famine, drought, etc. They are
few, hard to predict, and the losses incurred are very high. Low-variance
events are traffic accidents, work injuries, alcohol and tobacco consumption
injuries, suicides, etc. They are comparatively frequent, 1000 or 10 000 times
as frequent as the first kind of accidents, but the losses are much smaller, and
sometimes only a few relatives will really feel the loss. When people die one
at a time, society absorbs the accidents. But the number of fatalities per year
is probably higher for low-variance risks than for high-variance risks, so the
absorption of low-variance risks is regrettable.

Judgments of positive versus negative values

Much work has been done to measure the subjective utility of objective
amounts; the latter concept – the independent variable – is usually represented
by money. From these studies it is seen that the subjective utility function is
steeper on the loss side than on the gain side (see Fig. 6.3a), which means that
we are more sensitive to increases in loss than to increases in gains in relation
to the amount of wealth we are adapted to. The larger our gains are at a given
moment, the less we differentiate between them.

It is plausible, as the subjective utility function is steeper on the loss side,
that if we see a five dollar bill on the sidewalk, lean down to pick it up, but
are just that bit slower than somebody else, we will feel slightly poorer than
the moment before we saw the bill. The loss seems larger than the "same
amount" of gain, so we react with disappointment instead of indifference.
From behavior in organizations we know that reorganization during expansion
works better, in fact much better, than during decline, when diminishing
resources have to be distributed, or during stagnation. Allocation of limited
resources with the aim of evening out differences between people must be more
difficult than distribution of increased resources, not only because one has to
take away from some people to give to others more in need, but also, if the
slope differences are true, what is taken away from "the rich" is perceived as
much more than the same amounts given to "the poor." So the deprived's
suffering outweighs the recipient's pleasure.

The steeper slope on the loss side also means that ten bodies killed
simultaneously are more than ten times as dreadful as one dead body. This is

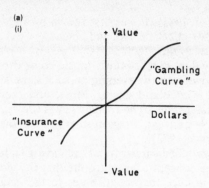

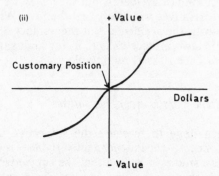

Figure 6.3 (a) Two well known utility functions for money. The left function (i) is suggested on the basis of comparisons of offers, the other (ii) is suggested after the notion that also very rich and poor people do gamble (e.g. commented in Lee 1971). (b) Value functions in real life, fancied by this author. Money cannot be everything,

how the effect interacts with the high-variance sensitivity. The values guiding our behaviour are more negative on the negative side than positive on the positive side. It would be disastrous for us if a lot of good could compensate for a value more closely attached to loss of single necessities. Many friends and books, for example, cannot compensate for a shortage of food and water. A value system with much emphasis on avoidance of negative consequences, and less emphasis on the "shoulds" to attain, gives us more flexible and adaptable guidelines.

The two functions in Fig. 6.3a were arrived at by different techniques where money was involved. It was pointed out in the paragraph on content of value that utility, equality and freedom are independent; therefore one might well assume that there are differently shaped value functions.

In accordance with some human values mentioned earlier, the functions in Fig. 6.3b were drawn by the present author to illllustrate the thought that there

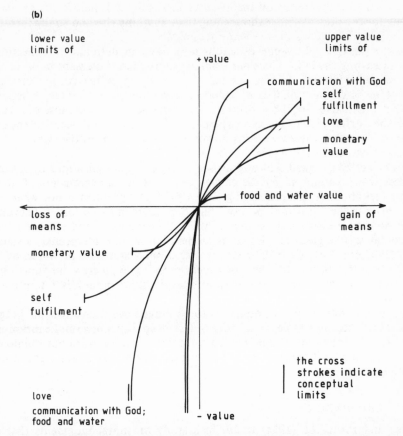

and neither can self-fulfillment if valued needs are missing, so upper and lower value limits are suggested – as are conceptual limits. The positive parts of the functions were cut at their optimal and conceptual limits. In the negative quadrant there should be losses which cannot be compensated for.

could be different shapes and different limits of value functions. The accustomed amount was chosen to be zero. Communication with God was the best thing that could happen to Augustine. Just because it seemed to be the best thing ever, at least for someone, it was allotted the highest limit in the hypothetical distribution of functions here. Self-fulfillment got the next highest value because it is fashionable. Food and water supplies probably have low values in our culture now, so they exemplify a low positive function. Refusal to communicate on the part of God should be evaluated very negatively, as loss of love, food and water, so these curves are very steep on the negative side.

As is further seen in Fig. 6.3b we assume conceptual limits to gains and losses. One person's gains and losses seem meaningful or comprehensible only to some extent. There are also ends to monetary value, and as money is not everything, money too got its upper and lower value limits. Basic needs very soon reach (vertical) limits on the negative loss side, and these limits are (we assume for the present) more threatening than anything else and so the threats have asymptotic effects on the value judgments.

On the positive side, some functions may have an optimum or inflection point preceding the limit. Consider drinking more than is pleasant in order to cure an inflammation of the kidneys versus being subjected to torture. Everything is of value if it is of value to something else of value, whether positive or negative. So, if one drinks more than one wants, the cause of it can make the surfeit either positive (when it is for a cure), or negative (when torture). Therefore the curve turns upwards or downwards to the right of the end-point chosen in the figure.

It is sometimes argued that utilitarianism requires quantifications of consequences which cannot always be carried out, such as measurements of how people feel about future events (e.g. Lee 1977). The problem is not whether emotions can be measured or not, but that there may be other relevant dimensions to measure than common utility. Let the gains and losses on the horizontal axis be gains and losses of money, but money interpreted as signs from God, proof of self-fulfillment, or means for acquisition of water, as it may be by different people. Then the functions in Fig. 6.3b are value functions of money, but have got very different shapes, since money is interpreted differently.

The interpretation of what quality is to be judged can thus affect the judgment. The functions can be made more or less steep depending on the meaning to the judge of the object to be judged. Moral indignation is, in our opinion, very sensitizing to judgments of loss of value, making the losses seem more negative.

MORAL INDIGNATION

Riskey and Birnbaum (1974) found in a study on moral judgments that a person described as capable of a very bad action was not judged as any better if other less bad attributes were ascribed to him. This finding suggests that moral indignation and other acceptance limits have asymptotic effects on the evaluation. If a value is assessed as being very, very large, then addition or substraction of other values does not greatly change the first assessment.

As we know from real life, some situations, at least to some individuals, seem completely impossible to accept or compensate for. Cut-offs or infinity assumptions should be allowed in utility models to cover such real-life judgments, and the absence of love, communication with God, and food and water in Fig. 6.3b, were drawn to show how we think intense threats should be depicted. Moral indignation, induced by suspicions of others' indifference or purposeful evilness which thus threaten the whole value system, add such strength to judgments that matters arousing moral indignation might be judged similarly to the threats depicted.

Moral indignation is utilized in political debate and in more vulgar quarrels to stop the arguments from the other part. Not wanting to insult any Swedish political leader, the author gives an example from her own circle of acquaintances. A friend found a new, modern, clean and bright, centrally located apartment with a functioning elevator for her aunt and also offered to help her move, and said, honestly but unthinkingly, that as the new apartment was slightly smaller than the old one, all the furniture (which was already stacked) would not fit into the new apartment. "Well", the aunt said, "may I still have my bed or shall I sleep on the floor? I cannot get up from the floor, you know", and then refused to go into details. The exploitative trick of moral indignation is to find an insinuation which is dirty enough to trigger an asymptotic effect on evaluation. In politics it is particularly effective if the alleged intention is damaging to a group that is inferior in any respect and requires care.

In March 1981, a working group within the Swedish Social Democratic Party considering present and future crises, made a small pilot study on evaluations of longer working spells and higher retirement age. Mass media immediately observed this, and the group received a lot of criticism. If these matters are evaluated, they might be considered negotiable and the thought of this causes indignation. If moral indignation is strong enough, working time and retirement age can be kept outside cost–benefit analysis, or can make cost–benefit analysis unsuitable by their allegedly immeasurable loss values.

During the late spring of 1981, a young Swedish girl was sent to London for a heart transplantation, a surgical operation that is impossible in Sweden since a person is judged to be alive as long as the heart is working, and so donators of functioning hearts do not exist. The operation would cost 60–75 000 dollars, money that of course had to be taken from other fields of the medical service, something the County Council did not want to allow at first. The decision makers changed their minds after much ado, including a radio program where the public could call them to tell them that no monetary value could be set on the young girl's survival, and so all discussion about how and whether to allocate money in her favor was absurd.

Riesman (1950) noted the explosive power of moral indignation, its power to activate the masses and make the politicians change their view. Green (1975) pointed out that many inconsistencies in the law seemed "emotional", for instance to forbid hashish but not cigarettes or to forbid small doses of chemical additives in food because large doses cause harm to animals. He hoped it was pragmatism. The present author believes that it is flirting with the public's moral indignation. Ideally the loss part of a risky option could be assessed as $p \times (-c)$, the probability of the risk times the loss (if no benefits or other costs are assumed). Some losses are very large. Nuclear power plant accidents or accidents with biological and chemical weapons (not to mention war) are complicated outcomes with costs hard to assess, so they can best be described with risk panoramas sketching possible outcomes. The probabilities attached to them are small, however. As the risks mentioned are man-made, their occurrence will cause indignation as well as damage. Many people have already warned against the devastating consequences. As this author strongly believes that (moral) indignation adds a negative attribute to these man-made risks, we think that those who are "negativists" as regards the kind of accidents now mentioned assign extremely large, practically infinite, negative values to them.

In experiments on gambling, small probabilities are overestimated by naïve subjects. If a nuclear power plant is estimated to have a core melt-down with a probability of 10^{-6} per year by experts, who knows what the naïve subject

imagines that number to be? Does it feel like 0.1 or 1 percent? Either the accident is impossible or it is possible; if it is possible, its probability is probably
imagined as many times larger than 10^{-6}. It is, of course, not the case that
people do not know that there are numbers as small as 10^{-6}, but we think that
when these numbers have to be used subjectively for an intuitive judgment of
$p \times (-c)$, the small p values cannot be imagined as small enough to compensate for the very large imagined negative values of c.

WHAT IS WORST AND WHAT IS BEST?

Is there a fate worse than death? There seems to be since some people commit
suicide. Others sacrifice their lives. It is not always irrational to challenge death
(Richards 1971). Death may be the price we accept in fighting for our moral
principles or for a society embracing threatened values. Also, during war,
people seem to be able to endure horrible circumstances and struggle against
death for more reasons than the value of life itself.

What loss of values, then, is most threatening to us? What is worst? In a
collection of "Poems from the People", a 12-year-old girl made her summary:

I fear
losing my friends
Margaret, Bridget, and you
I fear seeing all that's beautiful
destroyed
forests, lakes and mountains
I fear
there will be a war
that takes away everything I fear to lose

Everything I fear to lose ... she is foreseeing the uttermost risk. There is
a risk that we will lose what we hold in high esteem, and to lose what we most
of all fear to lose, that is worst.

Sweden's foreign debts, lack of oil deposits, unemployment, the reawaken-
ing of the cold war, the high frequency of racial and religious antagonism
(abroad), and consequences of nuclear power have been among recent risk
news. The less pressing risk panorama, but fairly current, is the suspiciously
dangerous industrial growth society, which is accused of causing alienation,
isolation, centralization, commuting, pollution, expert dominance, impoverish-
ment of the Third World and exhaustion of natural resources; in other words
it is amplifying psychoneuroticism and aggravating the ecocrisis. There is a
controversy between industrialism or the technical policy of expansion and
conservation of ecology, the latter accusing the former of ruthlessness and
short-sightedness. Which is best, the industrial growth society or the life
necessities (nature-balanced) society? Regardless of how it came about, hand
in hand with the anti-nuclear power movement, conservation formed its goals.
The discussion showed that the advocates of the advanced technology had
difficulty in explaining the benefits to the rest of society.

Swedes traditionally tend to vote according to their profession. Workers
vote for the Social Democrats and farmers and forest owners for the Center

party, etc. The parties are supposed to represent the interests of people according to their position in the society. So far, ecological interest does not
"belong" to any profession, but it has recently given rise to a political party,
and this has happened and will probably happen in other European countries
as well. France had a preservationist party entering the election in 1981, and
the same was true for Belgium. As the preservationists' goals are neither
utilitarian, egalitarian nor liberal, the consequences of new goals entering the
political discussions will be very interesting. The threats now causing the
permutation of values are damage to the environment, the shortage of energy
and a distrust in the ability (or aim) of technology to provide necessities and
wealth; "life necessities" or new possibilities looked for seem to be more
control over basic needs, both intellectually (understanding of complex causes)
and physically (decentralization of production), and also a wish for a healthy
(and healthy looking) body.

The water defences of the Netherlands protecting the countryside have been
adjusted to specified probabilities of not being submerged, after the government adopted a risk analysis method and accepted assessment of upper limit
in terms of probability estimates of flooding. Industrialists also seem to want
to be met with that complaisant attitude (TNO 1977). They want to be met
with admissions concerning percentages of pollution. As preservationists are
so doubtful as to the benefits of industrialism and so negative to growth
ideology, at least these two groups – the industrialists and the preservationists
– are not likely to come to any mutual agreement. For the latter group there
are almost no benefits against which pollution can be chalked up. And,
perhaps making it a growing dilemma, the industrialists do not realize well
enough that it would be fair and correct to discuss the dimensions and values
of benefits seriously, and not only costs (risks).

Technology can be described in a fairly objective manner, probabilities of
accidents can be calculated and countermeasures planned, but there cannot be
any production without intentions, since there cannot be any human actions
on that level of complexity without intentions. These intentions can be
evaluated from several perspectives. As pollution and damages are often more
local than the benefits, at least when it comes to power plants, plants for
destruction of chemicals and pulp mills, it is obvious that there is a need for
a thorough discussion of whose values and costs and benefits are to be
considered, and why. Industrialism has lost its promising aura, since it is now
evident that it will not make us rich forever, and thus is asked to give reasons
for its existence. It must let the production be allocated in such a way that the
benefits and the costs match, also, from a new point of view. The values are
changing. They help us to adapt to new circumstances, and if some people
think that the population is misled, they should argue and give reasons for
their standpoints, not just discard their opponents as "emotional" or
"romantic."

It is not only in this way, however, that the benefits of industrialism in the
situation of today are obscure, there is another point that differentiates between the flood that threatens the Netherlands and pollution or injuries that
are caused by manufacturing. Natural catastrophes do not cause moral
indignation. Moral indignation puts damage in another light, and the costs are
probably perceived as much higher when they are man-made disasters, or even

caused by a group of people whose willingness to avoid damages to other people has been doubted. The indignation is in the hands of the preservationists.

Problems with preservation that are overlooked are how to distribute necessities in a decentralized society and how to guarantee caring and education in communities with lower than average supply power; so far, societies with low centralization also seem to lack long-term planning. "Community-egoism" might develop too. Consequences of technological costs of reorganization and restructuring are neglected (already there are protests against demands that people should move to find new jobs). Are we smart enough to develop an effective and cheap small-scale technology? Who will estimate all low-variance risks caused by a lot of people wanting to manage their own production? How many Swedes can we really feed in the life-necessities society? What will happen to the equality principle if we change the production and the distribution of goods drastically? How will equality and justice be interpreted in a new life situation with new beliefs about necessities and causes, including the belief of a sound body as the result of sound living? How shall we redistribute arable land and organize small-scale food production? Will that decentralization be more or less efficient, or does that question not matter?

If these questions were discussed by the preservationists themselves, they would most probably lose the tool they have got now, the moral indignation over risks in the present society, since it would be apparent that there are costs to pay in a life-necessities society too. Maybe new waves riding on moral indignation have to sharpen their arguments all the time in order not to get trapped by the same method?

A third cause to doubt that there will ever be a serious cost–benefit analysis as to which of the two societies is best (including a debate on primary values), is that the alternative striven for by the preservationists has not yet been tried out, so there have not been any mishaps yet. As long as the drawbacks are not manifest, they will not be taken seriously. Things have to happen first (Green 1975); with a few exceptions, society never let purely hypothetical risks prevent its development. As long as decision analysis and risk analysis are utilitarian, as is economic reasoning on the whole, plans focus on utility calculated as monetary gains, and the negative consequences, diffuse and even more complicated matters such as increased vulnerability, do not in practice enter the analysis (Fischhoff 1977). But it probably works the same way, if a value other than utility is favored. When ecological balance is given priority, utility and other values come second. That seems inescapable. So, if goals change and advanced efficient technology or utilitarian goals, for example, are replaced by ecological goals, there will be new risks such as distribution problems, technological disarmament and over-confidence in "sound" food and "sound" habits as healers, that the "new society" will just TAKE.

Conclusions

Much of this chapter has described irregularities of value judgments. Values vary according to choice of perspective and environmental changes, interact with occurrence of events and purpose of events, are asymmetrical with regard to gains and losses, and are sensitized by threats, unfamiliarity or powerlessness. The observations of the irregularities may partly be due to misleading expectancies. Value should not be confounded with facts. Still, the way in which values are studied and debated, and thus also described here, shows that it is very likely that facts and values get mixed up. The most tempting confusion probably exists between facts, or objective measures, and utility, and sometimes it looks as if the difference between them is assumed to be only a matter of scaling.

Research on values has been carried on in the same tradition as research on perception. It has already been accepted that perceptual dimensions for cognitive analysis, such as numbers, height or order, do not perfectly map objectively definable and measurable environmental variables, and so it has automatically been accepted that value judgments and objective quantities do not perfectly agree either. However, the properties of the irregularities hint at a very bad match between objectively measured variables and preferences. As values are taught and learned and often concern postponement of benefits, the cognitive component of values of course is salient, but what seems to be most often forgotten is the motivation component. The match between objectively measurable variables and value judgments is so unsuccessful that one ought to question not only the possibility to define stimuli for value judgments objectively but the intentions of the respondents to judge those stimuli. There are thus two sources of errors in research on values: the one that traditional cognitive denotative identification of stimuli is inappropriate, and the other that it is inherent in value judgments that the intention of the judge interferes with the judgment, and both sources are linked to the motivation aspects.

The common assumption is that stimuli are first identified and then evaluated, but we do not know for sure that cognitive identification is prior to evaluation. It is just as likely that evaluation comes first and that cognitive analysis is motivated by the outcome of the value judgment. It is recognized that motivation plays its part in all mental processes, so it is logical that evaluation does not have to come second, and that evaluation is not dependent on mental structures identical with the cognitive mental structures.

To assign a value is often a performative utterance, and the giving of values aims to influence the relation between the judge and his audience. There is not much ground to assume that the values given should be chosen for no reason at all. Researchers and canvassers do not want to give their aims or intentions either, so everybody is cheating in this game.

That utility is easily confused with facts may have historical explanations. Utility has been a dominating value during the construction of the society and the institutions ruling us today. Now when this base is rigid and decisions habitual, the original motives are forgotten, and the causes believed to be matter-of-facts.

How should research on values develop and how can risk avoidance be improved? If it is so difficult to study values, what can one do: sit down and sense them? Introspection is probably not the worst way to learn about values, and could give clues to the dynamic processes behind evaluations. Anyhow, value changes, categorical depreciations, indignation and moral argumentation still have to be understood. The dynamic properties of value judgments have more to tell about the uniqueness of values than static preference judgments. And why not try to learn to argue in moral debates? Researchers do not seem to be very good at moral reasoning and cannot guide people around the hidden rocks they find. But practice makes perfect.

References

Allardt, E. 1979. *Att ha, att älska, att leva. Om välfärden i Norden*. Lund: Argos.

Blasi, A. 1980. Bridging moral cognition and moral action: a critical review of the literature. *Psychol. Bull.* **88**, 1–45.

Brown, R. and R. J. Herrnstein 1975. *Psychology*. London: Methuen.

Cason, J. 1930. Common annoyances: a psychological study of everyday aversions and irritations. *Psychol. Monogr.* **40**(2), 1–218.

Cohen, J. 1960. *Chance, skill and luck*. Baltimore, Md: Penguin.

Dreman, S. B. 1976. Sharing behavior in Israeli school-children: cognitive and social learning factors. *Child Dev.* **47**, 186–94.

Edvardson, B. and J. Vegelius 1976. *Livskvalitet*. Unpublished manuscript available from the Department of Psychology, University of Uppsala, Sweden.

Festinger, L. 1957. *A theory of cognitive dissonance*. Evanstun Row & Peterson.

Fischhoff, B. (1977). Cost benefit analysis and the art of motor-cycle maintenance. *Policy Sci.* **8**, 177–202.

Fischhoff, B., P. Slovic, S. Lichtenstein, S. Read and B. Combs 1978. How safe is safe enough? A psychometric study of attitudes towards technological risks and benefits. *Policy Sci.* **8**, 127–52.

Fischhoff, B., P. Slovic and S. Lichtenstein 1980. Knowing what you want: measuring labile values. In *Cognitive processes in choice and decision behavior*, T. S. Wallsten (ed.), pp. 117–41. Hillsdale, N.J.: Erlbaum.

Frankena, W. K. 1963. *Ethics*. Englewood Cliffs, N.J.: Prentice-Hall.

Gallup, G. H. 1976. Human needs and satisfaction. A global survey. *Publ. Opinion Q.*, **40**, 459–67.

Golant, S. and I. Burton 1969. *Avoidance response to the risk environment*. Natural Hazard Research Working Paper No. 6. Toronto: Department of Geography, University of Toronto.

Green, H. P. 1975. Legal and political dimensions of risk-benefit methodology. In *Risk-benefit methodology and application*, some papers presented at the Engineering Foundation Workshop, September 22–26, 1975, D. Okrent (ed.) ASILOMAR, California. Los Angeles: Energy and Kinetics Dept., School of Engineering and Applied Science, University of California, Los Angeles.

Haan, N. 1978. Two moralities in action contexts: relationships to thought, ego regulation, and development. *J. Personal. Social Psychol.* **36**, 286–305.

Hadenius, S. and L. Weibull 1972. *Press radio TV* (Rev. ed.). Stockholm: Aldus.

Hermerén, G. 1973. *Forskning inom filosofin beträffande värderingars förändring och spridning*. In Värderingars förändring och spridning. Ds Ju 1973: 20. Stockholm: Ministry of Justice.

Holmberg, P. 1972. Välfärds- och fördelningspolitikens förutsättningar och möjligheter. In *Värde, välfärd och jämlikhet*, G. R. Nordenstam (ed.). Lund: Studentlitteratur.

Kelvin, P. 1969. *The bases of social behavior. An approach in terms of order and value.* London: Holt, Rinehart and Winston.

Kinsbourne, M. 1981. The brain. Sad hemisphere, happy hemisphere. *Psychology Today* May, 92.

Krebs, D. L. 1970. Altruism – an examination of the concept and a review of the literature. *Psychol. Bull.* **73**, 258–302.

Lee, W. 1971. *Decision theory and human behavior.* New York: Wiley.

Lee, W. R. 1977. Some ethical problems of hazardous substances in the working environment. *B. J. Ind. Med.* **34**, 247–80.

LO, in press. *Krav på arbetsmiljön.* Rapport från LO:s arbetsmiljögrupp. Stockholm: LO.

Muson, H. 1979. Moral thinking. Can it be taught? *Psychol. Today*, **13**, February, 48–92.

Nordenstam, G. R. 1972. Folkmakt och elitstyre. In *Värde, välfärd och jämlikhet*, G. R. Nordenstam (ed.) pp. 19–47. Lund: Studentlitteratur.

Näätänen, R. and H. Summala 1975. *Road user behavior and traffic accidents.* Amsterdam: North Holland.

Otway, H. J. and M. Fishbein 1977. *Public attitudes and decision making.* RM-77-54. Laxenburg, Austria: International Institute for Applied Systems Analysis.

Peck, R. H. and R. J. Havinghurst 1960. *The psychology of character development.* New York: Wiley.

Rescher, N. 1969. *Introduction to value theory.* Englewood Cliffs, N.J.: Prentice-Hall, 1969.

Richards, D. A. J. 1971. *A theory of reasons for action.* Oxford: Oxford University Press.

Riesman, D. 1950. *The lonely crowd.* New Haven, Conn.: Yale University Press.

Riskey, D. R. and M. H. Birnbaum 1974. Compensatory effects in moral judgment; two rights don't make up for a wrong. *J. Exp. Psychol.* **103**, 171–3.

Sjöberg, L. 1982. Beliefs and values as components of attitudes. In *Social Psychophysics*, B. Wegener (ed.), pp. 199–218. Hillsdale, N.J.: Erlbaum.

Sjöberg, L. and A. Biel 1983. Mood and belief-value correlation. *Acta Psychol.* **53**, 253–70.

Slovic, P., B. Fischhoff and S. Lichtenstein 1979. Rating the risks. *Environment* **21**(3), 14–39.

Starr, C. 1969. Social benefit versus technological risk. *Science* **165**, 1232–8.

Svenson, O. 1981. Are we all less risky and more skillful than our fellow drivers? *Acta Psychol.* **47**, 143–8.

Swaton, E., R. Maderthaner, P. D. Pahner, G. Guttman and H. J. Otway 1976. *The determinants of risk perception: the active-passive dimension.* RM-76-74. Laxenburg, Austria: International Institute for Applied Systems Analysis.

TNO 1977. 10th International TNO Conference. *Risk analysis: industry, Government and society.* The Hague, the Netherlands: TNO.

Tversky, A. 1969. Intransitivity of preferences. *Psychol. Rev.* **76**, 31–48.

Tversky, A. and D. Kahneman 1973. Availability: A heuristic for judging frequency and probability. *Cognitive Psychol.* **5**, 207–32.

Tversky, A. and D. Kahneman 1981. The framing of decisions and the psychology of choice. *Science* **211**, 453–8.

Velimirovic, H. 1975. *An anthropological view of risk phenomena*. RM-75-55. Vienna, Austria: IIASA.

Zajonc, R. B. 1980. Feeling and thinking. Preferences need no inferences. *American Psychologist* **35**, 151–75.

Part II

REACTIONS TO RISK

7 *Human anxiety*

HAMPUS LYTTKENS

Introduction

A historical view of the development of risk (Odén 1982) seems to show that
our society has hardly become more hazardous during recent years. Rather,
the level of risk for the individual has remained fairly constant. The fact that
behind this constant level of risk there are hidden and varying forms of risk
is a different story and one on which we need not comment in this context.
Without doubt, the important thing is the total level of risk, and that, as has
been mentioned, is constant.

In spite of the fact that the level of danger in society has not been raised in
recent years, people are still worried; they still show signs of anxiety. We can
mark this worry at many levels in society. There are the dangers of atomic
power, risks that have to be taken in places of work and anxiety connected
with pollution. These are just three examples of areas that have intensively
engaged the minds of people, and where this engagement has had and still has
far-reaching social and political consequences.

Thus, even if the actual risks as they appear in statistics have hardly increased
recently, anxiety and confrontation with them have obviously increased. How
should we best understand this situation? Human worry is probably influenced
by real risks. The position maintained by quite a few researchers who
acknowledge that anxiety has increased in modern society is that the degree of
anxiety is also dependent on a series of other factors. Values and life-styles,
expectations that people have of life, the way society manages to fulfill these
expectations, the experience of one's own situation in the industrialized and
bureaucratic society, various threatening pictures that show dangers concerning the environment, threats of economic crises, and the (doubtful) ability of
religion and ideologies to give answers and security with regard to them, probably influence the experience of anxiety. But there is also a basic worry, one
that belongs to human existence itself in a world where death is the only certain
future. In the following discussion, we shall examine human anxiety from this
existential viewpoint, on the one hand, and on the other hand, we shall examine the sort of anxiety that could be called a structuralized anxiety produced
by a complex situation of cause and effect. In this way we hope to be able to
see points of view that will allow us to understand better something of the
forces behind the debate and engagement.

The fact that we have chosen precisely this perspective must not, however,
be understood as though we were considering anxiety as more or less im-
aginary, and the engagement mainly an expression of a diffuse dissatisfaction
and an existential anxiety. Rather, we shall regard the engagement caused by
processes at various levels as realistic fears concerning the development of
society and technology.

General considerations

CAUSES AND TYPES OF ANXIETY

Centralization and increased technical efficiency work for both good and evil. We all know that rapid economic growth has brought with it a tremendously increased standard of living. At the same time, however, the vulnerability of society has increased. Modern technological development in armaments especially has placed great power in the hands of responsible people in political systems that seem to be more and more unstable in many parts of the world. This is doubtless a situation that contains in itself the power to create anxiety. Anxiety can relate not only to risks of catastrophic disasters in large technical systems, but also the worry that oneself or one's nearest relations can develop cancer as a consequence of pollution or because one has been exposed to radiation by radon gas in one's home. Anxiety can be caused by natural catastrophes or by man-made events. Children often experience acute worry that we might be exposed to war. Anxiety has many shapes and forms. Perhaps the constantly increasing material standard of living has in itself been destructive because it has created hopes that have not been completely fulfilled. Many of the material advantages in society exist only in limited quantity. In spite of the fact that one runs as fast as one can, one is always at the same distance behind the "in" group. Furthermore, recent developments seem to mean a real lowering of the standard of living.

The main interest in this chapter focuses on human anxiety but, by way of an introduction, there are grounds for speculating a little on the possible further effects, apart from anxiety, the situation can lead to. Anxiety can lead to attempts to lessen the tension, for instance, with the help of drugs or other soothing or relaxing aspects of life-style (e.g. viewing the television). Sometimes there can also be a search for a destructive, exciting life-style. One looks constantly for new experiences and adventures in a more or less vain pursuit of enjoyment. Pascal describes extensively how man seeks diversions and to fill his life with nonsense in order not to be confronted with the emptiness of his life, with death, suffering and evil.

In the search for enjoyment there is naturally the central factor of increased material consumption. There seems to be no upper limit to what people can demand if they are given the opportunity. Only our own imagination can put a limit to fantasies as to our next desired object of consumption. It is the change which is decisive for positive (or negative) feelings. One very quickly becomes used to what one has achieved in a high level of consumption and considers it as one's right.

The question of the degree and extent to which people experience anxiety is many faceted. There is also a relation to the various areas of knowledge in the sciences. At this point, we shall distinguish between various kinds of anxiety. This may be done by using the causes of anxiety as a point of departure, and in this way social, economic and ideological factors enter the picture. One can also study, with regard to anxiety, whether there are differences between individuals, groups, classes, or sex, and in this way one can touch upon the fields of sociology, differential psychology and biology.

There is a distinctive difference between two kinds of anxiety. The first is simply fear and concerns concrete threats and dangers. The other sort is existential by nature; it is structural and often without external, provable causes, and it is often called "anguish" by psychologists. Fear is a signal of concrete danger that threatens one or more people. Fear functions in principle in the same way as pain, which is also a warning signal. As signals, both pain and fear make people aware of a threat and, at the same time, give out impulses to try to avoid the danger. Fear of this kind has concrete, identifiable external causes. When the danger is over, the fear disappears. One often finds that an attempt to annihilate or avoid danger already serves to oppose anxiety. This type of anxiety is also limited in time. When danger appears the fear arises. When the danger is over, the fear disappears. However, the boundary between worry or fear and structurally and existentially induced anxiety fluctuates. Anxiety expressed as fear can come close to the existential interpretation in certain cases. When it is a question of threat against entire groups or against the existence of the most important values in the life of a whole community, then anxiety easily acquires a deep and long-lasting character. Faced with such threats the individual often experiences impotence. The threat comes from forces and powers that the individual cannot master. Examples are anxiety in economic crises, anxiety about unemployment, destruction of the environment and war.

In the other kind of anxiety I should like to include, firstly, what I would call the structurally caused anxiety, an anxiety dependent on social factors. By this I mean a certain anxiety dependent on structures in society and on basic ideological and social systems prevalent in that society. One can ask oneself, for instance, as many have already done, whether the present technological, industrialized and capitalist-oriented society in the West contains factors that create anguish and anxiety. For example, research relating to the needs of psychotherapy shows that a large number of people experience psychological disturbances. At the same time, it is maintained, with a certain justification, that the causes of these disturbances are not to be sought in the individual but rather in the conditions in which they have grown up and in which they are now forced to live.

Closely related to anxiety caused by structures in society, there is the existential kind of anxiety. By this is meant the anxiety a person can experience because his own existence confronts him with a series of enigmas which no one can yet answer. Humanity is confronted with meaningless suffering, guilt and, above all, death that often and abruptly break into our existence; all humanity shares this same fate. This sort of anxiety is the eternal companion of humanity and is part of man's peculiar make-up and situation in the world both as a species and as a social being.

One can also say that existential anxiety has distinctive causes. Sooner or later death becomes a reality for all of us. But there is also a form of anxiety that has no substance, that cannot be explained by certain external factors. This anxiety is closely related to neurotic anguish. Such insubstantial anxiety has an important rôle to play in the human condition, above all other considerations according to the philosophers of existentialism. The success this interpretation of life and philosophy has had shows that the interpretation must have hit on something essential and which has worked as a means of expressing deep-seated anxiety.

ANXIETY AND VALUE JUDGMENTS

Regardless of what kind of anxiety one may speak about, it is doubtless the case that anxiety can vary in strength. It can be a feeble, unconscious anxiety or an anxiety that seizes the whole personality, creating tension and even having a paralysing effect. The degree of anxiety is very largely connected to those values in life that are threatened; it is also connected to the place in the hierarchy of values where a particular threatened value might be. In other words, anxiety is a problem that centrally touches upon our needs and values, those things we consider to be central and important in life. When a particular value is threatened anxiety becomes more intensive, especially when it is a value for which there is no alternative. One such value in modern times, for instance, is health which has become a religion. Factors that threaten our health are quickly and forcibly given attention, and people are inclined to make intensive efforts to protect themselves against those factors.

Much of the importance of the values related to anxiety is connected to the expectations people have of life. One's view of life and what one expects of it plays a rôle in human feelings of security and satisfaction. The possibilities for disappointment are great in our Western welfare society with its strong demands that life should provide us with both material and spiritual satisfaction. The anxiety that life is not going to give one those things generally considered to be a right, and that are preached about as the norm, receives ample nourishment, especially in a competitive society where the successful and efficient person is regarded as the ideal. It is obvious that, in a society where demands of this type are brought into political debate, published in the press, on the radio and television, in literature, etc., the risks to individuals and groups that they will not be able to experience the realization of the demands is increased, and the anxiety that life is running away from one is given ample nourishment.

In this context, an important question is to what depth and breadth those views of life and values that are accepted and propagated in society are well motivated and "correct." As an example, one could choose the general belief that increased welfare and a higher economic standard would give people more happiness and satisfaction. It appears that these values are, at most, necessary conditions but they are not sufficient conditions. It would really be an irony of destiny if a value whose nonfulfillment creates anguish were to show itself to be false, over-emphasized or far too simplified in the light of later psychological human knowledge. Such points of view doubtless remind one of classical Christian warnings against attaching too much importance to worldly goods rather than eternal values. We are reminded of Jesus' words about not storing up treasures on Earth where they can be destroyed but rather storing treasure in Heaven where it cannot be destroyed. The same thing is expressed by Father Augustine when he warns that one should not attach oneself to perishable things that lack that degree of reality which divinity alone possesses.

With these reflections in mind, we now consider the importance of the structure and climate of society for the birth and maintenance of human anxiety. This influence is, however, complex and many-sided.

SOCIETY AND ANXIETY

Two features are basic. On the one hand we have the rôle played by ideological and value factors. People have ideals, demands and dreams about their lives and environment. To a large extent these are determined by prevailing views of life; those that are accepted and advanced in society. We could, for instance, indicate the rôle played by the concept of the quality of life in the current debate about the environment. It is easy to show that the different meanings given to this concept are decided by ideologies and values.

On the other hand, we have the realistic conditions in society, its organization, its economic and technologically industrialized system, its law making, its class structure, styles of living, etc. It is not intended to discuss the relations between such social and ideological factors here. The relation between them is also an expression of a complicated interplay and a mutual interdependence within the situation. However, one can establish that an increasing number of analysts in society maintain that Western industrialized society robs more and more people of the possibility of experiencing self-respect and identity by its structure. If this is the case, and if such a loss creates anguish, there are factors creating anguish and anxiety built into the present Western society itself. The disappointments people experienced during the 1970s, as a result of promises given during the 1950s and 1960s failing to be realized, are a result of these in-built factors. Man has experienced how a society that promised increased welfare, health, increased consumption, increased leisure time and liberty has instead brought the opposite effect with threats to health, welfare and environment as well as risks to future generations. Instead of those bright dreams for the future, one sees before one a society with poisoned food and with an increased number of mentally ill. One of the factors creating anxiety in the industrialized society is the reports that are published regularly showing risks to life and health. It seems as though the industrial environment has an inherent chain of risks that is difficult to predict. We constantly receive new alarming reports. It is obvious that such reports have created and maintain a latent anxiety. The knowledge that economic interests often make business management less inclined to take the initiative itself in investigating problems, preferring to let business run on routine lines, does not help to lessen apprehension. Uncertainty about the possible risks involved in using various substances, and the new risks that are being discovered all the time, are creating anxiety and anguish in an age where health is given a high place in the hierarchy of values.

Thus, during the 1970s, a *knowledge* of real risks due to modern technology has been widespread. Previously only a few experts knew for certain what these risks were. It is obvious that this realistic knowledge contributes to the creation of anxiety. As a result of the debates about risks, many improvements have been made by means of new techniques that have been developed with less risk involved in them, and new laws and regulations have been introduced. However, the improvements are not as noticeable as the risks; and new risks appear to be endless.

There is often a relationship between the anxiety based on the structure of society and the existential anxiety. Ideologies and structures in society can influence the existentially motivated anxiety. The lack of answers in present-day society to a chain of existential questions can increase one's anguish. Because of the relationship between existentially based and structurally based anxiety, it would be better, in this part of the chapter, to discuss more deeply first the existentially based anxiety, and then to take up the structural relationships in society which seem to cause anxiety.

Existentially based anxiety

Existentially based anxiety has its origin in certain basic relationships which characterize man's existence. Many scholars in various fields of study are agreed that man, because of his biological development, has not only been endowed with important faculties but that these faculties hold in-built problems for man. This gives rise to a need to attain answers to the eternal enigmas of life, those that can never be fully answered and which will therefore always continue to cause anxiety. Here are some examples.

Erich Fromm (1973) maintains that that which characterizes man's situation is an inner contradiction. This is due to the facts that, on the one hand, man is much freer than animals and is less guided and programed by his instincts, whereas on the other, he has his large brain to compensate him for the lack of guidance by instinct. Fromm shows that three things follow from this: (a) man has an awareness of himself; (b) he has imagination which allows him the possibility of imagining things other than what he actually sees and knows; and (c) he is conscious of his own limitations and of his powerlessness in the face of death. Fromm maintains that the I-consciousness, reason and imagination have destroyed the "harmony" that characterizes the existence of animals. There is no inherited program which tells man what to do. Man is the only being who does not feel at home in his existence and who can feel expelled from paradise; the only creature who experiences his existence as a problem which he has to solve. Man is a part of nature and yet he cannot return to a total dependence on nature.

Thoughts like those of Fromm can be seen in many other places. Malinowski (1958) maintains that things that characterize man are the abilities of foresight and imagination. Malinowski stresses in particular man's consciousness of death. Similarly, Dobzhansky (1967) emphasizes the idea that that which differentiates man from animals is primarily man's self-awareness and his awareness of death. Man can foresee his own destruction.

Sociologists of religion who hold functionalistic theories point to three primary factors in man's existence which threaten to take away from him his satisfaction and happiness. Firstly, man's situation is characterized by uncertainty. He lives in uncertain conditions. The forces that decide his safety and welfare lie partly out of his reach and control. This uncertainty means that anything one undertakes can lead to failure. Secondly, man's situation is characterized by impotence. Impotence shows itself in the fact that man cannot obtain all that he wishes. It shows itself above all in the face of death and suffering. But it also appears in his powerlessness in the face of the development and compulsion which so many people are exposed to. The third factor is scarcity. The necessity to distribute scarce resources leads to the fact that some members of society experience need. In particular, uncertainty and powerlessness puts man in situations where the usual mechanism of adaptability is insufficient. In the face of these so-called breaking points "the question of meaning" is put with renewed clarity. One asks oneself: why should I die? Why should loved ones be taken from me? Why did I fail? Why is there sickness? (O'Dea, 1966).

All the authors mentioned above who describe the existentially based problems see a way to answer those problems in religion. Among contemporary theologians it is the existentialist-oriented theologians who have dealt with the existential form of anxiety more deeply. We may remember, however, that Augustine had already maintained that the human heart would continue to feel anxiety until it found rest in God, although he did this from a metaphysical point of view.

An interesting expositor among those theologians who discuss human anxiety is the American theologian Paul Tillich (1959). Tillich distinguishes between three different types of anguish: as an anguish in the face of fate and death; as an anguish in the face of emptiness and loss of meaning in life; and as an anguish about guilt and damnation. In all three cases the anguish is of the existential sort, i.e. it belongs to the bases of human existence. It is not dependent on, or an expression of, anything abnormal or sick in the state of the soul, as neurotic anguish is, for example.

All three kinds of anguish are existential. Yet Tillich thinks that in different eras different types have dominated. In antiquity, anguish in the face of death predominated; in the middle ages it was anguish in the face of damnation; and in our own times it is anguish in the face of emptiness and meaninglessness.

It is possible to argue against those who talk of an existentially based anguish that not everybody seems to experience it. In this case, there are several possibilities. One possibility is that there are individual differences between human beings. Some feel more plagued than others by an existentially based anxiety. Another possibility is that anguish is unconscious and shows itself in a way that is different from a direct experience of it. The first point of view is supported by certain findings made by Ingemar Hedenius (1959) and by a French psychologist, Ignace Lepp (1963). Hedenius distinguishes between religiously innocent people and those who cannot avoid involving themselves with religious problems. Lepp distinguishes between people who have and those who do not have a so-called metaphysical anxiety. By metaphysical anxiety Lepp means the anguish of those who are busy with metaphysical problems, the human questions of life and death.

We find another way to answer questions about anguish and the experience of anguish among existentialist philosophers. These maintain, as has been mentioned, that anguish is empty of content. The danger for which anguish is a signal cannot be specified in terms of its content. It is something purely internal and at the same time persistent. This does not mean that people always experience anguish. Anguish is something that appears and disappears again, apparently without grounds and reasons. Anguish itself, as a feeling, is a passing phenomenon. But the danger signalized by anguish is permanent. And it always exists because it belongs to an essential feature in the structure of existence. This permanent danger is a total threat to the entire existence of man, the threat of annihilation.

It is well known that existentialist philosophy is very complicated and this is not the place to enter into its apparatus of concepts and its reasoning. I shall, however, point to some features in the interpretation of anguish. What is contained in the concept of anguish is the meaninglessness and nothingness of human existence. There is also a problem regarding anguish in the face of death, but it is not the problem of the fear of death as a concrete future event. Anguish depends for its meaning on the idea of non-being and nothingness in death. Regardless of the different ways in which the existentialist philosophers describe, explain and interpret anguish, it is clear that they consider anguish as a basic factor in human existence.

There is an interesting psychological phenomenon in the view that anguish has no basis. Man has a tendency to transform such anguish into fear by focusing it on to a concrete object and in that way making it easier to endure. Perhaps part of the opposition to nuclear power can be interpreted in this way. Baseless anguish of this kind is difficult to endure. If man succeeds in creating the illusion that anguish is a fear of some object, that anguish becomes easier to cope with.

Having thus discussed existentially based anguish and anxiety we shall now return to present-day society, and one can conclude that in many ways this society seems incapable of giving man an answer to his anxiety problems and freeing him from the existentially motivated anxiety.

Anxiety in today's society

THE NEED FOR MEANING

Man seems to need to perceive his existence in a meaningful context, to see that that which happens to one in life is not the consequence of blind chance but an expression of intention and meaning.

The French Nobel prize winner Jacques Monod (1970) maintains that those ideas that prove to be most useful explain the human condition by giving man a place in a meaningful context. He also says that it is man's anguish when confronted with abandonment and loneliness that creates his need for explanation and his need to be placed in a meaningful context. Monod goes as far as maintaining that this need for a meaning and explanation is inherent in the genetic structure of man, and that the lack of such an explanation is the source of deep anguish. There is a chain of factors in today's society which makes it more difficult for man to discover and experience a meaningful context. In this respect, there is an obvious conflict with modern technological society. The view of nature that predominates up to the present day is dependent on factors chosen by chance and rejects the idea of systems guided by intention. The idea that there is, behind one's life, a personal intention appears to be an illusion against this background. Man experiences himself as living in an icy and desert-like universe. To the scientist, belief in a meaningful context is a leftover from an animistic tradition from which one ought to free oneself. If Monod is right in his hypothesis that man's need for explanations and meaning is inborn, then the conflict will remain.

Similarly, the well-known sociologist Peter Berger and others (Berger *et al.* 1974) maintain that what has happened in modern society is that a social homelessness has become metaphysical. Religion used to give people strength to carry on through illness and suffering by means of religious explanations. It provided a belief in and a hope for a better existence. In our own time these explanations have been questioned for various different reasons. Questions have arisen through intellectual criticism but, as Berger maintains, even social changes play an important rôle. The problem is that modern society has not succeeded in eradicating the experiences which have been calling for an answer and an explanation. People continue to be beaten by sickness and death, and to experience injustice and social abandonment. Modern ideologists have been notably incapable of presenting an answer to such problems. Our times have brought with them big changes in human existence but the weakness and mortality of human existence has not changed. The only thing that has happened is that we have weakened the religious view of reality which used to help people to live. The result has been an increase in anguish.

It is not only religiously motivated meaningful contents, however, that have lost their relevance in modern society. The possibility for immanently based meaningful contents to life has also been made more difficult. First, the complexity of our society means that not only religion but also all ideological systems are being questioned. The multiplicity of alternatives and points of view creates a fundamental insecurity and perplexity. What is right? What is one supposed to believe? Added to this, the institutions and politics of society have become increasingly abstract. People experience institutions as formal and distant from them and without the power to give meaning to the individual. The complexity of society implies that any fundamental meaning no longer exists. On the contrary, the individual is faced with competing and partly contradictory interpretations. Added to this, working life has lost its meaning for large groups of people. Work is seen as uniform and stressing. Work is done merely for survival but cannot give the individual personal self-satisfaction. That this is dangerous is clear when one considers that the need for self-respect and for personal worth is fundamental to man. When employment no longer functions as something that gives meaning, then one is left with leisure. This is supposed to give one the meaning which neither religion nor the institutions of society can any longer provide. But here, too, one finds the same factors for anxiety as in society. There exists no uniform structure in private life. The variety of choices exists even there. Teachers tell us that the number of deranged (and those becoming deranged) children has noticeably increased in their classes over the past years. Part of the reason for this could be the splitting-up of homes. The task of creating one's own life and one's own meaning seems to produce anxiety in some people. One escapes from the pressure of making too many choices only to become anxious that he might have made the wrong choice. The relativization that follows the multiplicity of choices even beats one in the individual sphere. This position of relativity gives neither a clear guide nor a feeling of security. The modern man's crisis of identity is a consequence of this.

THE LACK OF WORTH

Many psychologists maintain that the need to feel worth something and the need for self-respect are basic to man (e.g. Becker 1971, 1974). Becker stresses that it is this experience of having a certain worth which gives the "I" protection against anguish. It is the task of culture to make constant self-respect possible. If Becker's idea is correct — and there is much to be said for it — we can assume that just as in the case for a need for meaning, modern man is threatened by anguish for two reasons: partly because the religious dimension has been pushed aside and partly because modern society offers little prospect of finding compensation for the loss of the religious dimension. The need for self-respect and personal worth is closely connected to the need for forgiveness in Christianity. Many great theologians in Christianity have borne witness to the meaning of forgiveness, but few have done it more clearly than Martin Luther. Luther knew what liberating forces are hidden in the knowledge that one is loved, that there is somebody who cares about one in spite of all one's errors and failings. Luther's insight has been verified by modern psychology which stresses the idea that self-despising and feelings of guilt are a source of aggression, whereas a positive experience of the "I" and a secure feeling of self-respect create positive feelings and attitudes. Modern psychology therefore dreams of creating the harmonious happy man. But Luther had a more realistic view of reality. His view of man and the world finds its point of departure in the fact that no man can escape being touched by norms and demands, which he can only fail to fulfill, and that no man can escape being touched by sorrow and disappointment that give to him the feeling of being outside, not understood, not loved. Life is seldom so kind to man that he may develop in a positive atmosphere throughout life. The Christian dimension means that in spite of these negative factors there is a way of experiencing goodness and of being loved. In Christian language this is called belief in God's forgiveness.

If, then, the possibility of receiving forgiveness is essential in order for man to maintain his self-respect and his feeling of worth, we are led to say that the rejection of Christianity will have the result of lessening the possibilities for modern man to maintain his self-trust. We can make the same analysis we made with regard to the need for meaning. Modern ideologies seem incapable of giving man an answer to, or to liberate him from, his problems of guilt and to give him any form of forgiveness. Among other things, it has been said of Marxism that it lacks answers to the problem of guilt. However, we are still faced with the circumstances in man's life that threaten his self-trust and which give him the feeling of being worthless.

When everything is said and done, religion creates both feelings of guilt and a way of escape from them. Literature from earlier periods often speaks clearly about strong feelings of guilt with partially religious undertones. To achieve forgiveness and freedom from guilt was not simple. The question is whether the diminishing significance of religion in our society has not also brought with it the notion that religiously based feelings of guilt have considerably diminished. It is not meant by this that *all* sources of guilt have diminished in significance. All societies have norms and to break these can lead to feelings of guilt. Added to this, modern technological and bureaucratic society shows several features that mean that people experience a lack of worth rather than a feeling of being worth something. I shall point to two of them: first, anonymity and depersonalization which characterizes industry and, second, bureaucracy. Technologically industrial production brings with it anonymous social relations. The workers are looked upon, calculated and counted, as factors in the processes of production. If this were not so, then the mechanization and repetitiveness of the production process would not be possible. In mass production the worker becomes both an individual and an anonymous factor of production. The guiding factor is the technological process and this demands that one should be regarded as yet another cog in the industrial machine. The best example is the one given by Taylor (1947), who introduced the concept of equating man with a unit of output. Anonymity also exists in the relationship between workers. The colleague, too, is seen as a cog in the industrial machine, of whom it is demanded that he should function according to a given pattern. In thus dehumanizing people, one also diminishes their worth as individuals.

Within the field of bureaucracy this becomes even more obvious. One of the basic concepts of bureaucracy is impartiality, but the subjective consequence is sometimes that people find themselves being treated as abstract numbers. In itself, the attempt to give each person fair treatment implies depersonalization, and this constitutes a threat to the idea of belief in oneself. The more important the personal and individual values are, the more the person is going to feel that such treatment is an invasion of the individual's privacy. There are plenty of examples of this in the treatment people receive in our hospitals where the giving of a number, the impersonal form of address and treatment which is felt to be humiliating, all contribute to the feeling of depersonalization.

Against the background of the domination in our society of technology and bureaucracy it must be said that the chance for the individual to experience the feeling of personal worth is diminishing. People in this situation find it more difficult to fight anguish and anxiety and they become easier victims of them.

A special feature of anonymity among people within technology and bureaucracy is worth noting. It is part of working life within an industrial process that feelings have to be subdued. They may have some place but must be kept in check and controlled within the framework of what a working morality demands. The ideal person is the cool, efficient worker. Similarly, within the bureaucracy, there are demands for the control of feelings. One demands of the bureaucrat that he shall not be moved by personal considerations, that he must follow thoroughly the given procedures, and so on. The result is a gap in the emotional life of the individual. Certain parts of the individual are unimportant and almost harmful. In particular, those feelings that are considered to be of great importance for the creation of belief in oneself and the "I" security – namely, warmth, the ability to love, tenderness, personal involvement, etc. – are not desirable. The expression of rage, even justified rage, involves big risks. Taking into consideration the fact that there is an inclination among people to allow working life to influence, and to spill over into, other spheres of life, the danger of a certain coolness in human relationships generally becomes obvious.

Man's need for forgiveness, a need for help to appear, to be freed from feelings of guilt and to be able to develop a positive attitude are fundamental; so, too, are his feelings of responsibility and moral obligation towards somebody or something.

In this connection I wish to point to the demand for perfection in our technological and bureaucratic society. The reasons are obvious. Technical error may bring devastating consequences, including human victims, within many areas of our society. We need only think of medical care, aviation, navigation and the building of bridges in order to realize this. Bureaucracy requires that one should be efficient and have no failings. One error in bureaucracy can also bring unfortunate consequences. Injustice and economic catastrophe could be the consequence. The system demands that people working within technical and bureaucratic areas should make no mistakes. Machines and bureaucracy make no allowance for variation, they are not considerate, they do not show forgiveness. Industrial society demands efficiency. But, in spite of the demands for efficiency and perfection, it is a fact that it is people who control the system and we can never guarantee that people do not make mistakes and errors. Unfortunately, this faultless character of the system means that mistakes and errors are unforgivable. For many people this creates anxiety when they face the work in hand.

Because they are human beings with weaknesses and failings, however, many people have not been able to fulfill the demands mentioned above within technology and bureaucracy. There are in our society an increasing number of people who cannot keep up with the stress and demand for efficiency. Industrialization is about to create a society of unforgiven people, the so-called B league. We are creating, with this development, an increasing group of people who are bereft of the possibility of experiencing their worth and of keeping their self-respect. If it is correct that self-respect and the "I" security are conditions for protecting oneself against anxiety and anguish, this development in our society must lead to the point where an increasing number of people will lack protection against anguish.

We must conclude: belief in forgiveness which returns to people their dignity and self-trust, which helps them to experience their worth and gives them back the belief that there is somebody who cares about them has in our modern society difficulty in making itself heard. In addition to the repression of religion, there is the fact that society seems to lack the ability of providing compensation for this loss and, on the contrary, is developing in the direction where man's ability to experience worth and self-trust is receding more and more.

Change in the content of anxiety brought about by changes in systems of value

It has been stated earlier that values influence the nature of anxiety. The more a central value in life is threatened the more the anxiety increases. It is possible in our present-day society to find that, in relation to earlier eras, changes with regard to both values and ideologies have taken place. As a final comment, I shall now indicate some of these changes.

An important aspect of religions and life-stances is that they try to indicate to others a better situation than that in which man lives at present. The dream of a better world springs from the knowledge of the limitations and imperfections of human existence. The contradiction between what man is able to accomplish and what he has in fact accomplished compels the need to imagine a better existence. The dream of a better existence presumes that existence can be changed, that it is not set once and for all.

In earlier times, one used to put the happy life in a distant past, a golden age, or in an equally distant future. We may think of Plato's Ideal State, or of Judaism's and Christianity's belief in a Messianic happy age. The goal of Marxism, too, the classless society, is a Utopia. What characterizes the present is that the thought of a better human life is no longer placed in a distant past or in an equally distant Utopian future. It has become a program for the betterment of society and the creation of new possibilities for man.

It is obvious that such demands that life should now realize something of the Utopian dream has created both expectations and anxiety, for time goes on and the goal appears to be as distant as ever. In present-day society there appears to be a strange contradiction between, on the one hand, criticism of society, political programs and planning of the so called "good" society and, on the other hand, people's daily experience that the realization of the plans are increasingly pushed into the distance, and that the development of society seems rather to move in the opposite direction to what has been planned and preached.

Man's fear of the future has thus changed its character when compared with times past. In earlier times the fear of hell predominated and was maintained far into our century by "hot gospelers" and doomsday prophets. In our own time this fear has largely disappeared – and good riddance! In its place it is likely that one will have to reckon with an increased fear of the future. For more and more people the future has become uncertain and threatening. Fear is increased by the fact that the demands for a better world are directed towards the present. People are upset by various failings in society, and this is certainly being fueled by disappointment in the fact that the promised better conditions seem to take time. One could ask oneself whether the fear of death has increased because people are focusing on the present life as the only thing they have. Death becomes an even greater threat. Closely connected to the belief in a better society is the contemporary discussion about the quality of life. An increasing number of people are being given the impression that it is a fundamental human right not only to have material security, but also to be allowed to live a life that is friendly towards man with the possibility of attaining self-realization. When it is seen as a self-evident right to be happy, anything that happens to destroy that expectation is bound to create severe disappointment. And the more people have to experience the very opposite of the happiness program, the more the basis for anxiety is created that this present life – being the only one there is – should pass one by without any glimpses of the "real" life. It goes without saying that we should not cease to strive for a better society. But such as our nature is, one cannot escape the anguish-creating effects that come as a result of dreams of happiness. In earlier times, people were prepared in a very different manner for the fact that life was a "vale of tears."

Finally, one may ask oneself whether women do not feel the threat of the future more strongly than men. Research into anxiety about the political situation in the world shows that women in Sweden experience anxiety concerning the future at the thought of the risk of war to a higher degree than men. In most studies, women are shown to be more negative in their attitude towards nuclear power than men (even if the difference is sometimes small). To what extent this anxiety is justified no-one can decide. A hypothesis worth thinking about, however, is that people with greater emotional sensitivity than others, perhaps primarily women and artists, also perceive the dangers earlier and see what is happening in society more acutely. With this hypothesis in mind, one form of study of the future might be a study of what is going on in the arts. Another method hinted at by Rollo May (1972), among others, is to study the development and character of psychological troubles shown by the patients of the psychotherapists, because it is true that within this area, too, changes have taken place. Rollo May believes that he can show that the psychological troubles the psychotherapists encounter in their patients presage developments in society.

It would be interesting to compare the reasoning mentioned above with an empirical research into the anxiety actually experienced by people. It has to be stressed, however, that one cannot simply draw conclusions from research about experience concerning what people experience as anxiety and the factors of anxiety. Many people are probably not aware of the nature of the context in which their experiences lie. What they can give an account of is merely their personally experienced anxiety.

Anxiety and risk

What, then, is the relationship between anxiety and risk? A simple model is that the experience of a risk creates an anxiety close to the sense of fear. This can be called a realistic anxiety or fear. As such it has a positive effect on the ability to deal with the danger, if that is not too great. An intensive fear, however, can lead to a paralysis of action, difficulty in thinking sufficiently clearly, and to many unpleasant effects on the body.

We often learn to stop thinking about threats that we cannot control or influence. Nuclear war is a dreadful risk which we Swedes, at least, can do very little about. We cannot, and do not have the strength to, live with anguish within our consciousness decade after decade. We push away that fear, and perhaps create a new target for a fear which we can influence more easily. Before the referendum of 1980 in Sweden, many people probably thought that nuclear power was precisely one of those problems they could influence. But what is it like now? Is it possible that the lessened activity in the problem could partly be explained by the fact that one is now thought to be powerless?

Relationships, however, can be more complicated. A risk can be marked not only because it is dangerous in itself but also because of its inability to satisfy basic needs for security, community of feeling and meaningfulness. Some of these failings can be nearly impossible to fulfill; such is the case with man's anguish in the face of the enigmas of life and death.

In the debate about risks, one has to respect people's views for what they are as well as for what they pretend to be: concern with real dangers. This does not prevent one from understanding, sometimes, reactions to risks in wider contexts such as have been outlined in this chapter. Obviously such an understanding must not take precedence over a serious debate about risks as such. In this chapter our task has been, amongst other things, to describe and understand people's reactions to risks. We have therefore also considered it important to relate them to more general factors which have their origin in the character of human existence.

References

Becker, E. 1971. *The birth and death of meaning*. New York: The Free Press.
Becker, E. 1974. *Revolution in psychiatry*. New York: The Free Press.
Berger, P., B. Berger and H. Kellner 1974. *The homeless mind*. London: Penguin.

Dobzhansky, T. 1967. *Biology of ultimate concern*. New York: The New American Library.

Fromm, E. 1973. *The anatomy of human destructiveness*. New York: Holt, Rinehart and Winston.

Hedenius, I. 1959. *Tro och Livsåskådning*. Stockholm: Bonniers.

Lepp, I. 1963. *Psychoanalyse de l'atheisme moderne*. Paris: Grasset. [English translation: Atheism in our time. Translated by B. Murchland. New York: Macmillan. Macmillan Paperbacks Edition 1964.]

Malinowski, B. 1958. The role of magic and religion. In [W. A. Lessa and E. Z. Vogt, (eds)] *Reader in comparative religion*: *An Anthropological Approach*. Evanston, Ill.:Row Peterson.
Monod, J. 1970. *Le hasard et la nécessité*. Essai sur la philosophie naturelle de la biologie moderne. Paris: Editions du Seuil. [English translation: Chance and necessity: An essay on the natural philosophy of modern biology. Translated from the French by A. Wainhouse. London: Collins.]
May, R. 1964. *Love and will*. New York: Norton.

O'Dea, T. F. 1966. *The sociology of religion*. Englewood Cliffs, N.J.: Prentice-Hall.
Odén, B. 1982. Historiskt perspektiv. In *Risk och beslut*, L. Sjöberg (ed.), pp. 19–53. Stockholm: Liber.

Taylor, F. W. 1947. *Scientific management*. Westport, Conn.: Greenwood Press.
Tillich, P. 1959. *The courage to be*. New Haven, Conn.: Yale University Press.

8 *Valuation of personal injuries: the problem*

BIRGITTA JUÅS AND BENGT MATTSSON

Explicit and implicit values

Decisions affecting the risk for personal injuries are made in several sectors of society, e.g. in transport by sea, air and land, in nuclear power stations, in hospitals and fire departments and in factories as well as in everyday life at home. The decision maker could be the government, state or local, its officials, the corporation head, the employee, the car driver or the housewife.

Risks could be reduced at a cost. Each one of us is willing to take risks at the right price. We cross the street instead of using the subway beneath it, if we would lose too much time that way. So we could expect society (i.e. all of us together) to do the same: trade safety for other utilities. When resources are allocated between risk-reducing activities on the one hand and production of other utilities on the other, we need to know what society is willing to pay. Efficiency considerations alone would call for an allocation of resources between risk-reducing activities so that the cost, at the margin, of further risk reductions is the same in all activities. (We will modify that statement somewhat later.)

If the government, the Road Traffic Board or someone else decides that each saved life is worth $250 000 in calculations concerning road traffic safety measures we call that an *explicit* value. If we know that by spending $1 million on a road safety project we will save four lives (and there will be no other effects) and that the decision maker has turned down that project, we will say that the *implicit* value of a life is less than $250 000.

Implicit values could be calculated for all kinds of sectors (road traffic, aviation, hospitals and so on) but explicit values are not frequently used in all sectors. Particularly within road transport they use, more or less officially, an explicit price of different kinds of accidents in their cost–benefit analysis.

IMPLICIT VALUES VERSUS PREFERENCES

In our opinion it is possible – with the method described above – to estimate *values of accidents*. If we are to interpret those values as the preferences of the decision makers, further assumptions are required:

(a) The decision maker must have an opportunity to choose. Consequently there must be at least two alternatives.

(b) The decision maker must be informed of the dimensions of all the relevant facts. Thus, in the example cited, he must know the expected decrease in the number of accidents[1] and the other benefits and costs.

(c)   The decision maker acts rationally. Among other things, this means that he considers the risk of accident and always comes to the same decision whenever the circumstances are the same.

Willingness to pay in theory

How much does society want to pay (what cost[2] is acceptable) to reduce the risk of personal injury by, say, 0.0002? (By multiplying with the number of people involved we could find out the extra number of people we expect to save by a particular safety device.) The answer is: That depends. Let us discuss some of the factors that might affect the answer.

WHO IS THE DECISION MAKER?

Utility functions and budgetary restrictions differ, but as long as people are trading risks in the same markets they meet the same price, and in maximizing utility they arrive at the same willingness to pay. But governments, officials, firms, employees and households are buying different kinds of safety measures. They are "selling risks" in different markets. Therefore, we try to cover the various decision levels within each sector.

WHAT IS THE RISK LEVEL?

The willingness to pay is increased as the risk is increased and could very well be thought of as infinite at a high risk. I may be willing to pay infinite amounts to grasp at a straw, when I am almost certain that it is my only chance to survive. If we want to find out the willingness to pay in society, we ought to study decisions to reduce risks at different levels of initial risk. Also, we should bear in mind that if we use estimates of willingness to pay for marginal risk reductions to estimate larger decreases or increases, we overestimate and underestimate, respectively, the willingness to pay.

RELATIONS TO THOSE IN DANGER

Schelling (1968) stressed the difference between identified and anonymous persons: "Let a 6-year-old girl with brown hair need thousands of dollars for an operation that will prolong her life until Christmas and the post office will be swamped with nickels and dimes to save her. But let it be reported that without a sales tax hospital facilities of Massachusetts will deteriorate and cause a barely perceptible increase in preventable deaths – not many will drop a tear or reach for their check-books."

We agree with Schelling about the conclusions, but we are not convinced that they could be attributed entirely to identifiability. Without an operation the little girl was certain to die. The initial risk was very high and her, or her parents', willingness to pay may very well be infinitely high and so will the society's that includes her. Furthermore, a direct personal sacrifice was called for. The act of giving makes me feel good and I know that my conscience would torment me should I let the girl die. Then, it is not just the girl that I pay for, but the benefit of the act of giving as well. With tax-financed hospitals that transactionary benefit is not there. The implicit values, we may find, are to be used in calculations of, for example, hospital care and road projects. And there is no transactionary benefit there either.

Myself, my children, my aunt, someone I know, someone I have heard of, people in my home town, Swedes or someone red-haired like me or just some-one in danger...Of course, it matters who it is! The chances of getting to know people, from newspapers and magazines, may be greater the fewer they are. As a rule, there are more people in danger that could be saved by precau-tionary measures than by measures after the accident. Also the time to "get to know" those in danger may be important for the relations that may be established between us and them. Searching for people shut up in a mine is a lengthy process.

If we want to protect our neighbors, the risk they run should be included in our utility function. As is pointed out by Bergstrom (1974) that does not *necessarily* imply that we want them to take better care of themselves. Because to do that, they have to make sacrifices (e.g. of time and money). If we are really concerned about their well-being, we might come to the conclusions that they should not pay more than they themselves want to. In that special case, where our neighbors' utility functions (not their lives) enter our utility func-tions, the sum of what people are willing to pay for their own lives is equal to the sum the society wants to pay. Otherwise it is less (Bergstrom 1974).

CATASTROPHES OR JUST COMMONPLACE ACCIDENTS

Does the number of people killed in one accident matter? Are people willing to pay more or less to save 100 people from being killed in 80 accidents than from a catastrophe where all 100 are killed? The answer has to do with what we dealt with above. In a catastrophe all my family, friends and foes go with me. I am spared the agony of mourning. On the other hand, nobody will pass on my heritage. The politician (or bureaucrat) will perhaps be harassed by the press if 100 people are killed in a catastrophe. Eighty separate and trivial accidents will not attract that much attention. That might affect the decisions made by the politician, but then he has disregarded maximization of social welfare.

FEELING SAFE: ACTUAL RISK VERSUS PERCEIVED RISK

As pointed out (e.g. by d'Iribarne 1969), willingness to pay is determined not just by what you want to pay to prolong your expected life time; anxiety, the sense of insecurity or the thrill of risk-taking may also be involved. The fear of flying is very real although statisticians can prove that car driving is more dangerous. Then the utility functions should include not the actual risk but the perceived risk element as a component of the utility function.

VOLUNTARY AND INVOLUNTARY RISKS?

Starr (1969) has, in an oft-cited article, distinguished between voluntary and involuntary risks. According to Starr (1969, p. 1233) the distinction is the following: "In the cases of 'voluntary' activities, the individual uses his own value system to evaluate his experiences."... "Involuntary activities differ in that the criteria and options are determined not by the individuals affected but by the controlling body." According to Starr, dangerous driving is an example of a voluntary risk and earthquake is an example of an involuntary risk.

We see no reason for this distinction. We think that almost everything an individual does can be characterized as taking "voluntary risks." The individual makes, of course, a greater sacrifice if he drives a car at 130 km h^{-1} when there is a speed limit of 50 km h^{-1}, compared to no speed limitation at all. Even the risk of an individual being killed in an earthquake can be influenced. One way is to move from California, if you live there, eastwards in the USA. The cost of moving (including all types of costs; lower wages, a higher rent, transportation costs, etc.) or the cost of driving slowly (e.g. increased traveling time) could be called a transaction cost. The individual can, at a certain transaction cost, decrease the risk of being killed in a car crash but he can also, at a certain transaction cost, decrease the risk of being killed in an earthquake. What it comes down to in the end is not a difference in kind but in degree. You may say that "involuntary risks" are situations you have to "pay" *a lot* to get out of.

To clarify the discussion, we therefore recommend the use of the term high or low transaction costs to affect the risk of accidents.

Sometimes "voluntary–involuntary risk" is used in another sense. Raisbeck (1972) writes: "Some risks may now be involuntary simply because people are ignorant about them." If one does not know, for example, that the risk of dying from thrombosis is increased if one uses contraceptive pills, and if one does not know that the risk is positively related to some factors (e.g. type of blood) one could, of course, call it an involuntary risk when someone takes her pills. We think nevertheless that it is more clarifying to discuss it in terms of access to information. This is, on the one hand, a more correct labeling, on the other it makes it easier to understand that this is a question of degree and not of kind. Thus, in this case we prefer to speak of access to or lack of information at the moment of decision.

LIVES OR REMAINING YEARS?

When we "save a life" with some measure affecting personal fatalities we in fact make it possible for a person to live some years more. Instead of speaking of "saved lives" perhaps we should use the term "remaining man-years." If you "save the life" of a girl of 15 in Sweden you will on the average save about 63 remaining years. (For a boy of the same age it is 58 years.) If you "save the life" of a woman of 67 years you, on the average, save about 15 remaining years. (For a man of the same age the corresponding figure is 13 years.) In this chapter we try to use both concepts but, because of statistical difficulties, it is not always possible for us to show the value per remaining man-year.

HOW MUCH DO WE (OR SHOULD WE) PAY?

We have listed above a number of hypotheses about factors that might affect the attitude to risk. We have, more or less successfully, tried to find the data to test them. (Some general conclusions are reported later in this chapter.) From a normative point of view, we may take some of them into account when we determine the value to society of a risk reduction. Then, we should not call it "inconsistency" when the implicit values vary due to variation in those "admissible" factors. It is outside our field of work to make normative statements and therefore it is left to the reader to determine whether decisions are in fact inconsistent or irrational.

ESTIMATION OF IMPLICIT VALUES

From what has been said, it should be clear that the value of a reduced risk of accidents should be based on what society is willing to pay. Many different decision makers are involved, private firms and individuals, local and central authorities. In cost–benefit analysis it is common practice to determine what individuals are willing to pay for a commodity. What society wants to pay is then assumed to be the sum of what each individual wants to pay. Often, where human life is at stake (e.g. in the neighborhood of a nuclear power plant) individuals have left it to the authorities to make decisions on safety matters. The willingness of individuals to pay is then manifested in political decisions.

We will now deal with the theoretical problems one meets when one tries to determine the willingness of individuals and public bodies to pay (for whom the willingness to pay appears as decisions made by local and central authorities).

The individual's willingness to pay

First, it should be pointed out that the term "willingness to pay" should be interpreted in a broad sense: It could be money. You buy a more expensive safer car. You buy life jackets for your boat. Or, you choose a job with a comparatively low risk of accidents instead of a better paid but more dangerous job. It could be time. You drive slowly but safely. You choose the train instead of the car, although you would reach your destination sooner by car. It could be convenience. You wear a safety helmet although it makes you feel uncomfortable.

THE "PURE" DEATH-RISK[3]

For relevant references, see Conley (1973), Bergstrom (1974), Rappaport (1974), Usher (1973), and Jones-Lee (1969). Consider the following two lotteries: Lottery no. 1: Outcomes $0, 1, 2, \ldots n \ldots$ is the number of remaining years to live. P_n is the probability of having exactly n years left to live. Let q_n be the probability of dying in the year n provided you have lived for $n - 1$ years. Then

$$P_n = (1 - q_0)(1 - q_1)\ldots(1 - q_{n-1}) \cdot q_n$$

Lottery no. 2 has the same outcomes, but the probability of dying in n years is increased. An extra risk is added. The probability will then become P_n^*. How much do we have to pay a man to swap lottery 2 for lottery 1?

In the theory of consumer behavior we usually assume that a man's utility could be represented by a function of the consumed amount of commodities (Y) during different time periods (t). When life is over (in time period n) one cannot consume. Our risk taker, when still alive, could be allowed to take an interest in the well-being of generations to come, e.g. his heirs. We would then introduce the future flows of commodities as arguments in his utility function. (But he is probably not indifferent to commodities available before and after death.)

The utility function (U) of a person with n years left to live would be as follows:

$$U_n = U_n(Y_0, Y_1, \ldots Y_t \ldots). \tag{1}$$

Y_t may thus be commodities available after the person's death in the year n. On some, not very restrictive, assumptions about rationality the theory of expected utility is applicable (see e.g. Luce & Raiffa 1958). The expected utility of a lottery is the expected value of the utility of the outcomes:

$$E(U) = P_0 U_0(Y_0, Y_1, \ldots Y_t \ldots) + P_1 U_1(Y_0, Y_1 \ldots Y_t \ldots) + \ldots \tag{2}$$

We assume that a person will choose Y so that $E(U)$ is maximized subject to his physical and financial restrictions.

Now, we add an extra risk λ in time period 0. The probability of dying in period 0 will then be $P_0^* = \lambda + (1 - \lambda)q_0$. The probability of dying in period n is q_n as before and the probability of living for exactly n years would be $P_n^* = (1 - \lambda) \cdot P_n$. The expected utility:

$$E*(U) = \lambda U_0(Y_0, Y_1, \ldots Y_t \ldots) + (1 - \lambda)\Sigma P_n U_n(Y_0, Y_1, \ldots Y_t \ldots) \tag{3}$$

is maximized on the new assumptions. Let the maximum value be $\overline{E*(U)}$.

It can be seen from the utility function that an increased amount of Y, for example in period 0, could be a substitute for an increased risk. It is assumed that commodity Y_0 will bring a diminishing contribution to utility (marginal utility) as we consume more of it, which means that, as the amount of Y_0 is increased, we are more inclined to buy increased safety at the price of less consumption in, for example, the year 0. The willingness to pay is increased. By willingness to pay we mean in this context.

$$\frac{dY_0}{d\lambda} = -\frac{dE*(U)/d\lambda}{dE*(U)/dY_0} = \frac{(E*(U) - U_0)/(1 - \lambda)}{(1 - \lambda)\Sigma P_n[(\partial U_n/\partial Y_0) + (\partial U_0/\partial Y_0)]} \tag{4}$$

The value of human life used explicitly in, for example, traffic planning is usually based on the discounted value of future loss of production caused by the death of a human being. Let us compare that approach to Equation (4). In Equation (4) the future loss of consumption determines the value of a risk reduction. The more years I have left to live, the higher is $\overline{E*(U)}$ and the willingness to pay. Remaining length of life is thus a more relevant measure of the effect of safety arrangements than the number of lives.[3]

Suppose that the "market price" of the extra risk at unit level is $\overline{Y}_0$. The risk taker would then take a risk λ_0 so as to equalize Equation (4) to $\overline{Y}_0$. In so doing, he has revealed to us that he is willing to pay the price $\overline{Y}_0$ for a marginal decrease in risk. We now have the answer to the question we asked initially: how much do we have to pay to persuade a man to accept lottery no. 2? It should be observed, however, that the market price is relevant for marginal changes in risk only. He demands a better unit price[4] for larger increases and a lower unit price for larger decreases in the risk level. This asymmetrical behavior, which in our example is a direct consequence of the decreasing marginal utility of commodity Y_0, is in accordance with observations of behavior under gambling conditions. If all people in a society are faced with with the same price of risk, all of them, with a few exceptions, the suicider and the one who wants safety at any price, will reveal the same willingness to pay. Then we could claim to have found what we are looking for: what society is willing to pay for a marginal decrease in risk. This does not imply that all people are alike, but they have adjusted their behavior to the same set of prices. They have all reduced their risks to the point where the price of further risk reduction exceeds utility.

A person might not wish to lose his life for anything that money could buy. Yet, he could choose the car instead of the train, even though he knows that the train is safer. There is nothing contradictory about that: suppose, for example, that $dE*(U)/dY_0 = 0$ for $Y_0 > Y_0'$. That means that satisfaction is reached at a finite consumption level, and it would make the willingness to pay for risk in terms of Y_0 infinite. Besides, the absolute risk level is important to the value of a change in risk. For a person who is not concerned about the consumption of his heirs, the first term of Equation (3) equals 0 and the rate of substitution will become:

$$\frac{E(U)}{(1 - \lambda)\Sigma P_n(dU_n/dY_0)} \tag{4a}$$

and approach infinity as λ approaches unity.

We could thus conclude: the ambition to save a man from certain death at any price may be in accordance with what we would recommend on the basis of a cost–benefit analysis, where the benefit of a life is based on the individual's willingness to pay.

There could not (in the long run and on realistic assumptions about costs of producing increased safety) exist sectors side by side with different market prices for risk. Nobody would take the lower paid risk. Yet evidently there exist at the same time different prices of risk, for example the very high price of safety measures in nuclear power plants and airplanes and the much lower price on the road. There seems to be something wrong with our reasoning. We now introduce, as an explanatory variable, the feeling of risk.

THE FEELING OF RISK

Utility was expressed as a function of the consumed quantities of commodities. That does not mean that utility is independent of other conditions. Consider a person who is confronted with a risk but has an option to buy himself free from that risk. Should he choose to spend some of his budget on risk reduction, the utility U_n of each life span is reduced by the marginal utility of those other things that money can buy. The availability of intangibles like friendship is not affected by his decision so we do not have to bring them explicitly into the utility functions U_n. (Linneroth's (1975) apprehensions on that account are not well founded.) There is one qualification, however, the feeling of risk. There are reasons to believe that the utility of a given length of life depends on the risk. During the flight you may think about the dreadful things that would happen if all engines stopped working. You drive at top speed and enjoy playing with death. The circus performer enjoys the admiration of the audience of his contempt of death. So risk has utility in itself, be it negative or positive.

If we introduce the risk as an argument in the utility function of a given length of life, it would be as follows:

$$E*(U) = \lambda U_0(\lambda, Y_0, Y_1 \ldots Y_t \ldots) + (1 - \lambda)\Sigma P_n U_n(\lambda, Y_0, Y_1 \ldots Y_t \ldots) \quad (5)$$

Suppose that the value of this function is maximized subject to financial and physical restrictions. The willingness to pay will be:

$$\frac{dY}{d\lambda} = \frac{\overline{(E*(U))} - U_0)/(1 - \lambda) + (1 - \lambda)\Sigma P_n(-dU_n/d\lambda) + \lambda(-dU_0/d\lambda)}{(1 - \lambda)\Sigma P_n(dU_n/dY_0) + \lambda(dU_0/dY_0)} \quad (6)$$

It could be seen that the fear of death has added two terms, the value of which depends on the utility contribution caused by an increase in risk, $dU_n/d\lambda$. The terms are positive if the increase in risk decreases utility as it does with the nervous air passenger. The circus performer could give us some trouble. If the increase in risk increases utility the last two terms of Equation (6) are negative. Ultimately, the whole ratio could become negative. But hardly at high risk levels.

The theory of expected utility, which our utility function is built on, presupposes in fact risk aversion. It may seem contradictory to introduce people like the circus performer. When we derive the expected utility from the probability distribution of outcomes, we, however, assume a game which is quite different and in that game he could still be a risk averter. He likes to jump in front of an audience but not to run the risk of losing his life. The increased risk of death is the price he has to pay for the cheering of the audience.

There is no reason to believe that $dU_n/d\lambda$ should be equal in all social sectors involving risk (air and road traffic, nuclear power plants, factories). That is a possible explanation for the fact that different market prices of risk exist side by side. Risk is not a homogeneous commodity. The second and third term of Equation (6) differ between sectors.

THE LIFE OF OUR NEIGHBOR

The existence of a human being may bring joy or sorrow to others. A reduced risk of accidents then becomes a public utility, in the sense that it enters the utility function of at least two persons. People may be unwilling to finance by private means a commodity that gives other people utility to almost the same extent. Suppose that nobody (not even the person in danger) could pay for a reduction in the risk which my brother J runs. How much do I want to pay of commodity Y_0? My brother is confronted with a risk λ_j which is introduced into my utility function. It becomes:

$$E_i(U) = \Sigma p_n^i U_n^i(\lambda_j, Y_0, Y_1, \ldots Y_t \ldots). \quad (7)$$

I want to sacrifice:

$$\frac{dY_0}{d\lambda_j} = -\frac{dE(U)/d\lambda_j}{dE(U)/dY_0} = \sum \frac{p_n(-dU_n^i/d\lambda_j)}{p_n(dU_n^i/dY_0)} \qquad (8)$$

If I like my brother, Equation (8) will be a positive number which should be added to the estimate in Equation (6) (his own willingness to pay) to get what society wants to pay for brother J. (That is if I do not care about my brother's consumption of other commodities.) Now, suppose that I am exposed to the same risk factor as my brother. $dU_n^i/d\lambda_j$ in Equation (8) and my willingness to pay may well depend on the risk I run myself. But it is hard to tell whether it will increase or decrease as λ_i is increased. If I myself run a great risk of being killed, the chances are good that I do not have to mourn my brother. On the other hand, I may be anxious for someone in the family to carry on. Those relations are important to the valuation of catastrophes (earthquakes, nuclear explosions) which may annihilate whole communities.

Now, suppose that my brother J pays for his increased safety. Brother J will consume a greater amount of commodity Y if he chooses to take a greater risk. His consumption of commodity Y may be a public good as well as the risk. That would mean that I rejoice at my brother's consumption. In order to arrive at the social willingness to pay, the value in Equation (6) should be adjusted not only for my willingness to pay for my brother's risk but also for my willingness to pay for his consumption.

The former term is positive, the latter negative. Now, suppose instead that what gives me joy is not my brother's consumption directly and the safety he enjoys, but the utility that my brother derives from it. My utility function will then become:

$$E_i(U) = \Sigma p_n^i U_n^i(E_j(U_j), Y_0, Y_1, \dots Y_t \dots). \qquad (9)$$

If, besides, my utility function is additive we get:

$$E_i(U) = a_i E_i(U) + a_j E_j(U_j) \qquad (10)$$

where a_i and a_j are weights.

My brother J is fully compensated for an increase in risk by the amount in Equation (6). (He moves along the same indifference curve.) If I have an additive utility function I am thereby also fully compensated for a change in my brother's safety. Thus, what society wants to pay for a decrease in risk is then the value of Equation (6) unadjusted.[5] It may seem paradoxical that the most "altruistic" form of my utility function will lead to my not paying anything to reduce my brother's risk. The truth is, however, that I do "pay" by the thought that my brother will consume less.

Empirical investigations alone could decide between the shapes of our utility functions. We could get a hint if we consider how we treat suicidal attempts. Do we try to "save" the suicider even though we know that it is against his wishes? It is not evidence enough that we in fact try to prevent suicide, unless we are convinced that the attempts are meant seriously.

It may be that I want to pay one way or the other to reduce the risk to my brother, but do we want to pay to reduce the risk to total strangers? I could hardly mourn the death of people of whose existence I am not aware. Yet, I might contribute a minor sum of money to reduce the risk of an accident in a factory in another part of the country, although I do not know who works there. Maybe my contribution would be less if the factory were abroad but more if it were in my home town. I would certainly pay more if those who are exposed to danger were portrayed in newspapers. If I knew that an accident would happen if I did not contribute, I would be more generous. It could be of some importance if many people were to be killed in a severe accident than if there were many accidents with only one person killed in each.

But why do I want to pay for a stranger? In order not to have the life of a human being on my conscience? To feel that I have done my good deed for the day? To be saved myself (with some vague idea of being rewarded)? In all three cases it is the monetary transaction that gives me satisfaction: as I have been given the option to contribute or not I have a responsibility that lies heavy on my conscience. I find satisfaction in the voluntary contribution. I feel safer when I think I have a claim of gratitude. The answer will decide whether we are to add the willingness to pay for unknown people to the value in Equation (6). We should not do it if the hypotheses of our motives are correct. What we want to pay for is connected with the voluntary contribution. And it is not relevant when the authorities collect information of the willingness to pay in order to decide on the taxes that should be used to prevent accidents. Schelling described vividly in his article of 1968 the willingness to pay for a six-year-old girl with brown hair who needs money for an operation that would prolong her life until Christmas, as discussed above. He wants us to compare that sum to what we would pay in the form of sales tax for a hospital in Massachusetts. According to Schelling the difference in generosity depends on the fact that the girl has been identified to us. It is true that it might be one of the reasons. Another reason may be that the girl must certainly die now, the patients of the Massachusetts hospital might survive. The third reason is the difference in the financial arrangements, a voluntary contribution or a sales tax.

The willingness to pay of government authorities[6]

An authority has physical and financial restrictions to consider. An increased safety must therefore be bought at the price of other commodities. The costs would be the loss of private consumption if the safety measures are financed with increased taxes, or the cost could be other commodities produced by the authority within a given budget. The cost of producing safety is probably increasing as a function of the safety level already reached.

We introduced a utility function for an individual which should represent his preferences for different commodities, among them safety. The authority's preferences could be represented by a function, but it cannot be derived in the same way as the utility function of the individual. To mark the difference we call the function of the authority "preference function." We could say that the authority (as did the individual) consumes a certain level of safety and pays a certain price for it. The safety level chosen by the authority will be that which maximizes the values of the preference function, subject to physical and financial restrictions. Alternatively, we could say that the authority produces safety at a cost. (The choice of the individual could also be reformulated as a production problem: one produces safety by buying a life jacket and putting it on.)

If the commodities were sold on the market place, the authority would be faced with fixed prices, p_λ and p_y. A profit-maximizing authority would produce so much that the cost of a marginal change in risk (as measured in commodity Y_0) is equal to p_λ/p_Y which is equal to the individual's willingness to pay as given in Equation (6) before we introduced neighborliness. But the authority does not market its safety measures and there are no price signals to follow. The authority must base its opinion on how much people would sacrifice for increased safety on something else. Theoretically, the preference function could be derived from the individual utility functions, provided among other things that utility is measurable. When we described a person as maximizing his expected utility, we, in fact, used the same assumptions from which we could derive measurable utility. An impartial authority could, however, feel obligated to take care of the interests of future generations. It could, for example, be willing to pay more to prevent genetic changes than would individuals. So far we have regarded the authority as a welfare-maximizing machine. But the authority is a decision maker with his own views on how much to produce of different commodities. The preference function is personal. The decision maker could take his own good conscience into consideration, or give way to public opinion roused by a sensational accident.

Let $f(\lambda, Y_0)$ be the preference function of a centrally planned community. λ is an extra risk, as before, and Y_0 represents other commodities. The risk could be affected by several activities $x_1, x_2, \ldots x_m$. The restriction on resources is:

$$C(x_1, x_2, \ldots x_m, Y_0) \leqslant R \tag{11}$$

An optimum condition would be:

$$\frac{dY_0}{d\lambda} = \frac{C'_1}{\lambda'_1} \cdot \frac{1}{C'_{Y_0}} = \frac{C'_2}{\lambda'_2} \cdot \frac{1}{C'_{Y_0}} = \ldots = \frac{C'_m}{\lambda'_m} \cdot \frac{1}{C'_{Y_0}} \tag{12}$$

That is, the marginal sacrifice of resources (= marginal costs) of increased safety should be the same for all activities affecting safety and equal to the willingness to pay. If we measure the consumption of other commodities (Y_0) in monetary units we will have the willingness to pay expressed in monetary units.

Now, let us return to a decentralized community where there are many decision makers. Suppose that different sectors (e.g. sea rescue, air traffic and hospitals) appear to have different marginal costs of increasing safety. Could we then draw the conclusion that the latter difference indicates different willingness to pay? The answer is yes if we could assume that resources were optimally allocated between the private and the public sector and between the different public authorities. As that is not the case, we are confined to comparing the rates of substitution between the variables entering the preference function of each authority. We could, of course, use the monetary unit in comparing the values of one decision maker who is responsible for several sectors. We must, however, remember that on a lower level the costs in monetary units are not comparable between different decision makers. We could study the values of the Parliament by comparing marginal costs of the Board of Occupation Safety and the Board of Road Administration. We could study the preferences of the Board of Road Administration by comparing the marginal costs of making the road broader and improving the surface of the road, but these marginal costs should not be compared to the costs of inspecting factories. The preferences of the Board of Occupation Safety and Board of Road Adminis- tration could be the same even if the marginal costs are different, if their budgets differ by mistake or because the parliament, which decides on their budgets, values safety measures in the two branches of administration differently.

Inconsistencies among authorities could also be caused by lack of inform- ation of the consequences of their decisions or the alternatives open to them at the time of the decision. It seems difficult to discriminate between incon- sistencies caused by lack of information and those caused by different prefer- ences. To do that, we have to know the degree of information available at the time of the decision. If we give up that ambition, the implicit values are still useful. The decision maker should be confronted with his implicit values and then he has a chance to decide whether they are in accordance with his prefer- ences or not.

Problems of estimation

THE RISK CONCEPT

We have deliberately postponed a definition of the concept "risk." A willing- ness-to-pay approach calls for a definition of risk, so that it corresponds to the payer's experiences, be it a private person or an official, acting on his own behalf, or as a representative of the public will.

Newspapers pay attention to the total number of accidents, and sometimes a drop in that figure is regarded as an increase in safety. The number of acci- dents must, of course, be viewed in relation to something, but what? We could with Katz (1971) group the denominators into two families, a static family and an activity family. Examples of the static family are accidents/number of inhabitants, accidents/number of cars and accidents/number of road- miles. Examples of the activity family are accidents/production volume, accidents/number of landings and accidents/number of passengers.

Now, safer cars may not decrease the number of accidents per 1000 cars. Households cannot afford two cars when the cost of the safety equipment is added to the purchase price. Each car is used more frequently and the number of accidents per 1000 cars may actually increase. The number of accidents should be related to an activity variable, such as car-miles instead. Although we acknowledge the superiority of activity variables, when it comes to it, we are not always able to measure activity.

Hypothesis number 2 (p. 132 "What is the risk level?") above was that the initial risk level was a factor determining the willingness to pay for a change in it. Hence, we must somehow measure the absolute risk levels.

CHANGES IN RISK

Controlled experiments, the method for studying causes and effects, so widely used in behavioral and natural sciences is often an unattainable ideal in social sciences. In a few cases, controlled experiments could be used to find out how the risk of, for example a collision, is affected by a particular safety device. But, as a rule, we have to rely on time series (e.g. compare the number of accidents on roads with and without speed limits). The trouble with both methods is that it is not only the safety measures that differ, so causal inferences are difficult.

THE "PRICE"

By the word "price" is to be understood not just payment in monetary units but, for example, time and discomfort as well. Safety measures seldom have a pure effect, a decrease in the number of deaths. Should we restrict our study to those cases, our report would be thin indeed. Improving the roads in a district will diminish the number of people who die in road accidents, but the number of people who are injured, seriously or slightly, and the number of properties damaged are affected as well. Travelling time and vehicle repair costs are changed. To get the "price" that has been paid to avoid deaths we must, somehow, value in monetary units the benefits of fewer people getting injured, of less vehicle repair costs, of shorter traveling time, and then deduct that sum from the costs of road improvements. That means that the techniques, developed in cost–benefit analyses, must be used.

To buy safety devices is one way of reducing risks. Another way is to give up risky activities such as motor racing, sailing and mountain climbing. The price paid to reduce risk by giving up sailing is the joy foregone (valued in money) by doing something else less the cost of keeping a sailing boat, the so-called consumer surplus.

Assigning money values to such things as discomfort and traveling time is easier said than done. In some cases it is possible to evade the problem by confining ourselves to "at least" values or "at most" values. Suppose, for example, that people are known to accept a 12-second delay in order to cross a road by using a subway. Suppose also that we are certain that it is more comfortable to walk in the subway (no chilly wind, nice posters to look at, etc.), then, we could say that people will pay at least the value of 12 seconds to reduce the risk. But if there were a bridge instead, and if we knew that not only is the bridge pass longer, but it is less comfortable as well, then neither "at least" nor "at most" values could be derived.

THE SUBSYSTEM

A decision maker who maximizes (or who should maximize) some social utility function will consider all costs to society of safety measures. When we estimate social costs we must see to it that the subsystem is large enough. Traffic restraint schemes may decrease the number of people and accidents in one part of the town but people may prefer a shopping center in another part of the town and the number of people and accidents will increase there.

MIXED OUTPUT

We have three problems to solve concerning the output:

(a) To define the output of a certain measure.

(b)   To separate the "safety effect" from other effects.
(c)   Within the "safety effect" to separate the willingness to pay for different kinds of injuries.

The problem of how to define the output is dealt with above. The other two problems we will try to analyze here.

Besides a greater safety we usually have other effects from "safety measures." (We gave examples above.) If market prices for these effects are available (e.g. if stricter rules for occupational safety would mean that the production process is delayed), and if they are not too poor estimates of the social value[7], they can be used. (In the empirical work reported below we will, to a great extent, study decisions of authorities in the public sector and therefore here we will discuss the problem from a social point of view. Individuals and enterprises have problems in defining and quantifying effects. They are less interested in the social effects.) If you do not have a market price for the shorter traveling time, less noise etc., or if you do not accept the market price as a measure of the social value (e.g. the price of gasoline in Sweden is about twice the importing cost of the commodity) you have to construct a "shadow price."

As to traveling time there is extensive literature and quite a lot of empirical work for a summary, see Harrison and Quarmby (1969) and Bruzelius (1979). It is also possible to find some estimates for noise (see, e.g. Walters 1975). For other effects, for example other environmental effects (pollution of different kinds), the empirical foundation is weak. Our investigation aims at giving information of maximum and minimum values and, because of that, environmental effects do not necessarily mean problems as long as we can tell if the sum of them is positive or negative. You get a minimum value when somebody decides in favor of a proposal of a "safety measure" and a maximum value when the proposal is rejected. For the intangibles (environmental effects in our example) you get the following possibilities:

(1)   maximum value + positive environmental effects;
(2)   maximum value + negative environmental effects;
(3)   minimum value + positive environmental effects;
(4)   minimum value + negative environmental effects;
(5)   maximum or minimum value + unsettled environmental effects.

The impact of our values of the five cases are:

(1)   The mentioned maximum value is not biased but with better information you could calculate a lower value.
(2)   The maximum value is too small.
(3)   The minimum value is too high.
(4)   The minimum value is not biased but could with better information be raised.
(5)   It is unsettled if the values are biased or not.

Items (2), (3) and (5) above thus mean problems to us, although item (5) is perhaps rather unusual. One possible solution is to choose examples where you can decide in advance that the environmental effects can be neglected.

A problem that is quite common and not of marginal importance is the last of the three problems mentioned above, that is how to separate the willingness to pay for deaths, disablements, other serious injuries and so on. Let us discuss some possible ways to "solve" that problem.

(a) Suppose that fatalities, disablements, other serious injuries and so on occur in almost fixed proportions. In such cases you could discuss the implicit value per "unit of accident," which, for example, is composed of one person killed, three people with serious injuries and ten people with slight injuries.
(b) You can use implicit values per types of injury from other sectors. If, for example, you can isolate a value for the risk of death from a sea rescue it could possibly be used in other sectors.
(c) You could use explicit values from Sweden or abroad and use them for average relations of persons killed, serious and slighter injuries.
(d) You could start with explicit values for accidents (including deaths, serious injuries, slight injuries and so on) and use them for extreme compositions of injuries and in this way get intervals of values.
(e) If you have the values for all types of injuries but one, you get that value with the standard procedure for implicit valuation.

It is difficult to evaluate these methods in general. Which of them to use depends on what kind of data you have, if you already have some estimates of values in the sector, if the sector is very similar to other sectors etc. In our empirical work we therefore have to decide what method to use for each case of evaluation.

Applications

SUMMING UP

We do not expect a decision maker to be willing to pay the same amount for a given risk reduction under all circumstances:

(a) We are prepared to pay for avoiding the feeling of danger, not just for the chance to survive. The feeling of danger is essentially different in the sectors we examine.
(b) The willingness to pay for a given change in risk is higher, the higher the risk.
(c) Who is exposed to danger? Age, connections with the decision maker, identification with the exposed (which may depend on the publicity of the case) are factors of importance.
(d) The number of people killed in each accident varies.
(e) Information of the effects of safety measures is imperfect. We will try to find out what knowledge the decision maker had at his disposal at the time of the decision. Where this cannot be done, we must admit that we cannot say anything about the decision makers' valuation. We get a value that could be compared with implicit values in similar situations.

We would like to compare values in different sectors (e.g. different kinds of transport, nuclear power stations, hospitals), when other factors are held constant, compare accidents with different degrees of disaster, other things equal and so on. Our data do not allow us to isolate the factors of importance to the willingness to pay. The hypotheses will therefore not be tested to our satisfaction. Within each sector there are several groups of decision makers: private persons, firms, government officials and parliament. We try to find out valuations and values for all of them.

We have predicted considerable problems in the empirical part of our study due to mixed output (particularly injuries of different degrees of severity) and for want of controlled experiments. In several cases we have confined ourselves to establish "at least" or "at most" values or a value of an output which is admittedly mixed, for example a standard accident. In a few cases our values are to be regarded as no more than a demonstration of method. We have sometimes pointed out how a value could be computed or in what kind the payments are made for the decrease in risk.

QUESTIONNAIRES

In some cases it has turned out to be almost impossible to derive implicit values from past decisions. One reason is the problem of mixed output. Another is that people are not informed of the risk they run. Sometimes, for example, in what concerns nuclear power, we may find out the implicit valuation of government officials or our representatives in parliament, but we do not know the willingness to pay of private persons. They have not had the opportunity to choose between projects with different risk levels. Then, the idea of finding out their private valuation simply by asking people presents itself.

To our knowledge there have been very few surveys or interviews on how we value a change in the risk of personal injury (Hedgran & Lindell 1970, Acton 1973, Cohen 1970). It is not an easy task. The questions must be hypothetical if they are to fill the gap left when we have done our best to derive implicit values from past decisions. The interviewed person may find it difficult to abstract from facts as the question presupposes. The risk may be very small and it may be hard to grasp the meaning of, for example, 1 in 25 000.

We have tried to overcome these problems in the following way. We do not ask, directly, about people's willingness to pay, but they are asked to make decisions on allocation of resources between safety measures in different sectors and some other budget items (e.g. old-age pension and day nurseries). To make the questions less hypothetical we allow mixed output, i.e. diminished number of deaths, serious and slight injuries and less property damage.

The subjects of the interview consisted of 36 students of economics who were just about to begin their first term. Groups of four people have answered the question together. We expected the members of the group to give an account of their reasons for paying a particular sum of money. By observing their discussion we hoped to find out whether they were able to abstract from "irrelevant" facts the way we wanted them to. Psychological experiments (see e.g. Kogan & Wallach 1971) have demonstrated that groups are more inclined to take risks than are individuals. The absolute level of the willingness to pay may, therefore, be underestimated, but intersector comparisons are not affected.

Our questions were not hypothetical in that we asked about safety measures that had been planned or, at least, seriously discussed. All decisions could actually be made by the central government. The costs and what we told them about the risks were approximately correct. The questions were hypothetical in that the budget was largely fixed from the start and that safety measures and a few other budget items were to be decided upon. But, above all, we put the subjects of our interview into a government position.

We tried to make information of costs and risk more accessible by asking the groups to allocate resources between the budget items in two rounds with only three safety levels to choose between in each. Risk estimates are uncertain and to convey that fact to the decision makers they had to draw a lottery ticket between the first and the second round. The outcome could be above, below or just as expected. Some of them who got an outcome, as was expected, were given a description of how some of the accidents happened. The students seem to agree on a value of death in a road traffic accident of about 1.8 million Swedish Kr. (400 000 dollars in 1981 prices).

Suicide is special (except in one group) in that its value is extremely low (less than an eleventh of the value of deaths in road traffic). With two exceptions, they accepted a low value for people killed in industrial accidents (less than a third of the value of deaths in road traffic). The two exceptions wanted to raise its value. A high value of people killed in air traffic (more than 1.5 times greater than deaths in road traffic) was accepted. Again there were two exceptions, who wanted to lower the value. The initial value of nuclear power accidents was extremely high (25 times that of road traffic). One-third of the groups wanted to lower it. Whether the outcome in the lottery was better or worse than expected does not seem to have affected the decisions in the second round. But those who got results as expected, but were given a description of an accident, in general raised the sum allocated to that budget item.

INTERNATIONAL VALUES

In the spring of 1975 we made an inquiry to officials in the sectors of public administration in several countries [8] that handled safety matters. [9] We asked (a) whether values were used explicitly in, for example, cost—benefit analysis of public projects and (b) whether they knew of data that could be used to compute implicit values.

Of the 63 replies received, many contained comments on the usefulness and feasibility of studies of the kind we planned. Out of politeness or whatever the reason, most of them seemed to approve of the idea of making valuations explicit. A notable exception is air transport in France. Their spokesman found the idea interesting from a theoretical point of view but feared the practical consequences. They preferred to formulate a goal, a particular safety standard. Then, the most efficient way of reaching that goal could be computed.

In road transport explicit values are generally used. Exceptions are Austria, Norway, Canada (in some provinces), Switzerland and The Netherlands. In other sectors, they often referred to calculations made in road transport. Values of risk are used explicitly in cost—benefit analysis by the Federal Aviation Agency, but it has not yet reached the official status of values in road transport. With the exception of Great Britain (see e.g. Goss 1971) accidents at sea do not seem to be the object of economic calculations, although in some countries there seems to be an interest in the matter. In sectors dealing with accident prevention in factories they seem least inclined to use a value of human life in their calculations (or were least aware of how it can be done). There are a few studies of the cost to society of industrial accidents, but so far as we know the values have not been used in computing the social profitability of safety measures. Within railroad transport, they mostly referred to departments that handled safety matters from the point of view of the staff, not the passengers.

Some general conclusions

(a) Explicit values are not significantly different from implicit ones. The explicit values are evenly distributed between 180 000 Swedish Kr. (1981 prices) and 3.6 million Swedish Kr. The distribution of implicit values are bimodal with the intervals 0–500 000 and 2 000 000–3 500 000 as peaks.

(b) Implicit values of individuals range from 350 000 to 3 500 000 half of them below 1 000 000. The range of government values is somewhat larger: 90 000–9 000 000 (location of nuclear power stations at 5 billion are excluded): 75% of the values are below the 1 000 000 level. Government officials made decisions implying values from a few thousands to 90 million Swedish Kr., 60% below 1 000 000. The narrower range of values of individuals is notable.

(c) The high values (explicit as well as implicit) of nuclear power support the hypothesis that people are prepared to pay more to avoid catastrophes although the expected number of victims is the same. The high values of aviation safety might point in the same direction. The feeling of insecurity (as opposed to the objective probability of death) might be a contributing factor in explaining the high values in the aviation and nuclear power sectors.

(d) Low (even negative) individual willingness to pay (and an acceptance of consumer sovereignty) explains the low values of suicide prevention.

(e) Some evidence that publicity increases willingness to pay is given by the results of the interview experiment.

(f) The age of the victims is approximately equal in all the cases so there is not much ground for conclusions. If motorcycle helmets are made compulsory, we might conclude that values are higher for young people since measures preventing or curing heart attacks are considerably cheaper.

(g) The initial risk level (which is modified by safety measures) is high in medical care and suicide prevention.

Explanatory notes

1 In the expected decrease in the number of accidents the variance can be of importance. We leave this problem for the moment and will discuss it more in the following sections.

2 By cost we mean the utlities foregone by allocating resources to risk-reducing activities. To achieve comparability we have to measure costs in monetary units. Where decision-making units are working under different budgetary restraints or other restrictions the costs are not comparable between sectors unless resources are optimally distributed.

3 Loss of production, which is frequently used as a measure of the value of life, varies with the length of remaining productive life but loss of consumption for the entire remaining lifetime is a better measure if we take the individual's willingness to pay as our guideline.

4 By unit price we mean price/λ.

5 Bergstrom (1974) has pointed out this result.

6 In this context we use the term government authorities to represent elected bodies (parliament, local authorities), government, local and central, and administration.

7 A discussion of market failures of the different kinds one can have are discussed in the cost–benefit analyses of Mishan (1975) and Dasgupta et al. (1972).

8 In Australia, Austria, Belgium, Canada, Denmark, Finland, France, Great Britain, Italy, Japan, The Netherlands, Norway, Switzerland, United States, Western Germany.

9 The sectors were: transport by sea, air and land (road and railroad) and factory inspectorates.

References

Acton, J. P. 1973. *Evaluating public programs to save lives: the case of heart attacks.* Rand Corp., Report R-950-RC. Los Angeles: Rand Corporation.

Bergstrom, T. C. 1974. Preference and choice in matters of life and death. In *Applying cost–benefit concepts to projects which alter human mortality*, J. Hirschleifer, T. C. Bergstrom and E. Rappaport (eds), UCLA-ENG 7478. Los Angeles: Rand Corporation.

Bruzelius, N. 1979. *The value of travel time: theory and measurement.* London: Croom Helm.

Cohen, J. 1970, J. N. Plowshare, 1970: New challenge for the health physicist. *Health Phys.* **19**, 633.

Conley, B. B. 1973. *The value of human life in the demand for safety.* San Diego: Research Report, Center for Public Economics, California State University.

Dasgupta, P., A. Sen and S. Marglin 1972. *Guidelines for project evaluation.* New York: United Nations.

Goss, R. O. 1971. *Costs and benefits of navigational aids in port approaches.* London: Department of Trade and Industry.

Harrison, A. J. and D. A. Quarmby 1969. The value of time in transport planning: a review. In *Theoretical and practical research on an estimation of time-saving* pp. 173–208. Report of the Sixth Round Table, Paris. European Conference of Ministers of Transport.

Hedgran, A. and B. Lindell 1970. *PQR–A special way of thinking?* SSI: 1970:028. Stockholm: Statens Strålskyddsinstitut.

d'Iribarne, P. 1969. A la recherche de politiques rationelle de santé et de sécurité. *Anal. Prévis.* **4 (12)**, 17–28.

Jones-Lee, M. 1974. The value of changes in the probability of death or injury. *J. Pol. Econ.* **82**, 835–49.

Katz, A. 1971. Towards a methodology of traffic safety measurement and program evaluation. *Acc. Anal. Prev.* **3**, 15–43.

Kogan, N. and M. A. Wallach 1971. *Risk taking.* New York: Holt, Rinehart & Winston.

Linneroth, J. 1975. *The evaluation of life-saving: a survey*. Wien: International Atomic Energy Agency.

Luce, R. D. and A. Raiffa 1958. *Games and decisions*. New York: Wiley.

Mishan, E. J. 1975. *Cost−benefit analysis*. London: Allen & Unwin.

Raisbeck, G. 1972. Problems in the rational analysis of transportation safety. *Acc. Anal. Prev.* **4**, 1−22.

Rapparort, E. 1974. Economic analysis for life-and-death decision-making. In *Applying cost−benefit concepts to projects which alter human mortality*, J. Hirshleifer, T. C. Bergstrom and E. Rappaport (eds.). UCLA-ENG 7478. Los Angeles: University of California.

Schelling, T. C. 1968. The life you save may be your own. In *Problems on public expenditure analysis*, S. B. Chase, Jr. (ed.). Brookings Institution. London: Allen & Unwin.

Starr, C. 1969. Social benefit versus technological risk. *Science* **9**, 720−23.

Usher, D. 1973. An imputation to the measure of economic growth for changes in life expectancy. In *Measurement of Economic and Social Performance*, M. Moss (ed.) pp. 85−97. New York: (National Bureau of Economic Research).

Walters, A. A. 1975. *Noise and prices*. London: Oxford University Press.

9 *Collective risks and the environment*

EVA SELIN

Introduction

In risk analysis and the general discussion of risk, attention has so far been paid almost exclusively to the individual risk, that is, the risk for an individual person of being hurt or dying. However, people sometimes also experience and take precautions against collective risk, that is, risks for the whole of mankind or, in certain cases, for a group or a society. Collective risks are more difficult to quantify than individual risks. This makes people who are accustomed to working with figures (often economists and technologists), less inclined to take them seriously. They may, however, be regarded more seriously by ordinary people. Many people experience environmental risks as both individual and collective. In my view this is justified because many chemical substances have been shown to be carcinogenic (and thus harmful to the individual) and to cause mutations (and thus be harmful to the species). The question of where the individual human being would place his priorities if he had a chance to make a conscious choice between increasing the collective risk and increasing the individual risk has been very little studied. And yet a large part of the current discussion about environmental risks and complicated technological systems is concerned with this problem. It would therefore be interesting if behavioral scientists analyzed the conflict between those who believe in unrestricted economic growth and those who are concerned about the environment as an example of a conflict between individual and collective risk.

Individual and collective risks

In common with other biological creatures, man has a powerful and deep-seated instinct for survival, both as an individual and as a species. The desire for individual survival we satisfy daily by eating and drinking, resting, seeking shelter in our homes and, as far as possible, avoiding danger. The desire for survival as a species probably finds its strongest expression in the procreative urge, but there are many other phenomena that are indirectly linked to the need to perpetuate the life and specific character of the species. It seems probable that the driving force behind much creative activity has such an origin, whether it be artistic, scientific or technical. We wish to create something for a time period that stretches beyond our own life span, to communicate with, and make a positive contribution to, those who will come after us. The creation of societies and the development of cultures and religions are probably powerful manifestations of the need to further the life of the species.

When we assess risks in society, however, we concern ourselves almost exclusively with the individual risk, that is, the risk that a certain individual will be killed or injured. This is natural enough since our assessments are often made on a statistical basis and it is not easy to produce statistics for the risk of whole cultures or the entire human race being obliterated through a single catastrophe or a series of catastrophes. Collective risks – risks that an entire group may be wiped out – have in most cases not been identified, let alone analyzed. Since these play on what I take to be a basic human instinct (that of survival as a species) they often arouse powerful reactions in those exposed to the risks, as witness the intense involvement of the conservationist or the nuclear disarmament supporter, which is strongly reminiscent of religious fervor.

I believe it is necessary to complement the traditional risk–benefit philosophy, which is concerned with individual risks, with a similar philosophy for collective risks. We should not assume that we can assess such risks in numerical terms; we may rather be obliged to resort to qualitative and intuitive arguments. We also need to arrive at a philosophy of *comparative* risk for all those cases where we have to choose between exposing a limited number of people to individual risks and exposing a large group (the public, future generations) to a collective risk. Problems of this kind are already to be found in the chemical and nuclear industries, where in certain cases one can choose between penalizing the inner and outer environments respectively.

Similar problems are to be found in connection with the setting up of environmentally sensitive industries where one group, for example employers and employees, derive the benefits while the risks are borne by another group, for example people living in the vicinity. A problematical example of conflicting risks is that where the same individual is faced with a choice between an individual and a collective risk, or between a collective risk and deprivation of personal benefit.

Studies have been made of species of animals where each normal individual has a tendency to prefer individual to collective risk and thus give priority to the survival of the species above the life of the individual. The question is how will Western man act if faced with a conscious choice of this kind? In my opinion, such choices are already here for us to make. I shall try to clarify this point by giving a brief survey of the risk situation as regards environmental issues.

Environmental risks

Most of the books written in recent years on the subject of the environment and man's exploitation of the Earth's natural resources (land, vegetation, water, air, minerals and energy resources) convey a similar message: the attitude of industrial man towards nature and its resources is exposing both the human species and many other living creatures to the risk of total annihilation. Different writers will give somewhat differing figures as regards land despoilment, air pollution and squandering of resources, but the trend is always the same.

Every year hundreds of millions of tons of air pollutants are belched out into the atmosphere. These consist of thousands of different chemical substances, most of them with effects on living organisms that have as yet been poorly mapped. Discussion has centered largely around carbon monoxide, carbon dioxide and the problems of acidity, but recently increasing attention has been paid to the effects of heavy-metal particles, sulfur oxides and radioactivity in industrial waste.

Apart from the direct problems caused by air pollution (e.g. through reduction in the amount of light reaching the Earth's surface and the fact that these pollutants are inhaled by many living organisms), certain of the chemical components, when deposited on the soil and in the water, are assimilated into ecological chain systems, there to be successively multiplied in many living organisms. The effects of this are sometimes damaging and may even be disastrous.

In the long term, the Earth's heat and oxygen balance will be affected by the umbrella of air pollution and by the processes (e.g. combustion) through which pollution is produced. In their book *Population, resources, environment*, Ehrlich and Ehrlich (1970) state that a UNESCO conference in 1968 reached the conclusion that within a few decades the Earth would be uninhabitable on account of air pollution. Here and there the authorities have reacted by requiring a reduction in the volume of industrial waste and car exhaust, but at the same time the number of people, industries and cars continues to grow. We are fighting an uneven battle: it is difficult to check that the authorities' regulations are followed – in the case of many of the pollutants we do not know the paths along which they spread or the effects they may have on the ecosystem – and, finally, we have only limited means of measuring the presence of the various foreign substances in nature.

The waters of our planet are involved in a constant process of replacement, in which roughly the same amount of water evaporates from land, lakes and oceans as is replaced in the form of rain and condensation. Of this water, about 3% is fresh water, of which in turn 98% is in the form of ice. As a result of man's ever-increasing requirement for fresh water, many scientists fear that the world will soon be faced with a water crisis. In a number of countries, especially in certain developing ones, there is already a definite water shortage. The human body itself has a water-consumption requirement of two to three litres a day, but people in the heavily industrialized countries (e.g. the USA) actually use 7000 litres a day per head. In many places the groundwater level is sinking as a result of exorbitant amounts of water being drawn off and the subsequent upsetting of the natural process of replacement. Pollution is a threat here too, since many of the chemicals that are deposited on the soil are washed away by the rain and eventually find their way into the groundwater.

Rivers, lakes and the oceans have long been considered legitimate "recipients" and have been deliberately subjected to pollution in the belief that through dilution poisonous substances would be rendered innocuous. Millions of tons of industrial waste and municipal waste from boats (e.g. oil spill) are dumped in the sea every year. This includes pesticides, hydrocarbons, acids, mercury, lead, cadmium, arsenic, radioactive waste and oil refinery waste. It is hardly surprising that DDT and PCB have been found in fish in the Atlantic, that increased lead concentration has been measured in the surface water of the Atlantic or that animals high up in the nutrition pyramid, such as the seals in the Baltic Sea, are threatened with extinction through poisoning (the Baltic has low water replacement). The vast majority of the airborne pollutant particles which are expelled into the atmosphere every year also land eventually in lakes and in the oceans; well-known examples are acidification of thousands of Swedish lakes as a result of high sulfur contents in the rain and the occurrence of plutonium-239 in fish in the Atlantic originating from atmospheric nuclear tests.

The Earth is affected by airborne pollutants in the same way as the water, but cultivatable areas are also threatened in a number of other ways, the most widely discussed of which is probably deforestation with its concomitant erosion, flooding, drought and climatic changes. According to *World conservation strategy* published by IUCN-UNEP-WWF in 1980, the forests of the Earth are shrinking by many hundred square kilometers and the barren areas (deserts and the like) are growing by 160 km^2 every day! It is predicted that by the year 2000 one-third of the cultivatable soil will have been eroded or made barren.

An increasing portion of land is consumed by roads and buildings or is required for storing household refuse and other waste. The wild animals are forced back into smaller and smaller reservations, and numerous species on land and in the sea are threatened with extinction, as a result either of wholesale methods of hunting and fishing (see e.g. the threat to whales, herring, cod, tuna, haddock and hake) or of their inability to cope with the poisons that we have introduced into their environment. According to *World conservation strategy* some 25 000 plants, 1000 vertebrates and between a half and one million smaller animals may be extinct by the year 2000. This will, among other things, mean a very serious depletion of the gene banks, from which nature would have otherwise derived new material for the evolution of new species.

TRACE ELEMENTS, CANCER AND GENETIC DAMAGE

I would like to mention here just one of the risks that man may have to face as a result of the situation described above, namely the risk of slow – or sudden – extermination by one or other of the poisons in our environment. Let me first point out that, in common with all living creatures, we are dependent on the steady supply of certain substances in very weak concentrations. Thus we have in our blood serum roughly one-millionth part of copper and zinc and one ten-millionth part of the element selenium. The effect of both too high and too low a content of certain trace elements is very serious, and in either case sickness or death will follow. Pasture land, for example, must contain between one ten-millionth and one-millionth part of selenium if animals that graze on its vegetation are to be healthy. Certain substances (e.g. heavy metals like lead, cadmium and mercury) are highly poisonous even in weak concentrations. Through the spreading of chemicals (e.g. in pesticides and fertilizers) man has in many places succeeded in disturbing the Earth's natural composition of trace elements and replacing necessary substances with harmful ones.

Trace metals often fulfill a vital function in biological molecules, and if the right metal is replaced by another, the whole biological molecule may cease to function properly. Research into trace elements has not progressed very far, partly because there are thousands of different types of molecules to be studied, but the connection between altered trace-element concentration and, for example, heart attacks and cancer has already been noted. According to one of WHO's reports, heart attacks and cancer (as well as some mental disorders) are among the diseases that are increasing most rapidly in the industrialized countries. A strong suspicion can therefore be entertained that there is a link between our chemical manipulation of the environment (both by the introduction of poisonous substances and the alteration of trace-element concentrations) and these diseases. Some scientists assert that four-fifths of all cancers could be prevented if it were possible to track down and eliminate the carcinogenic substances.

Although the risk of getting cancer is an individual risk, there is a clear link between the carcinogenic properties of a substance and its ability to cause genetic damage, that is, to threaten the survival of the species as a whole. Many scientists believe that the same mechanism that produces cancer in a body cell will in a sex cell cause damage to the genetic code. The following table (Table 9.1) is taken from the findings of Professor L. Ehrenberg, Stockholm. It is interesting to study the time scale in Table 9.1. Thus it takes 5–50 years after an "event" on the molecular level, which we cannot register with our five senses, before cancer develops. How can one then say anything about cause and effect? The answer is that it is extremely difficult to demonstrate such a connection by means of studies of people suffering from cancer. This is possible only in isolated cases, namely when the cancer develops in a special organ (e.g. the lungs) and there is a group of people who differ from others in sharing a special environment (e.g. smokers or miners working in mines with radon). The causal connection for genetic injury over a timescale of several generations is, naturally, still more difficult to establish. One can easily imagine what would have happened, for example, in the case of thalidomide if it had caused cancer and genetic injury, but not such typical kinds of malformation that could be discovered at birth: thalidomide would probably still be in use.

Every year some 250 000 new chemicals are added to the two and a half million which are already in use. A good many of these are carcinogenic and therefore also constitute a genetic risk, but the harmful effects can be difficult to identify because of the timescales involved. It is true that certain scientists are trying to discover methods other than biological and epidemiological ones to determine the carcinogenic and mutagenic properties of a substance, but in

Table 9.1 The effect of genotoxic substances on various organs, from Ehrenberg, personal communication.

Organ affected	Effect	Timescale for effects to appear
reproductive organs	mutation (genetic change)	several generations
mature body cells	cancer, leukemia, shortening of life expectation	5–50 years
foetal cells	malformation	at birth or later

view of the great number of substances and the small number of researchers, the prospect of success is poor. One must also consider the extremely complex combination between the different chemical substances, as well as between these and substances in the human body.

One can perhaps sum up the situation thus: we know that by devastating land and introducing pollution into the ecosystem and disturbing the trace-element concentrations in the plants and animals, we are taking risks. We have indications that something is wrong in the increased frequency of cancer, allergies and cardiovascular diseases. But we do not really know how great the risk is for irreparable collective damage. The situation is so complex that we cannot measure the risk in figures.

Difficulties in quantification

The psychological need to be able to quantify risks varies a great deal from one person to another. Many animals have instincts which tell them when a situation is dangerous; we sometimes say that animals "smell danger." One can assume that people react in a similar way. Most mothers do not need to take statistics as a basis for warning their children about traffic or dangerous wells. Sometimes intuition can play a similar rôle. One can have a feeling that a situation may entail risk without directly being able to say exactly what the risk is, still less to quantify it. Many scientists, however, especially economists and technicians, are used to describing their results with the help of figures. For them it feels more reliable to be able to quantify a risk as, for example, probability multiplied by damage. There is, however, an excessive belief in figures in this connection. The fact that a figure in itself is exact does not necessarily mean that the assumptions on which the figure is based are reliable. There are plenty of examples of risk estimates which are often quoted (e.g. the risk of a disaster at a nuclear power plant) which can very well be uncertain by a factor of 100 or 1000 but as soon as the figure is given, many people tend to forget this and accept the figure as a fact.

Growth philosophy and collective risk

As mentioned earlier, a large number of people feel that the misuse of natural resources and our manipulation of chemicals in the natural environment, together with industrial effluent, chemical waste and spraying, expose us all to a collective risk which, owing to the complexity of the problems and the many unknown factors, is difficult to quantify. The factors behind the problems are industrialization, the mechanization of agriculture and forestry and the demands for efficiency and rationalization in working life. Conservation of nature and environmentalism often stand in opposition to industrialization, production and consumption. In the existing economic models, factors such as people's health, clean water, fresh air and an undisturbed ecosystem are not generally regarded as assets. On the contrary, the gross national product (GNP) increases if more people are taken to hospital; there is greater turnover, more growth. Biologists have pointed out that perpetual growth is something which is quite impossible from a biological point of view; instead of growth it is balance which we should strive to achieve. But economists cling to their models and politicians, consciously or unconsciously, deceive themselves and others by talking about "room for increased consumption," without mentioning that increase in consumption (at least goods) nearly always leads to an increased strain on the environment and/or an increased exploitation of limited natural resources. One can naturally imagine the development of another kind of technology which conserves resources and spares the environment, but today this technology is not to be found except in isolated cases, and it is far from certain that it will be "profitable" in the short-term economic perspective.

Since it is our present patterns of production and consumption which lead to the environmental risks and disturbances in the ecosystems which threaten us, more and more people have begun to question these patterns. But even so, is each individual person consistent? Who thinks of waste problems every time he opens his packet of coffee with its three or four outer covers? Who thinks of dwindling water supplies when she buys new clothes made of synthetic materials or allows herself to be manipulated by the fashion industry? Yet I believe that many people, if faced with a conscious choice between increasing environmental strain (and thereby the collective risk) and refraining from over-consumption would, in fact, choose the latter alternative.

A new morality

In the tension between environmentalists and supporters of growth there are threats and persuasion on both sides. Environmentalists warn people about the long-term ecological risks and supporters of growth issue warnings about unemployment, poverty and want. One might perhaps say that environmentalists "threaten" us with collective risks whereas supporters of growth "threaten" us with individual risks. Obviously there is exaggeration on both sides. The concept of moderation seems to have been forgotten.

One interesting issue in this connection is the question of work. We have an old-fashioned protestant work ethic, probably inherited from Luther, which considers any kind of work better than "inactivity." Even work ultimately of a destructive nature (e.g. manufacturing weapons, poisons, carcinogenic chemicals, etc.) is considered better than lying on the grass and looking up at the sky. To be unemployed is a social stigma: it is better to hurry mankind along the road to destruction by destructive work. There are, however, especially among young people, certain signs that the old saying about the sanctity of labor and its ennobling effect on the worker is losing its hold. People are beginning to demand that work should have a meaningful purpose. This could be interpreted as a sign of spoilt behavior but it could just as well be a result of the higher level of education and consciousness of the youth of today. Sometimes, perhaps, it is, on a subconscious level, a sign of a new morality which requires that we refuse to participate in activities that increase the collective risk. Enthusiasm for industrialization and trust in technical development have, in certain cases, been replaced by suspicion and doubt.

In the above chapter, I have tried to show that this is not only an emotional reaction but one founded on rational considerations. Undoubtedly there is a need for a new technology which does not have economic usefulness as its only criterion, but which meets ecological demands. But it is also necessary that behavioral scientists and those engaged in spreading information should work actively to open people's eyes to the partial contradiction in demanding *simultaneously* a reduction in the misuse of the environment and an increase in consumption and production. The interrelation between individual and collective risks should be shown from several viewpoints so that people become conscious that they are often placed in situations where they have a choice. Then they can choose with their eyes open, without falling into the hands of the kind of people who try to mold public opinion and who often drive home their views in a very one-sided manner.

References

Ehrenberg, L. Personal communication.

Ehrlich, P. R. and A. H. Ehrlich 1970. *Population, resources, environment*. New York: W. H. Freeman.

WHO 1980. *World Conservation Strategy*. Report by IUCN-UNEP-WWF. Geneva: WHO. Also available in a popular form by Robert Allen: *How to save the world*. IUCN-UNEP-WWF 1980.

10 *Public transportation fears and risks*

ANNA-CHRISTINA BLOMKVIST

Introduction

In this chapter fears and risks concerning public transportation are described with the aim of comparing their influence on choice of means of tranportation. If fear avoidance counteracts risk avoidance in this context, the theme is a serious one. If fear avoidance has little impact in comparison to risk avoidance, fears are still an urgent topic since it is reasonable to try to minimize them in daily affairs, such as, say, travels to and from work.

Intra-city or intra-county traveling is less well documented than longer journeys, therefore much of this chapter will concentrate on train and airplane journeys. We want to stress, though, that obstacles to such collective means of transportation discussed below are worthy of consideration in the context of commuting and intra-city traveling as well. The discussion refers to a great extent to Swedish conditions.

Transportation and choice of means

Some people do not use public means of transportation. In a study by Norges Markedsdata AS (1976), 33% of the Norwegian sample reported traveling more than 500 km by train less than once a year, and 24% said they never traveled by train: 50% had never traveled by air. In a study for Finnair (Mäkelä 1975), 54% of the men and 66% of the women had never traveled by air.

As regards journeys of more than 500 km, twice as many Swedes travel by car as by train (Statistical Reports 1977), and when journeys are longer than 100 km, three times as many travel by car as by train. When journeys are shorter than 100 km, 80% travel by car, 12% take the bus and only 3% take the train, as estimated by the Nordic Institute for Studies in Urban and Regional Planning (Engström 1981). The reason why trains are used at all in the last case is that in Sweden and the other Scandinavian countries, trains are relatively cheap and convenient and are thus a good alternative for shorter journeys.

The automobile is the most frequently used means of transportation and corresponds to 75% of all person-kilometers traveled (Statistical Reports 1980). The drawback with the popular car mode from the national point of view has been one of the incitements for research into choice of means. Car accidents and the augmenting oil bill could be reduced if public transportation were to be utilized more effectively. (1) The reasons why people travel are better known than why they do not travel or how they choose among the means available. (2) Choice modeling has been attempted to predict demand for traffic alternatives and to make speculations in changes of possible choices. (3) However, aggregation of analytically derived results has the disadvantage of losing a large proportion of the inherent population and transportation system variance and thus of losing explanatory power. (4) Choices might be influenced not by frequency of trams, for example, but by the exact time of one special tram or by details such as being accompanied by spouse or child. (5) The lack of behavioral hypotheses then results in models which may be fairly suitable for prediction at *status quo*, but grossly inadequate if changes are brought into the transportation system as, for instance, when economical conditions change (Stropher 1977).

For many people, the prime goals of life are probably not the often studied aims to save money and time and to avoid risks, but to allocate pleasure and displeasure in more sophisticated ways, holistic from the individual's actual point of view as well as idiosyncratic. As an example, Recker and Stevens (1976) found that people traveled to the same destination by different means depending on the reasons for the journey. This means that if you are going to buy something very expensive or meet a pop star, you might travel by more expensive means. Other subjective attributes studied by the authors were: for buses, convenience, personal safety, service and status; and for automobiles, autonomy, cost and safety. For buses, cars, taxis and walking, safety was regarded as salient when the modes were described. It seems, from Recker's and Stevens' (1976) data, as if "walk safety" had some influence on choice when the journeys' goals were least urgent such as shopping for odds and ends and personal items, but safety had relatively low explanatory power for modal choice.   In a study by Paine *et al.* (1969) on "auto versus public transport mode," safety was again given a high degree of importance. "Arrive without accident" was the most important item in the sample; the "safety factor" was second in importance for nonwork trips and third for work trips (where arriving on time was second). Safety, however, did not differentiate between the two modes. Paine *et al.* (1969) concluded that "persuasion campaigns" based on safety should not alter choices, since safety was not decisive.

Surveys made in Norway covered the aspects of safety, necessity, convenience, luxury, entertainment, accessibility and speed. During the years 1971–5, the profiles of these dimensions for train, car, airplane, boat and bus have been converging, i.e. the differences in value attributes between these means of conveyance are diminishing (Informationskonsult AB 1971, 1972, 1973, 1974, 1975). As long as no new drastic changes are introduced in traveling means, differences between mean values might come to matter less and less.

The studies now mentioned indicate that the attributes of means are not good predictors of choice. This can also be inferred from the differing travel patterns of men and women (Hanson & Hanson 1981). Besides, research on choice strategies (Tversky 1969, Montgomery 1977, Tyszka 1983) has demonstrated that decision rules made up by individuals may be such that no unambiguous goal is reached. Supposedly, it is not even aimed at!

When or if one uses decision rules, one does not need a goal that is a composite ideal. When using rules, one only needs to decide systematically or habitually among some attributes at hand. One way to manage life is to admit to cut-offs or rules; to be a bit rigid. Louviere and Norman (1977) saw that when one factor (fare, frequency, or proximity of bus transportation) was low in desirability, the other aspects had a smaller effect. Probably many travelers, when they know of one bad factor, do not try to find out about other factors.

Phobias and strong feelings of unpleasantness may work as cut-offs, and decisions or avoidance reactions are often declared by affected people themselves as being irrational, but they "cannot help it," they probably say. A study by Otway and Fishbein (1977) underlined the possibility that "negativists" do not consider positive information. This is not identical to perceiving the negative factors as more negative than do "non-negativists" – it just means that benefits are uninteresting.

In conclusion, risk avoidance and features of means do not clearly determine choice of traffic means and many people may avoid public transport means since they do not use them. This renders it possible that factors other than risks, such as pleasurable or unpleasurable anticipations, are among the decisive causes. We will now review some common fears, then obstacles of means of transportation, and try to estimate their frequences and influence on choice or avoidance.

Common contents of fears and phobias

At first fears develop in a fairly stereotyped way and are thus common to us all at an early age. Cautiousness regarding heights is regularly seen at an early age in children. At about six months of age, infants start to show signs of experiencing fear and have, by then, developed an ability to recognize some fear-arousing stimuli. During the first two years of life, for instance, children are easily frightened by sudden noises or strange objects. Pre-school children often get very upset by threats of injury or thoughts about death. The latter fears depend on imagination, like fear of darkness which develops at about three years of age. Wood (1976) mentions death, someone close dying, animals, house burning down, being followed by a stranger and being kidnapped, as fears experienced by the majority of children.

When fears become profound and very unrealistic the word phobia is applicable. Phobias are intense fears focusing on certain objects, places or situations. From the behavioristic point of view, phobias are conditioned fears more or less accidentally associated with a stimulus. From the psychodynamic point of view, they are not conditioned but displacements of unconscious strong threats or desires.

When Hebb (1965) speculated on the development of fears and phobias, he chose strangeness as being an explanatory factor. He exemplified his theory with fears of snakes, death masks and toy animals in artificially bred chimpanzees, suggesting that the objects mentioned are unnatural compared to the chimpanzees' ordinary surroundings and bodies.

Findings in studies on avoidance reactions have led to several suggestions concerning dispositions that associate fear with some selected stimuli rather than with others. A modified behavioristic approach was proposed by Seligman (1975) who postulated that we are pre-programed to sense some dangers more easily than others, and that after an unpleasant conditioning is established, potentially phobic stimuli paired to brief electric shocks cause slower extinction than neutral stimuli (Öhman *et al.* 1977). This means that when we experience danger in a potentially phobic situation, the fear conditioned in that situation will probably be prolonged. Also, lower animals (such as rats) do not learn to avoid neutral stimuli, such as pieces of wood, as easily as strange places in conditioning experiments (Hebb 1965).

Shettleworth (1975) suggested an incentive-motivational mechanism, a model implying that behaviour appropriate to anticipation is reinforced rather than simply a single response. She found that behavior appropriate to food expectancy was more readily conditioned by food reinforcement than inappropriate behavior, and she also noted interaction effects in experiments on conditioning due to animals' prior experiences. This makes expectation and imagination, in the case of humans, more salient, along with pre-paired associations directing anticipation. As will be exemplified below, people seem to associate slightly unpleasant stimuli to great danger in a fear-evoking context. Testa (1974) suggested that the structures of the brain will channel events to "appropriate" central locations, which would imply that some cues are more readily related to each other than others. Animals may avoid food of certain colors after induced illness, if visual cues are the most salient to them (Garcia & Koelling 1966, Rozin & Kalat 1971, Wilcoxon *et al.* 1971). If we feel sick, we are often inclined to blame it on something we have eaten.

In a fear survey, Wolpe and Lang (1964) reviewed reactions to various stimuli on the basis of 15 years' work with behavior therapy. They grouped the stimuli into six classes: animals, tissue damage, classical phobias, social stimuli, noises and miscellaneous. Among the classical phobias mentioned were loneliness, heights, open spaces, crossing the street, the sight of deep water and crowds. Noises causing fear or other unpleasant feelings were those of vacuum cleaners, sirens, sudden noises and loud voices. Examples of fear-arousing social stimuli included speaking to an audience, entering a room where others were already seated, authorities, angry, sick, insane or deformed people, strangers and being ignored.

It is evident that these components of fears which have caused people to seek the aid of specialists, severely hamper a person's capabilities. If one cannot cross the street or meet strangers and avoids crowds, one will not reach a railway station or an airport. Consequently "travel" and "aircraft" are included among the classical phobias on Wolpe's and Lang's schedule.

Darkness, enclosed spaces, heights, being alone, noises at night, crowds, snakes, sharks, bees and wasps, rats and mice, moths, spiders, dogs and birds were the 14 most frequently reported examples in a study by Wilson and Priest (1968) where normal undergraduates were instructed to list fearful objects and situations. This means that there is no substantial difference in content between the schedule used for clinical purposes and a list of fear-inducing situations or objects stated by students, though the rank order of the most avoided situations varies.

Social stimuli and tissue damage were the largest categories found in a study of approximately 1 000 teenagers, also based on a scale developed by Wolpe. For girls, the most repellant categories were social rejection, tissue damage, unpleasant things, small animals and traveling, in that order, followed by social isolation, unpleasant people, stormy weather, acrophobia (phobia of high places) and medical treatment. The order for boys was about the same, with "fighting" as a relatively frequent stimulus as well (Bamber 1977).

Apart from the subclasses chosen by Wolpe and Lang, Marks (1969) suggested a clustering on the level of perceptual description: strong stimulation, irregular stimulation, sharp corners, abrupt changes (like falling), heights, motion parallax, high speed towards the subjects, and so on. Strahan (1974) emphasized three broad factors: potential bodily harm or discomfort, social situations and disorder or disruption.

Travel distress

There are not many inquiries in psychological literature focusing directly on train journeys as far as the present author knows. Nor have the Scandinavians (or the German or Dutch railway companies) looked upon their undertakings from a point of view which would demand questions concerning possible aversions. Some things we have all noticed, however. The first obstacle is finding out about time schedules, ticket prices and location of train stations. Appalling moments might be: to miss the train, get on the wrong train and get lost, lose valuable luggage, be separated from friends or the family, have the wrong ticket and so appear stupid, or not notice where to get off and then not know what to do, as well as the factors of meeting strangers, being in a crowd, hearing noises, being set in motion, etc. These are the kind of elements which are classified among phobic elements. For elderly people, very young or handicapped people, changing trains can be an alarming part of the journey as they have to rely on fellow travelers.

In an experiment at Pennsylvania railroad station in mid-Manhattan, subjects were asked to carry out some common relevant tasks at a less, and a more, crowded time of day (Mackintosh et al. 1975). Subjects experienced more negative effects in the crowded conditions and male subjects experienced more feelings of aggression and elation. Almost one-third of the subjects' own explanations were classified as describing feelings of inadequacy.

In a study carried out for Lufthansa, overcrowded trains during vacation peaks as well as long ticket lines and lack of hygienic facilities were mentioned as drawbacks of train transportation, along with the disadvantage of fixed times of departure, as compared to private cars. The same kinds of classical drawbacks were mentioned among the disadvantages of bus travel: the possibility of crowded buses, and the possibility of offensive people. That one need not put up with unpleasant people was one of the five most important advantages of traveling in one's own car (GETAS 1977). Stress and unpleasant feelings co-vary with crowdedness or social and ecological factors rather than with distance covered and time spent on the train; a statement also confirmed by studies using subjective ratings and measurements of catecholamine secretion (Singer et al. 1978, Lundberg 1976).

What are the unpleasant moments of an air journey? Among GETAS' (1977) reports of unpleasantness of flying were anxiety when flying, feelings of increased risk of injury despite a rational knowledge of safety on board and the dependency on the weather. The feelings of uncertainty were more difficult on charter flights, and increased with delay of departure, but the study by GETAS with only 60 respondents is not very extensive.

Gruen (personal communication 1977) asked 600 air passengers with different flying experience how they felt before an air journey: 41% felt worried, 27% felt discomfort before an air journey and 11% felt scared; 32% said that the uneasiness continued during the flight. From his own and others' experiences, Gruen (1977) chose items covering the journey from leaving for the airport until the landing, asking what parts of the journey were worrying, fearful or unpleasant (see Fig. 10.1).

The fear-eliciting elements Gruen used were not related to what is actually dangerous. Being locked in, safety demonstration, waiting before take-off and so on, and especially safety belts, do not make an accident more probable. There is a small danger lurking in the air but what makes the passengers think of this danger are unpleasant incidents that should be familiar to them since they are of an everyday—everywhere nature. One might be reminded of one's vulnerability as a passenger, wonder what is going on and be reminded that the technology is beyond one's control. What was not mentioned by GETAS or Gruen is unpleasant people. Either the air passengers do not feel crowded together or they have more positive expectations of each other than do bus and train passengers.

Among the headlines in Swedish newspapers on September 16 1977, was "Dead Woman on Airliner." A captain on an SAS plane first refused to take off when he learned that a passenger had died in transit and, according to the SAS legal representative, he had a legal right to do so. The other passengers were not told why the take-off was delayed. One of the airport officials said, according to an evening paper, that he had never heard of a plane starting with

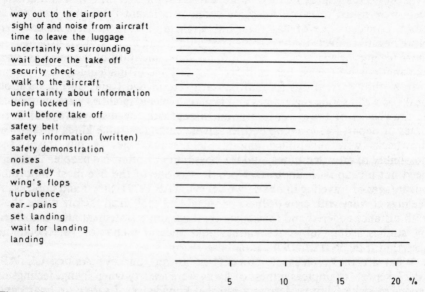

Figure 10.1 Moments of unpleasantness. Data for 600 passengers, showing which percentages get frightened when (from Gruen 1977).

a dead passenger before, a statement that is strange even if true. Apart from the extravagance of transporting a dead body by airplane, the fuss was probably due to the symbolic value: a dead body on an airliner has nondesired associations. We use this example to bring this paragraph on distress to a close: travels easily *elicit* displeasure and thoughts of threats.

Aspects on avoidance responses to trains and aircraft

In a study for DSB (the Danish State Railways) by OBSERVA (1970), about 300 people who had gone by train on their most recent long-distance journey were asked why they had chosen this means of travel. Some 12% said they could not stand flying and/or were too scared to fly. If 12% of railway passengers cannot stand flying, at least that proportion of the total population would probably avoid flying.

Among air passengers asked at the end of a flight if they would fly again, 14% said they were eager to, 64% would undoubtedly fly again, 13% were hesitant and 8% would prefer not to fly again (Richards & Jacobson 1975). We do not know what happened during those flights, but the authors said that the best predictor variable for willingness to fly again was the rated comfort on the actual flight.

Gruen (personal communication 1977) asked experienced air passengers if they had thought of canceling a journey because of their fears, 29% said they had considered it and 10% said they had done so at least once. In the Richards and Jacobson (1975) study, there was no correlation between unwillingness to fly again and the number of previous flights, but the sample was very uneven with regard to the frequency of experience.

With reference to the notions that phobic situations constitute a part of train and air journeys and that the avoidance responses seem to refer to fears or unpleasantness rather than to dangers, frequencies of phobias give some idea as to frequencies of avoidance of train and air journeys. In an often cited study, Agras *et al.* (1969) estimated the prevalence of mildly and severely disturbing phobias to be about 77 per 1000 in the population at large. Relevant phobia-evoking examples were crowds, height, enclosures, strangers and separation. The prevalence of different ages was estimated from information on the ages at which each person in the sample admitted to having suffered from the phobia. A peak of 17% was reached around 50 years of age. Being in a crowd was one example that grew more frequent with age. Solyom *et al.* (1973) referred to the study by Agras *et al.* (1969) saying that the latter authors found intense fear of flying in 10% of their sample, and mild fear in 20%. Although we have not found these values in the original article, we do believe they are reasonable.

Probably at least 12% avoid flying and less than 7% avoid trains; avoidance reactions which thus would push people in the direction of less risky choices. This is satisfactory. Our point of view is that, as trains are relatively safe, one should also take care to make them more pleasant than buses and cars in order to make people prefer that means to buses and cars as well as to planes.

During the 1970s, new railroad carriages were planned in Sweden. First SJ (the Swedish State Railway) suggested less space for each passenger and only one toilet per carriage. This was criticized by newspapers and the disabled people's association, and plans were changed. However, on September 10 1977, Sweden's largest morning newspaper wrote an article stating that still only one exit was planned – "and what will happen if a fire starts in a crowded carriage at the (only) exit end." Was SJ not challenging the phobias?

From the Government monopoly's isolated point of view, it might be convenient to persuade more people to go by their buses. Buses require less central administration than trains linked together by time schedules and bound to the same rail system. If the highways get crowded, SJ will not be held responsible for that; accidents would increase but they would be more evenly distributed and the responsibility diluted.

The possibility of traveling by airplane has a drawback of its own: the increase in accident potential due to journeys being so easily accessible, for instance to Bangkok, Mallorca or the Canary Islands, which would otherwise not be undertaken. Among domestic flight passengers, 5% on business and 15% on private affairs would not have gone at all if it had not been possible to fly (Resvaneundersökningen 1973). Also relevant to avoidance responses is the fact that the acceptance levels for risk seems to differ according to the risky objects. Green and Brown (1977c) said people seemed more concerned with fires and train accidents than with plane accidents, though flying is feared more. Fischhoff *et al.* (1978) inquired about perceived benefits, perceived risks and acceptance. Perceived benefit was higher for trains than for planes, but perceived risk was lower for trains than for planes and risk acceptance was also lower for trains. Trains *should* be safer than planes.

Trains are probably felt to be home-like. They resemble apartments and elevators more than other means of conveyance, and homes (houses) should be "absolutely" safe. Stability of our houses is highly overemphasized, and safety devices and safety planning for trains had better be overemphasized too, to correspond to people's expectations.

After the accident

What happened? How and why? Blomkvist and Sjöberg (Ch. 13) comment on the immediate demand for explanations of severe accidents in mass media. A scenario covering the verisimilitudes, and plausible and popular details, must be presented by the reporter in order to make the accident front page news. "Everybody" wants to know how it happened and again some things are of more concern than others.

When "it" happens, although it should not have happened, the immediate demand for explanations leads to "post-hap" investigations, though the reliability of evidence found after the event might be overemphasized. There have been some explorations of the change in perception of casualties after the outcome is known. Walster (1966) proposed that the more momentous an outcome, the greater the tendency to think we knew better than we did. Fischhoff (1975) stressed the cognitive-psychological explanations for the overconfidence in causes in post-hap evaluations: the outcome knowledge facilitates access to knowledge attached to the known outcome, and the knowledge that it did happen also becomes a biasing anchor. Fischhoff calls it a creeping determinism since further evidence that an accident need not have happened only slightly modifies our trust in the causes found. The more serious the outcome, the more it demands our commitment. Studies show that subjects deceive themselves, believing they would have made better predictions from information at hand once they heard stories of the outcome afterwards (Walster 1967, Fischhoff & Beyth 1975).

Walster (1967) suggested that one feels more secure if the world is an orderly and predictable place. Bulman and Wortman (1977) interviewed victims of severe accidents who were paralyzed from the neck or waist down. "I should have know better" or "things had been going too well for some time, so ..." were common statements. Victims exaggerated their own causal power, attributed more blame to themselves than seemed warranted and/or restructured the world so that the sum of events of a special class no longer seemed random or unintelligible. Few subjects were inclined to make probability-resembling statements. The very few who did, seemed less religious and more educated than the rest and also attributed more blame to environmental factors. Reactions towards natural and non-natural hazards were similar (Schiff 1977). Too much causal power was attributed to the victim in any case. In the same context, it was noted that expectation of hazard did not inspire adjustment though experience of hazard was significantly related to adjustment.

As long as no accident occurs, neither private persons nor government will adjust (Green 1975). However, if there is a train or airplane accident we attribute it to a few corporations: SJ and the airline companies flying within Sweden. The denotation is unambiguous. Consequently, if there were a train accident, say, SJ has had an accident for which they are responsible and they assume responsibility for investigation and preventive actions. The concern is nationwide and there is an identifiable goal for the moral indignation of mass media and the public. If there is a car or truck accident, on the other hand, this will seldom lead to preventive actions. There is no unifying target for accusation. It could depend on a mistake by local planners, the driver, the road-maintenance companies (local or national), other drivers ... or the weather. Road accidents are local news in the local newspapers and the circumstances are not regarded as generalities. Only in rare instances when constructional faults, such as faults of steering or brakes, are suspected, does the accident turn into real news. Most often the human factor is stressed. Blame and self-blame then free the rest of us from constructive measures. It is a tragedy that individuals are blamed in single accidents, but it is even more tragic that individuals too easily accept that burden.

Perceived risk rates

In studies on perception of, and attitudes towards, risk, Green and Brown (1977a, b) attempted to find measures for perceived safety. They also tried to determine if perceived safety would be brought into line with statistics when subjects were confronted with frequences of deaths and injuries. Green and Brown concluded that personal safety was found to be related to perceived voluntariness of the specific activities. The perceived hazardousness was found to be related to perceived probability and to perceived degree of personal lack

of control. Furthermore, the results suggested that the subjects defined accidents so that they included deaths and severe injuries but not, for instance,
accidents without injuries. Perceived safety was not unambiguously influenced
by objective data, but some influence from the actuarial probability of an accident and the number of deaths annually in one's own country were noted.

There are different ways of presenting or collecting objective data about
accidents; for instance, in percentage of man-hour exposure or length of
journey, number of accidents per journey or per inhabitant and so on. When
somebody makes a choice between traveling by rail or air from Gothenburg
to Hong Kong, it might be wise to consider that, including different kinds of
obstacles, flying is safer. Safely on the aircraft the danger of the moment might
be the only interest. So there are, in fact, different ways of subjectively perceiving accident rates too.

What are the "general" perceived risks of rail and air travel? Table 10.1
presents some naïve risk judgments, mainly collected for market research and
by stratified sampling. The rest of the judgments were collected for risk con-
ceptualization analysis. For comparison, judgments of the prime means of
transportation, private cars, are also presented. Apparently travel by train is
perceived as safer than travel by car or airplane. The order between car and
aircraft is not as clear. This might well correspond to differing connotations
of safety, as exemplified above.

According to Green and Brown (1976), objective statistics that should apply
to the knowledge of their subjects held the rank order in Table 10.2. It is
evident that there is no objective rationale for having one single opinion about
safety.

For Sweden, also, the rank order train, airplane and car, holds for deaths

Table 10.1 Subjective ratings* of risk or safety of means of conveyance mainly
collected for marketing research 1966–76.

| Year | Mode of transport | | |
	Train	Car	Plane
1966	1.6[†]	3.3	3.5
1971	1.85[‡]	3.55	2.85
1972	1.95[‡]	3.75	2.85
1973	2.2[‡] 1.6[§]	3.65 2.8	2.8 2.7
1974	1.85[‡] 2.7[¶]	3.55 3.9	3.0 3.7
1975	2.05[‡] 2.7[¶]	2.9 3.7	3.1 3.4
	737"	247	52
1976	2.7[¶] 1.6[**]	3.9 4.0	3.4 1.91
	(1.88)[**]	(5.0)	(2.9)

* The lower the rating, the lower the risk.
† Averages of ratings from 1–5 in Giscard (1966) France.
‡ Answers on 1–6 point scale for NSB by Informationskonsult (1971–5) Norway.
§ Answers on 1–6 point scale in Reisenanalyse (1973) Germany, supplied by Lufthansa.
¶ Answers on 1–7 point scale for NSB by Norges Markedsdata AS (1976) Norway (inverted
here).
" Geometrical means of magnitude estimates in Fischhoff et al. (1978). USA.
** Answers on 1–10 point scale in Green and Brown (1977a) England. Numbers in parentheses
are judgments of hazard.

Table 10.2 Rank order of actual number of deaths and injuries that should be the rational background for the results of Green and Brown (1976) presented in Table 10.1 (1 indicates the smallest number.)

	Per trip		Per hour of exposure		Per passenger mile
	Deaths	Injuries	Deaths	Injuries	Deaths
train	1[1]	2	1	1	1
car	3	3	2	3	3
plane	2	1	3	2	2

per trip and passenger miles, but is reversed for car and airplane when calculated per hour of exposure.

DANGERS IN TRAIN AND AIRPLANE JOURNEYS

There are international goals for civil aviation safety but not for trains. Trains are domestic affairs. Sweden has its own goal for aviation safety in the 1980s: a safety level of at least 10 million flight hours per fatal accident.

Air accidents have decreased since 1967 until the present day; safety at airports has increased. Probably emergency operations are now as well developed as we can reasonably afford. Safety during flight, take-off and landing has changed less. The most dangerous part of air traffic is landing. Ramsden (1976) wrote that it is "statistically debatable" whether the safety during the last 1 000 ft is improving at all. He attributed a clear majority of accidents to human error, and he seemed pessimistic.

SJ could allocate resources to provide protection against accidents. Road and rail level crossings are the only areas where effects of investment in increased safety could be guaranteed, possibly along with the prevention of doors opening when the train is in motion. At the moment, SJ is developing an automatic train control (ATC) system and, as is often the case when things are going to be better "after that", demands for co-drivers from engine drivers fearing "micro-sleep" are rejected with the argument that when the automatic system is completed they will not have to face any problems when driving alone.

If dangerous operations for railway employees (causing death and injuries) are disregarded, the next dangerous operation is level crossings. The number of accidents is often stated according to presence of gates, light signals, warnings signs, etc. There should also be factors like optimal density of traffic, changes in time schedules and changes in road surface influencing the accidents. Derailment is the third class of accidents. Derailments are as frequent at stations as out on the line, but at stations passengers are often standing at windows or in the aisle and are more exposed to the effects.

Derailment and train collisions are the main dangers to passengers followed by jumping on or off (or falling) at stations when the train is moving or standing still. Nobody seems to fear this latter danger and we believe that most passengers underestimate the risk for derailments at stations.

The probabilities of the events enumerated do not seem to have changed much during the past ten years. It is likely that the railways are operating at a high level of safety and that there are no drastic improvements in sight.

Final comment

It is apparent from the results on choice of means of conveyance, that people do not focus on minimizing risks, and that there are several idiosyncratic factors influencing a choice. Furthermore, the means discussed here did not differ enough on the risk aspect from the individual point of view to make risk a choice variable. On the other hand, there were some instances of fear avoidance determining choices. As the alternatives were not clear, one should neither draw the conclusion that fear avoidance stimulates nor counteracts risk avoidance in this context, but it is a potential factor. We would prefer to stress the point that it is human to try to minimize fears, and as there are fears that many people have in common, the task is not impracticable. Only about 7–12% would avoid train rather than air journeys. But the fact that situations intolerable to a few people also seem to be unpleasant for many people, means that common fears most probably are common stress factors.

Apropos of choice between means of conveyance, the most intense debate has been occupied with reference to private cars over public transportation. There is too much commuting by private car. Drawbacks often mentioned are accidents, delays due to traffic jams, pollution, fuel import expenses and the barrier effect of jammed highways through villages and countryside. These latter costs to the community and the environment probably do not enter into the individual's choice attributes at all.

Decentralization of housing has been supported by the Swedish government and costs for private car commuting are so far often deductable from income taxes. These measures amplify the drawbacks mentioned, but increased costs of commuting by private car (higher taxes) might result in a return to centralized housing, which is not desirable. The next conclusion is, thus, that there have to be new forms of commuting, if new benefits are to be gained; new forms of commuting where possible avoidance because of unpleasantness is counteracted, at the same time as the premise that public means of transportation may have to absorb twice, three or ten times as many passengers as is the case today.

The new forms of commuting will have to be decentralized to be attractive and flexible enough, and pick up the new passenger categories. As already mentioned in Chapter 6, moral indignation is a strong factor. The fact that there are central targets for indignation in rail and air traffic is considered to stimulate setting of high safety goals. Decentralization of organization of transportation has a weakness from this point of view. Dispersed accidents may receive less attention. If there is a train accident, every potential traveler can feel threatened and most Swedes belong to that group of potential travelers. If there is a bus accident, say in the community where the buses are run by company Y, members of communities where the buses are run by company X and Z might feel neither threatened nor indignant.

When transportation is decentralized and made more effective from the consumers' point of view, some people – previously train passengers – may travel by bus instead. Some car drivers might choose to travel by bus too or join a car pool. When there are car pools operating, some previous bus travelers change to car pools (Asplund 1981). As trains today are ten times safer than buses, and buses twice as safe as cars (per mile and traveler, Engström 1981), the exemplified changes due to preference of means will not imply higher safety. Rather, these changes would make pleasure preference counteract risk avoidance. In order to take local needs sufficiently into account to encourage commuters to use public transportation, new risk potentials are introduced which will not easily be noticed by the passengers. Therefore these risks have to be traced centrally and watched carefully.

References

Agras, S., D. Sylvester and D. Oliveau 1969. The epidemiology of common fears and phobia. *Comp. Psych.* **10**, 151–6.

Asplund, Ö. 1981. Samåkningen utvärderad: Kollektivt färdsätt bättre än samåkning. *Gatan* **5**, 7, 23.

Bamber, J. H. 1977. The factorial structure of adolescent responses to fear survey schedule. *J. Genetic Psychol.* **130**, 229–38.

Bulman, R. J. and C. B. Wortman 1977. Attributions of claim and coping in the "Real World": Severe accident victims react to their lot. *J. Personal. Social Psychol.* **35**, 351–63.

Engström, M. 1981. Market analysis for the Swedish Railways.

Fischhoff, B. 1975. Hindsight–foresight: the effect of outcome knowledge on judgment under uncertainty. *J. Exp. Psychol.: Human Percep. Perform.* **1**, 288–99.

Fischhoff, B. and R. Beyth 1975. "I knew it would happen". Remembered probabilities of once-future things. *Org. Behav. Human Percep.* **13**, 1–16.

Fischhoff, B., P. Slovic, S. Lichtenstein, S. Read and B. Combs 1978. How safe is safe enough? A psychometric study of attitude towards technological risks and benefits. *Policy Sci.* **8**, 127–52.

Garcia, J. and R. A. Koelling 1966. A relation of cue to consequences in avoidance learning. *Psychonomic Sci.* **4**, 123–7.

GETAS 1977. (*Marketing research for Lufthansa*) *Studie 1970: Reisen – motive – Bedingungen – Abläufe – Bedürfnisse.* Through agency of Lufthansa, Köln.

Giscard, P. H. 1966. *Conduit automobil et sécurité.* Arceuil, France: Organisme National de Sécurité Routière.

Green, C. H. and R. A. Brown 1976 *The perception of, and attitudes towards, risk.* Preliminary report: E2, measure of safety. Dundee: School of Architecture, Duncan of Jordanstone College of Art.

Green, C. H. and R. A. Brown 1977a. *The perception of, and attitudes towards, risk.* E3, Stability of perception under time and data. Dundee: School of Architecture, Duncan of Jordanstone College of Art.

Green, C. H. and R. A. Brown 1977b. *The perception of, and attitudes towards, risk.* Final report: E2, Measure of safety. Dundee: School of Architecture, Duncan of Jordanstone College of Art.

Green, C. H. and R. A. Brown 1977c. *Life safety: What it is and how much it is worth.* Dundee: School of Architecture, Duncan of Jordanstone College of Art.

Green, H. P. 1975. Legal and political dimensions of risk-benefit methodology. In *Risk-benefit methodology and application*, D. Ohrent (ed.), pp. 273–90. Some papers presented at the Engineering Foundation Workshop, September 22–6, 1975. ASILOMAR, California. Los Angeles: Energy and Kinetics Dept., School of Engineering and Applied Science, University of California.

Gruen, H. 1977. Trygg med kunskap. *Vindstruten* 25, 16–17.

Hanson, S. and P. Hanson 1981. The impact of married women's employment on household travel patterns: a Swedish example. *Transportation* 10, 165–83.

Hebb, D. O. 1965. *A textbook of psychology*. Philadelphia: W. B. Wang.

Informationskonsult AB 1971. *Rapport över NSB's grundundersökning Mars 1971.* Täby, Sweden: Studievägen 2.

Informationskonsult AB 1972. *Rapport över NSB's uppföljningsundersökning Mars 1972.* Täby, Sweden: Studievägen 2.

Informationskonsult AB 1973. *Rapport över NSB's uppföljningsundersökning Mars 1973.* Täby, Sweden: Studievägen 2.

Informationskonsult AB 1974. *Rapport över NSB's uppföljningsundersökning Mars 1974.* Täby, Sweden: Studievägen 2.

Informationskonsult AB 1975. *Rapport över NSB's uppföljningsundersökning April 1975.* Täby, Sweden: Studievägen 2.

Louviere, J. J. and K. L. Norman 1977. Applications of information-processing theory to the analysis of urban travel demand. *Environ. Behav.* 9, 91–106.

Lundberg, U. 1976. Urban commuting: crowdedness and catecholamine secretion. *J. Human Stress* 2, 26–32.

Mackintosh, E., S. West and S. Sargent 1975. Two studies of crowding in urban public spaces. *Environ. Behav.* 7, 159–84.

Mäkelä, I. 1975. (*Marketing research*) *Markkinaanalyysi No. 3 b.* Helsinki, Finland: Finnair.

Marks, J. M. 1969. *Fears and phobias*. London: William Heineman, Medical Books.

Montgomery, H. 1977. A study of intransitive preferences using a think-aloud procedure. In *Decision making and change in human affairs*, H. Jungerman and G. de Zeeuw (eds), pp. 347–62. Dordrecht: Reidel.

Norges Markedsdata AS 1976. (Marketing research for NSB). *Fra en undersökelse vedr. transportmiddler, 05 14/76.* Oslo: NSB.

OBSERVA 1977. (Marketing research for DSB) *Befolkningens rejsevaner og instilling til forskillige transportmiddler — Tabelvaerk, 1970.* Through agency of DSB (Danish State Railway), Köpenhamn.

Öhman, A., M. Fredriksson and K. Hugdahl 1977. *Towards an experimental model for simple phobic reactions*. Report 203. Uppsala, Sweden: Department of Psychology, University of Uppsala.

Otway, H. and H. Fishbein 1977. *Public attitudes and decision making*. Working group paper for the 6th Research Conference on Subjective Probability, Utility, and Decision Making, Warsaw, Poland, 6–9 September, 1977.

Paine, F. T., A N. Nash, S. J. Hills and G. A. Brunner 1969. Consumer attitudes toward auto versus public transport alternatives. *J. App. Psychol.* 53, 472–80.

Ramsden, J. M. 1976. *The safe airline*. London: Macdonald and Jane's.

Recker, W. W. and R. F. Stevens 1976. Attitudinal models of modal choice: the multinormal case for selected nonwork trips. *Transportation* 5, 355–75.

Reisenanalyse 1973, 1977. (Marketing research for Lufthansa). Through agency of Lufthansa, Köln, Germany.

Resvaneundersökningen 1973. *Enkät på svenska inrikesflyget.* Swedish Board of Civil Aviation, Financial Department.

Richards, L. G. and J. O. Jacobson 1975. Ride quality evaluation 1. Questionnaire studies of airline passenger comfort. *Ergonomics* **18**, 129–50.

Rozin, P. and J. W. Kalat 1971. Specific hungers and poison avoidance as adaptive specializations of learning. *Psychol. Rev.* **78**, 485–95.

Schiff, M. 1977. Hazard adjustment, focus of control, and sensation making: some small findings. *Environ. Behav.* **9**, 233–54.

Seligman, M. E. P. 1975. *Helplessness: on depression, development, and death.* New York: W. H. Freeman.

Shettleworth, S. J. 1975. Reinforcement and the organization of behavior in golden hamsters: hunger environment, and food reinforcement. *J. Exp. Psychol.: An. Behav. Processes* **104**, 56–87.

Singer, J. E., U. Lundberg and M. Frankenhaeuser 1978. Stress on the train: a study of urban commuting. In *Advances in environmental psychology*, A. Baum, J. E. Singer and S. Valins (eds), pp. 41–56. Hillsdale, N.J.: Erlbaum.

Solyom, L., R. Shugar, S. Bryntwick and C. Solyom 1973. Treatment of fear of flying. *Am. J. Psych.* **130**, 423–7.

Statistical Reports T 1977:5. 1977. *Long-distance journeys by private car during July 1975–June 1976: Journeys covering a distance of at least 50 kilometers.* Stockholm: Liber.

Statistical Reports T 1980: 21.1 1980. *Swedish travel patterns 1978.* Part 1: Main tables. All travels in Sweden. Stockholm: Liber.

Strahan, R. 1974. Situational dimensions of self-reported nervousness. *J. Person. Assess.* **38**, 341–52.

Stropher, P. R. 1977. On the application of psychological measurement techniques to travel demand estimation. *Environ. Behav.* **9**, 67–80.

Testa, T. J. 1974. Causal relationships and the acquisition of avoidance responses. *Psychol. Rev.* **81**, 491–505.

Tversky, A. 1969. Intransitivity of preferences. *Psychol. Rev.* **76**, 31–48.

Tyszka, T. 1983. Contextual multiattribute decision rules. In *Human decision making*, L. Sjöberg, T. Tyszka and J. A. Wise (eds), pp. 243–56. Lund: Doxa.

Walster, E. 1966. Assignment of responsibility for an accident. *J. Personal. Soc. Psychol.* **3**, 73–9.

Walster, E. 1967. "Second guessing" important events. *Human relat.* **20**, 239–50.

Wilcoxon, H. C., W. B. Dragoin and P. A. Kral 1971. Illness-induced aversions in rats and quail: relative salience of visual and gustatory cues. *Science* **171**, 826–8.

Wilson, D. W. and H. F. Priest 1968. The principal components of phobic stimuli. *J. Clin. Psychol.* **24**, 191.

Wolpe, J. and P. J. Lang 1964. A fear survey schedule for use in behaviour therapy. *Behav. Res. Ther.* **2**, 27–30.

Wood, J. T. 1976. *What are you afraid of? A guide to dealing with your fears.* Englewood Cliffs, N.J.: Prentice-Hall.

11 *The asbestos debate in Sweden*

LENNART NORDFORS

Introduction

In autumn 1975 the "asbestos alarm" shook Sweden. Reports of the cancer-provoking qualities of asbestos dominated the news. A heated discussion followed. Accusations were made in all directions. Earlier, asbestos had been perceived as a useful insulating material. Now it was just another occupational hazard. The National Board of Occupational Safety and Health (ASV) reacted by revising its newly issued instructions for the handling of asbestos, and in February 1976 the use of asbestos cement was forbidden.

It was not the first time that a widely used substance had proved dangerous, and numerous cases were to follow. Every year many new substances enter the market, even though our knowledge of the materials already in use is still far from complete. To cope with the hazards inherent in this situation, we need more thorough research into the facts.[1] Increased knowledge is not enough, however. We must also determine the limits beyond which a risk becomes *unacceptable*. This is, of course, a question of evaluation. The spontaneous reaction to the discovery of a risk would normally result in the demand "Stop it!". Unfortunately, reality is seldom so simple. We are often faced with conflicting values, where some may be at least as important as "health."

A case in point is vinyl chloride. In 1974 the substance was found to be carcinogenic. At the same time it is an ingredient in about one-fifth of all plastics produced. Vinyl chloride is, in other words, an important part of our economy. A ban would result in far-reaching consequences of various kinds (Stråby 1977, pp. 29–61). What knowledge of risks do the political actors possess? How are hazardous phenomena evaluated? What measures are taken? The present study deals with these questions. The object is to *describe* the arguments that occurred in the asbestos debate. The actors' standpoints will be interpreted and clarified. A second and subordinate task is to present an *explanation*. We will generate a few hypotheses about why asbestos cement was forbidden. Was the asbestos alarm a genuine "alarm" in terms of that it revealed previously unknown facts? To put it differently: was it new knowledge that produced the ban? Or was the decision made for other reasons, for example a need to satisfy a newly aroused and highly concerned public opinion?

In order to understand the discussion in all its details, one must know something about the different types of asbestos, their qualities and economic importance. A short description of what was known in 1976 – the year when the ban was imposed – is given in the section below. Then follows the main body of this essay: the account and analysis of the debate. Finally, a tentative answer is offered to the questions concerning possible explanations.

Background: the qualities and uses of asbestos

Asbestos is the name given to a variety of fibrous silicate minerals, the three most important ones being crocidolite ("blue asbestos"), amosite and chrysotile ("white asbestos"). The last is predominant, constituting at least 90% of the asbestos used in Sweden in the mid-1970s (Grimvall 1976). Blue asbestos is generally viewed as most dangerous, i.e. it has the strongest cancer-provoking effects.

Asbestos is known for its durability and flexibility. It has excellent insulatory qualities: Table 11.1 lists a few of its uses. Sweden imports asbestos. The annual import during the period 1972–6 was roughly 16 000 tons of pure material (Leijon & Norbäck 1976, p. 21), about two-thirds of which went to the asbestos cement industry. There it was manufactured into asbestos cement, one-fifth of which was exported abroad (Leijon & Norbäck 1976, p. 24).

At the time of the alarm, three plants were producing asbestos cement. Two of these, owned by Euroc, a large Swedish company, were situated in the towns of Lomma and Köping. Together the plants employed 520–570 workers. The third plant, which was controlled by Germans, lay in Varberg: 147 persons worked there in 1975 (Leijon & Norbäck 1976, pp. 28–9). Asbestos reaches the organism through the inhalation of dust. As a result, the

Table 11.1 Examples of the uses of asbestos in 1976 (from Grimvall 1976, p. 19).

Product (example)	Per cent asbestos	Important or unique qualities	Comments
asbestos cement for pipes, roofing, etc.	10–16 (short fibres)	durable, fire-proof, is not affected by insect or plants	blue asbestos is sometimes added in order to facilitate production
as an element in asphalt, vinyl plastics in flooring, etc.	10–30 (short fibres)	durable; resistant to oils, grease	
brake linings, friction surfaces in clutches, etc.	30–70 (long fibres)	frictional resistance is not lessened by protracted use	
fabric, filters for beer, wine, medicine	80–99 (long fibres)	Weavable material	also blue asbestos because of its resistance to acids
paper in electric equipment, insulation of cables	(long fibres)	low electric and thermal conductivity; positively charged fibres (yields good binding to cellulose and color pigments)	

following complaints and illnesses may occur: (a) pleural plaques, (b) asbestosis, (c) lung cancer, (d) mesothelioma, (e) cancer in other organs, such as the larynx or rectum, (f) pleuritis. The following account is based on Thiringer (1976).

PLEURAL PLAQUES

This sort of irregular thickening of the pleura is benign. The connection with asbestos was first shown in 1943. Pleural plaques can also occur for other reasons, but asbestos is the explanation in most cases. The frequency of this illness may well exceed 25% among asbestos workers. Pleural plaques do not generally produce any symptoms, and reduction in respiratory capacity cannot be found in most cases. It should not be seen as a preliminary stage to other asbestos-related complaints.

ASBESTOSIS

This is a sort of fibrosis of the lung. Even though it was first described in 1906, it was officially pronounced an occupational disease by Swedish authorities only in 1953. Generally, a long-term exposure is necessary to produce the disease. Close contact with the material for a period of 10 to 15 years is often required. Asbestosis manifests itself through respiratory troubles in connection with strenuous activities. A relationship between asbestosis and common lung cancer was first claimed in 1935, and proved conclusively in 1955.

MESOTHELIOMA

This is a very rare form of cancer. It arises in the pleura and peritoneum. A connection between this form of cancer and asbestos was first reported in 1943. Mesothelioma is known as a very dangerous form of cancer. Its consequences are nearly always fatal. Concerning other types of cancer, a correlation with asbestos was first reported in 1960. Asbestos workers seem to contract these diseases more often than other categories. However, up to 1976 medical research had not been able to find any definite evidence of a close connection.

A relationship between asbestos and pleuritis has also been demonstrated. This was shown during the last years of the 1960s. The complaint is not coupled with diminished lung function, and is usually self-healing within a few weeks or months.

A relevant question is whether asbestos cement produces the same illnesses as pure asbestos. It is always possible that the combination of asbestos and cement leads to lower or different risks. There was no certain answer to this question in the mid-1970. Check-ups of the workers in Lomma, Köping and Varberg had been undertaken, but no conclusive results could be presented. Different doctors were involved in different places, and there was a possibility that they interpreted the data according to disparate standards.

Smoking has a strongly aggravating effect as regards the risk of lung cancer. The asbestos fibres attract and concentrate the carcinogenic substances in tobacco smoke. According to certain investigations, the risk of a smoking asbestos worker getting lung cancer is 92 times that of a nonsmoker, who does not work with the substance. The corresponding difference between a smoking asbestos worker and his nonsmoking colleague is 23 times the risk. In cancer caused by the occupational environment it typically takes a longer time for the tumor to develop. Periods of 20–30 years are not unusual. The risk is also greater the longer one has handled the material. In other words, cancer mainly strikes people who have worked with asbestos for a long time (Thiringer 1976).

The asbestos debate

Let us start this section by introducing a few conceptual points of departure. These will later be used as a means of describing and comparing the actors' arguments. In the analysis of political ideas a division into three parts is frequently employed. The ideas are said to consist of: (a) a description of reality, (b) an evaluation of what reality ought to look like and (c) a recommendation concerning how to act (see e.g. Björklund 1968, Levine 1963). These three categories will be applied to the asbestos debate. They are related as follows to the questions of the essay:

(a) Description: what knowledge of the risks do the actors possess?
(b) Evaluation: how are the hazardous phenomena evaluated?
(c) Recommendation: what measures are taken?

It happens very rarely, however, that politicians and others gratify us scholars by arguing in this ideal way. Central parts of an argument are often left out. In many cases, for instance, the evaluation remains implicit. The reason for this may be that it is regarded as obvious. Often a reference to certain trends is argument enough in favor of a measure: everyone understands the speaker's view even if no evaluation is uttered. It may also happen that the recommendation is left out. This is frequently so when discussions have gone on for some

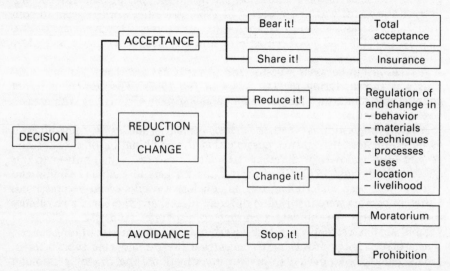

Figure 11.1 A classification of conceivable measures for coping with risks.

time. It is sufficient to present certain descriptions and evaluations for people to understand "which side" one advocates. This essay will, through the employment of systematic interpretation,[2] try to give the clearest possible picture of the arguments involved. The category "recommendations" may in turn be divided into a number of subgroups. When coping with risks, the following reactions are possible (Fig. 11.1)[3].

BEFORE THE ALARM

So far the preliminaries. Let us now turn to our case in point: the asbestos debate. As implied above, it has a long history. A convenient starting point for our investigation is 1964. This is the year when the National Board of Occupational Safety and Health (ASV) issued its first instructions for handling asbestos. The publication commenced by describing asbestos and its risks. Only one of the complaints listed above was included: asbestosis. The ASV declared that in most cases it was difficult to tell under what circumstances asbestos proved to be risky, and how serious the risks were. All this depended on the type of asbestos, the period of exposure and individual sensitivity. The Board noted that a long term of exposure was usually required, (ASV 1964, p. 3).

The ASV then proceeded to the actual instructions. First of all they called for a satisfactory level of safety in connection with the handling of asbestos, and continued by demanding that asbestos should be replaced with other less harmful or completely safe materials "wherever this is reasonably possible in view of the general circumstances" (ASV 1964, p. 4) and employers were charged with informing the workers of the risks. A number of ways of preventing asbestosis were described. The formation of dust was to be restricted by moistening the material or impregnating it against dust. The ASV also wanted machines and tools to be encapsuled and provided with extractors. The Board insisted that these rules should be followed wherever possible. Where it was not, the workers were to wear protective masks so as not to inhale the dust. Furthermore, the premises were to be designed so as to permit a specified cleaning procedure (ASV 1964, pp. 4–6). The publication closed with two points referring to existing legal paragraphs. Minors were barred from jobs handling asbestos and the workers were to be given medical check-ups whenever this was demanded by the ASV (ASV 1964, p. 6).

The Board gave a very incomplete description of the risks. The connection between asbestos and cancer was not mentioned at all. All the same, there was a general awareness of the dangers of the substance, and the ASV was willing to initiate action to protect the workers. Their determination had its limits, however. The general utility of asbestos was also taken into account. Consequently, the instructions represented three levels of ambition: primarily, the ASV wanted asbestos to be abolished. If this goal could not be achieved, the Board prescribed an adaption of machines and tools. But this, too, may be asking too much. There remained a minimal measure – to provide the workers with masks. The ASV did not demand an ideally safe environment for all workers.

As we shall see, the entire debate was dominated by this type of argument. A description of the dangers of asbestos, together with an evaluation of the type "everyone's health should be protected", was balanced against an implicit or explicit argument about the general utility of the material. The result was a recommendation in the category "Reduce the risk!".

In 1969 fresh information concerning the dangers appeared. The Swedish Institute of Occupational Health,[4] conducting inquiries into the risks of asbestos,[5] issued a newsletter where, amongst other things, mesothelioma was described. The same year, the Institute organized a conference about the question. One of the participants was Anders Englund, who reported on his studies of the Cancer Register, indicating unnaturally high rates of mesothelioma in certain occupations and geographical areas (Stråby 1977, p. 70). Research was also in progress elsewhere. The Construction Industries Organization for Working Environment, Safety and Health initiated studies of asbestos handling. One of the conclusions was that the insulation of houses by spraying asbestos was highly objectionable from a health point of view (Byggnadsarbetarförbundet (The Builders Workers' Union) 1972). The following year, 1970, the Building Workers' Union wrote a letter to the ASV suggesting that asbestos should be avoided whenever possible on building sites. They wanted the substance to be replaced by other materials. The Board agreed and referred to the current investigations at the Institute of Occupational Health. The letter did not prompt any other action from the ASV (The Builders Workers' Union 1972).

In 1972, the question was raised in parliament. The Communist Party (VPK) made a motion demanding a "categorical ban." They pointed out that the dangers of asbestos had been known since the turn of the century. The Party wrote of the risks of lung cancer and mesothelioma, and claimed that the dangers were not just occupational hazards. The risks encompassed society as a whole. The VPK quoted experts who claimed that mesothelioma was likely to become just as common as lung cancer: asbestos particles were commonly found in the lungs of city dwellers (Motion 1972/480 to Swedish Parliament). The Communists concluded their motion by claiming that substitutes for asbestos could be found in a number of areas, maybe even in all areas. This fact in combination with the risks spoke for the urgency of a ban.

The VPK clearly advocated the demand "Stop the risk!". For them the question was very simple: Asbestos is highly dangerous to both workers and the general public and at the same time superfluous – substitutes exist. There was thus no conflict between health and utility: everything stood to be gained and nothing lost by forbidding the substance. The motion was referred to the Parliamentary Standing Committee for Social Policy, which in turn circulated it amongst a number of organizations and authorities for comment. An overwhelming majority rejected the motion. Here follows an analysis of a few points of view.

The National Board of Occupational Safety and Health opened with a description of the dangers of lung cancer, mesothelioma, asbestosis and pleural plaques. However, the Board was uncertain of how closely asbestos was connected with the two types of cancer. Concerning lung cancer, asbestos might just be a transporting medium for the actually harmful substances. In mesothelioma, too, other causative factors besides asbestos might be involved. The Board's conclusion was that there was "not enough knowledge of the carcinogenic qualities of asbestos to establish the extent ... of (asbestos-related) tumors with absolute certainty" (ASV comments to motion 1972/480). The ASV pressed for further information and research. However, in the same communiqué they also noted that the only way to prevent the diseases was by keeping the amount of asbestos dust at a low level. The Board concluded that a general ban was neither called for nor possible. There were no substitutes for asbestos in many areas. However, it was to be abolished wherever other materials were available. The best way to regulate the situation was through instructions issued by the Board.

We note that the ASV's awareness of the risks involved has developed since 1964. But they are still not sure about the degree of danger. We recognize the remainder of the argument from the first instructions: health and utility are balanced. The Board wants to abolish the material, but in spite of this they accept the use of it: they want to "reduce the risk".

The Building Workers' Union felt that there was "conclusive medical evidence of the connection between asbestos and the very serious disease asbestosis and other lung diseases." Cancer was also mentioned. Concerning the building industry, the Union had no objection to a categorical ban. Quite the contrary: the demand had been backed by the Union for several years (The Builders Workers' Union 1972). The motion was, in other words, supported by the Union when it came to construction sites. Satisfactory substitutes could be found in this area, it was claimed. The Union continued by stating that if the authorities did not agree, the very least they could do was to forbid asbestos in its free form (e.g. spraying) on the working premises in question. Lastly, demands were made for more medical check-ups, absolute limits of dust concentration and compulsory measurements of dust.

The Association of General Contractors and Housebuilders claimed that the risks in connection with asbestos spraying and other use of the material in its free form were clearly established. Further, it was pointed out that the combination of smoking and asbestos was dangerous. The risks were assessed as so great that the Housebuilders supported a ban on the material in its free form in connection with building. However, they opposed a prohibition of asbestos in its bound form (e.g. asbestos cement). This type of product was not considered dangerous. Nevertheless, stricter measures were demanded against this material, too, in order to decrease the risks at the building sites.[6]

The Association of Chemical Industries wrote that asbestos was a thoroughly investigated material. The reported illnesses at the beginning of the 1970s could be explained by obsolete occupational environments. This was so because of the long time it took for the diseases to manifest themselves. It was also claimed that substitutes for asbestos were lacking in a large number of areas. Finally, the chemical industries stated that asbestos was completely safe if handled according to the instructions. Consequently the Association opposed a ban.[6]

The Swedish Shipbuilders' Association reported that they had exchanged free asbestos for other materials in all areas. However, they found it more difficult to avoid the material when it came to fireproof tiles, and they could not see any substitutes for asbestos in its bound form. They maintained that shipbuilders were trying to find such materials, even if they did not see any risks with bound asbestos. A total ban was rejected. It was claimed that such a decision could, among other things, result in unemployment.[6]

The three representatives of industry tried to tone down all talk of risks. They claimed that it was possible to handle asbestos without danger. The builders and shipbuilders made this claim only in connection with bound asbestos, whereas the chemical industries spoke more generally. The first two organizations seemed more sceptical than the last-named: they accepted a need for replacing the material, and the builders even talked of "reducing the risks." As far as the chemical industries go, the situation was quite plain. Their standpoint was completely opposed to that of the Communist Party. Asbestos was safe if correctly used. At the same time, the general utility of asbestos was emphasized. Everything was to be won and nothing lost if asbestos was admitted.

After referring to the three reactions just analyzed, the Federation of Swedish Industries pointed out that a ban would be most unfortunate. Among other things, such an action would result in decreased road safety, since asbestos was indispensable in brake lining. Another case in point was fire safety. The Federation also claimed that the VPK had exaggerated the risks. It had proved possible to keep the concentration below the prescribed limits by rather simple means. This was so in all Swedish asbestos plants. However, where substitutes could be found these would be employed (Industriförbundet (The Federation of Swedish Industries) 1972).

How did the Parliamentary Standing Committee for Social Policy react in its report? Concerning the risks, they pronounced asbestos to be dangerous. Radical measures were required. However, the Committee also felt obliged to declare that substitutes were lacking in certain areas. The Committee saw two ways of action: (1) a ban combined with wide possibilities of exemption and (2) general instructions for protection, where the risks in different situations could be weighed against the importance of asbestos.[6] The first alternative was rejected on grounds of principle. Furthermore, the Committee stated that good results could be achieved through strict instructions and standards in combination with severe control of the implementation. The demands for a ban of free-form asbestos at the building sites was backed. Concerning free asbestos in other situations, as well as the material in its bound form, stricter instructions were requested. Such instructions were at that time being drawn up by the National Board of Occupational Safety and Health.[6]

The Communist representative in the Committee lodged a protest against the report. He felt that the risks were so great that a ban with possibilities of exemption was the appropriate action. In order to obtain an exemption, a user should prove that no substitutes for asbestos could be found in his case and that all prescribed safety measures had been taken.[6] During the parliamentary debate the VPK enlarged upon this view, presenting a ban as more effective than instructions. The current instructions had not been satisfactorily implemented. The debate ended by parliament rejecting the Communist motion.[7]

The majority in the committee thus unmistakeably represented a standpoint of the type "Reduce the risk!". It was made clear that compromises between health and utility were acceptable where necessary. However, more rigorous instructions were called for. The risk must be reduced more effectively than before. Regarding the Communists, we can note a change of policy. The "categorical ban" previously demanded has been replaced by "a ban with possibilities of exemption." The general utility of asbestos was no longer uninteresting: the Communists were willing to accept trade-offs. The VPK now wants to "reduce the risk." It should be noted, however, that they stood for far stricter measures than others belonging to this category.

Asbestos was subsequently discussed in parliament during each of the two years that followed,[8] the Communists repeating their demand for a ban with possibilities of exemption. The contributions resembled those in 1972.[9] The VPK and the Social Democrat government were the only speakers in the debates. According to the Communist Party the basic principle in deciding whether or not to permit dangerous substances should be the workers' safety. Materials that harm the workers must be banned. However, it was possible to moderate this demand if satisfactory working methods were found. Recommendations like the instructions from the ASV were not viewed as a productive solution.[10] They were difficult to implement. For example, it was not easy to conduct measurements at the building sites. Concerning substitutes, the VPK claimed that the only case where such could not be found was brake linings.[11]

The Social Democrat government considered a hazardous working environment unsatisfactory, but added that substitutes had to be found before the risks could be eliminated. The Party claimed that a ban would be ineffective, since a large number of exemptions would have to be accepted. More research and stricter instructions were the methods that the Social Democrats advocated.[12] While these discussions were going on in parliament, the ASV was busy revising the asbestos instructions. The new instructions were to be published in 1973, but were in fact not ready until two years later. At this point they had been redrafted at least twelve times (Stråby 1977, p. 72).

A number of organizations, among them the Confederation of Swedish Employers and the Trade Union Confederation, were invited to comment on the draft proposal for new instructions. A notable answer came from the Employers, who demanded that asbestos cement be classified as dust-free, and guaranteed exemption from instructions that applied to other types of asbestos. The Employers also wanted the instructions to put more emphasis on the aggravated risks in connection with smoking. Their response was based on a reaction from Skandinaviska Eternit, the asbestos company in Lomma.[13]

The revised edition of the instructions was issued in June 1975, and was intended to take effect from the October 1 that year. The introduction contained a description of illnesses presented in section two of this chapter, and clearly stated the connection between asbestos and pleural plaques, asbestosis and lung cancer. The risks of smoking when working with the substance were also pointed out. Concerning mesothelioma, the wording was more cautious: "reports indicate that the risks of mesothelioma are intensified" (ASV 1975, p. 8). They stated that the illness was seen as mainly connected with blue asbestos, but "may also" be a result of contact with other sorts of asbestos. The publication also contained a few paragraphs about asbestos cement. The Board classified the material as producing dust. It was noted that products of asbestos cement were prefabricated, but the ASV nevertheless felt that they could cause dust. The instructions themselves primarily demanded that asbestos be avoided wherever possible. Blue asbestos was not to be used without consultation with regional inspectors of occupational safety. Furthermore, the spraying of asbestos was forbidden except with sealed equipment. Spraying was thereby stopped on building sites, aboard ships, etc. Asbestos was not to be used in insulation other than that of tools and equipment against strong heat. Products of asbestos cement were also accepted provided the maximum asbestos content did not exceed 10%. A condition for these exemptions was that substitutes were not available.

Exact limits to the concentration of asbestos in the air were also defined. In the beginning of 1975 the maximum had been set at two fibres per cm^3 of air, a value that had earlier been used unofficially, and which in turn was based on a British standard from the end of the 1960s (Stråby 1977, p. 66). This limit was now made a part of the instructions. If it were exceeded, more effective prevention of dust was demanded. Examples of such prevention were moistening of the material, encapsuling machinery, introducing extractors and improving the ventilation. The Board also issued regulations for personal protection and cleaning procedures (ASV 1975, pp. 13–19). Further, the ASV demanded dust measurements and controls of safety equipment at regular intervals. The asbestos was to be labeled upon delivery and import and the employer was to report the occurrence of dust-producing work to the regional inspectorate. Another point was medical check-ups of the workers. It was, among other things, demanded that these should continue also after the asbestos workers had left their employment.

The new instructions were far more stringent than those of 1964. The Board presented a more complete description of the risks, and stricter action was prescribed. Similarities in the principles put forward may also be found in the two editions, however. The ASV still stands for different levels of ambition. As earlier, the primary goal was the abolition of asbestos. Where this was not possible, the ASV permitted a qualified use of the material. The lowest level of ambition in 1964, the use of asbestos with masks as the only protection, was no longer accepted, and demands for preventive measures in the environment were stronger. Open-ended phrases of the type "if possible" were less frequent and exemptions were specified in most cases.

THE ALARM AND AFTER

New discoveries were made in September 1975. Anders Englund, who now worked for the Trade Union Confederation, had concluded his studies of the cancer register reported at the asbestos conference of 1969. He had found eight cases of death from mesothelioma among asbestos workers at the industry NOHAB in Trollhättan and 20 cases of the same disease among workers insulating engines at the Swedish Railways. The Board contacted the Metal Workers' Union, who had organized these workers. When the news hit the headlines on September 9, 1975, it provoked an immediate outcry among the public. The "asbestos alarm" was a fact (Stråby 1977, pp. 73–4).

The ASV was severely criticized by the media. The Metal Workers' Union demanded a tightening up of the new instructions, just being printed. The Board of Occupational Safety and Health reacted by appointing a special "asbestos group" to supervise, discuss and, if necessary, amend the instructions. It consisted of officials from the Board and representatives of affected parties, whose composition varied (Stråby 1977, pp. 74–5). Present at the first meeting were representatives from the ASV, the Metal Workers' Union, the State Employees' and the Factory Workers' Unions, the Plastic Industry and the Engineering Employers' Association. Later, the group was enlarged to include among others the Trade Union Confederation and representatives from the plants in Lomma, Köping and Varberg.[14]

At the first meeting, on September 24, a letter from the Metal Workers' Union was discussed. The Union demanded investigations into the extent of exposure of its members to asbestos. Medical check-ups of all the workers concerned were urged and reliable methods of diagnosing injuries exacted. The Union demanded a ban on asbestos wherever substitutes could be found. In remaining areas, asbestos could be used only with a special permit from the ASV. Another possibility was a system of authorization for companies with special protective equipment (Metallarbetarförbundet (The Metal Workers' Union, 1975). At this introductory meeting, it was decided to forbid blue asbestos, the substance responsible for the cases resulting in the alarm. The question of limits was also discussed, and the ASV was asked to consider the question.[15] The controversial point was what to do about asbestos cement. The issue was raised at the second meeting of the group, but it was decided to shelve it until the group could be enlarged with representatives from further involved parties.[16]

The asbestos cement question was the only point on the agenda at a subsequent meeting. Employers, trade unionists and safety controllers from the three asbestos plants were present. The plant in Köping only sent the shop steward of the local trade union. The employers' representatives from the two other factories pointed out that substitutes were lacking for asbestos, and that their plants lay below specified limits. An employers' representative from Varberg requested that his factory be allowed to continue production, claiming that new methods of work were under way. The trade unionist from the same plant said that conditions at his place of work were good and about to improve. A safety controller from Lomma attacked the Building Workers' Union for dealing too harshly with his company's products when demanding a ban on asbestos cement.[17] The Board of Occupational Safety and Health expressed disagreement with the safety controller. The Factory Workers' Union, which organized the workers at the three asbestos cement plants, underlined the urgency of the factories improving their environments. Attention should be paid to the question of substitutes. The Trade Union Confederation maintained that a ban was not immediately indicated, but that a reasonable schedule for winding up asbestos could be discussed. The Metal Workers' Union was critical: they felt that the producers were shirking their responsibility.[17]

The safety controller's attack on the Building Workers' Union was not the only case of conflict between local workers' representatives and the trade unions. At the end of October, the local trade union in Lomma sent a letter to the Factory Workers' Union expressing distress about the state of affairs. They claimed that the workers were not so much worried about their health as about the danger of losing their jobs. The local section urged their union to pay attention to this aspect and not be too much influenced by the debate in the media, which was described as "hysterical" (Boglind & Eriksson 1976). The Union replied that they understood the workers' concern, but that the health of the members was more important than the preservation of an industry solely for reasons of employment. They therefore pressed for stricter instructions, and advised the people in Lomma to try to find substitutes (Boglind & Eriksson 1976).

At a meeting on December 8, the ASV presented a draft for new instructions. This said that products from Varberg and Lomma need not be viewed as dust-productive as long as they fulfilled certain norms concerning, among other things, asbestos contents. The employers were charged with seeing to it that the materials were handled as little as possible on building sites and elsewhere. It was also announced that the factories involved were developing asbestos-free products.[18] A heated debate followed. The Building Workers' Union considered the draft a step backwards. The Factory Workers' Union repeated that asbestos must be abolished. A further lowering of the concentration in air and other improvements to the environment were also important. The Building and Metal Workers' Unions demanded that the instructions be provided with a time limit for terminating the use of asbestos cement. They claimed that the Trade Union Confederation also backed this idea. The ASV opposed a time limit. Such a decision might have negative effects. The risks were slight if the instructions were followed, they maintained. The Board also raised the question of employment: 600 workers in the production of asbestos cement were in danger of losing their jobs.[18] The Confederation of Swedish Employers said that it was impossible to abolish asbestos. There was a risk that substitutes would prove deficient. Consequently, the employers preferred a policy of protective measures in the handling of asbestos. Company representatives from Lomma said that dust from asbestos cement was far less risky than pure asbestos dust, if there was any risk at all. The firm considered its products to be dust-free. They had not found any signs of ill-health among their workers.[18]

Later, the ASV returned with a revised draft for new instructions including a time limit. Asbestos cement was permitted until January 1, 1979. But this version, too, was rejected.[19] Finally, on February 26, 1976, a communiqué came from the ASV prohibiting the installation of asbestos cement products from June 1, 1976. Certain exceptions were made, however. For the purpose of fireproofing, the material was permissible until January 1, 1977 (ASV 1976, No. 8). The ASV also decided to lower the permissible concentration in air from two fibres to one fibre per cm^3 of air (ASV 1976, No. 9). Two weeks after the decision concerning asbestos cement, it was announced that asbestos was to be banned in dyes, glue and jointing material from June 1, 1976 (ASV 1976, No. 7).

The Eternitrör company in Varberg appealed against the decision. Early in June 1976 the ASV decided to grant it an exemption for its production of pipes. These were allowed to be used on condition that they contained no more than 12.5% asbestos. The Board motivated its decision by pointing out that the company had improved its products, and that substitutes were to be introduced by 1980 at the latest (ASV 1976, No. 21). The Varberg section of the Factory Workers' Union opposed the exemption. They wrote a letter to their head office, demanding an official statement of opinion on the ban. The Union replied that it had never backed a ban. They had advocated a fast but gradual removal from working life and improvements to the occupational environment. This was best achieved through a lowering of the permissible concentrations in the air and attempts to find substitutes (Boglind & Eriksson 1976).

On December 12, 1976, asbestos was prohibited in flooring and walling. The manufacture of such products must cease from September 1977, and from September 1978 they could no longer be installed (ASV 1976, No. 39).

The Board of Occupational Safety and Health had thus made the following decisions:

September 1975 : prohibition of blue asbestos
February 1976 : prohibition of asbestos cement
February 1976 : maximum concentration lowered from two fibres to one fibre per cm^3 of air
March   1976 : prohibition of asbestos in dyes, glue and jointing material
June   1976 : products from Eternitrör in Varberg exempted
December 1976 : prohibition of asbestos in flooring and walling

The asbestos alarm did not result in anything new as far as arguments go. We recognise all these from earlier stages in the discussion. A large part of the debate concerns descriptions. The actors argue about the health hazards of the substance, and there is conflict concerning the availability of substitutes. We can also note dissent when it comes to evaluations. One of the topics debated is how much importance should be attached to the threat of unemployment among asbestos workers.

Concerning the recommendations, our categories stop–reduce–accept the risk to bring out what was common to the actors. All who agreed on the existence of risks also agreed that "reduce the risk" was best. No one advocated a total ban regardless of the possibilities of finding substitutes. For instance, no actor wanted to forbid the material in brake lining or in heat-protective equipment. Within these boundaries the debate was lively, however: the category "reduce the risk" had plenty of room for controversy.

At the same time as the decision making was going on at the ASV, the issue was debated in parliament. The first reaction after the alarm was a question raised by the Communist Party. The Party criticized the newly issued instructions, which they considered weak, and asked the Minister of Labor whether he might be prepared to back a ban with possibilities of exemption. The VPK claimed that such action would result in a quicker emergence of substitutes.[20] The Minister answered that the ASV was currently deliberating with trade unions and employers about a possible ban on certain floor materials. A restriction of the use of asbestos cement was also being discussed. The Minister considered the method of drawing up and implementing instructions together with the labour-market organizations far more efficient than a ban. The 85 000 industrial safety controllers together with the regional inspectors of the ASV guaranteed a practical implementation of the instructions. The Minister also agreed with the basic principle contained in these, that asbestos should disappear at the same pace as substitutes could be introduced. The past showed that the authorities could act with determination: blue asbestos had recently been forbidden.[21] The Center Party (formerly the Agrarian Party) also participated in the debate. One of their MPs felt that asbestos should be avoided "as far as posssible", but that they could not back the ban. Such a decision would result in ineffective action and a large bureaucratic apparatus, it was claimed. Furthermore, there was a risk that substitutes more dangerous than asbestos might be introduced. The MP felt that the supervisory authorities should be given a chance to function effectively. He called for more resources to be invested in occupational medicine, the ASV regional inspectorate and the training of workers and their safety controllers.[21] The Conservative Party also opposed the ban. Their speaker agreed with the point made by the representative of the Center Party. He added that the part played by smoking should be emphasized, and pointed out that a ban would lead to the dismissal of 700 workers in the Factory Workers' Union alone. Substitutes were lacking, he said, and claimed that too quick a development might result in the introduction of other dangerous materials.[21]

The alarm gave the Communist Party the opportunity to reiterate their demand "a ban with possibilities of exemption". This, the Social Democrat government parried with an argument slightly different from the one used on previous occasions. Gone is the idea that health should be balanced against utility. Instead another aspect, earlier subordinate, now played the dominant part: the demand for effective implementation. Instructions coupled with negotiations with unions and employers were put forward as more effective measures than a ban. The Social Democrats thus did not show any divergence from the Communist Party in their view of the risks of asbestos or their evaluation of these risks. The government wanted to show that the goal "everybody's health should be protected" was best realized through the measures it proposed. Another novelty was that nonsocialist parties also participated in the discussion. The Center Party's standpoint was similar to the Social Democrats, but the Center Party went a step further by claiming that the VPK's proposal might result in a *worsened* environment. The Conservative Party agreed with this, but differed from the others by stating that health should be balanced against other values. The Conservatives were the only party once more presenting this argument, which was used against the Communist Party motion of 1972.

The VPK had also tried to introduce a motion about asbestos at a point in the session when this was out of order. The Party claimed that the alarm was to be judged "an event of major importance", and that their motion could thus be accepted for discussion. However, the Speaker disagreed and the motion was dismissed.[22] The question was also brought up in the Committee for Social Policy, which, as a parliamentary standing committee, has the right of initiative and can introduce issues at all times. Thus it discussed whether to take action and demand a ban with possibilities of exemption. A number of closed hearings were held with representatives from the ASV, the Trade Union Confederations for blue and white collar workers, the Employers' Federation and medical experts. These resulted in a decision to let the matter rest.[23] The Committee for Social Policy motivated their decision by pointing out that none of the parties consulted had advocated a ban. The importance of getting rid of asbestos where substitutes were available had been emphasized, however. The committee pointed out that asbestos was a highly dangerous substance. Radical action was therefore motivated. The target was the disappearance of asbestos. However, a ban was inadvisable, since it could give rise to red tape and the introduction of dangerous substitutes. The committee was thus for working within the framework of the existing laws. Moreover, they pointed out that the new instructions meant stricter measures than earlier. Reference was made to the work of the asbestos group, which was just discussing the prohibition of asbestos mats and restrictions on the use of asbestos cement.[23] Criticism was also directed against the ASV's instructions. The committee felt that these were difficult to interpret in certain parts, and that they ought to contain a recommendation to asbestos workers not to smoke. The communists' representative in the committee lodged an objection. He argued that the results of the hearings strengthened the case for a ban with restrictive possibilities of exemption.

During the regular notice period (January), two motions were made. One came from the Communist Party, who once again demanded a ban with exemptions, and specified how the latter might work. Every imported asbestos consignment should be dealt with separately, and detailed descriptions of the techniques for handling the material should be submitted to the trade union and the regional inspectorate for approval. The Communist Party indicated personal protective equipment as an article that could be declared exempt.[24] The other motion originated from the Liberal Party, who requested that a few words concerning the rôle played by smoking should be inserted into the instructions.[25] The latter motion was approved by the Committee for Social Policy, who, however, felt that parliamentary action was not required. The Communist Party's demands were met with the same arguments as earlier, and the Committee pointed to the ban on asbestos cement as an example of practical measures to restrict asbestos.[26]

It is interesting to note how the parliamentary majority constantly lagged one step behind the Board when arguing against the Communist Party's proposals. First the ban on blue asbestos was used as an argument. When the Committee for Social Policy later rejected demands to initiate action, they did it, among other things, on the grounds that the ASV was considering a limitation of the use of asbestos cement. Finally, the VPK motion was rejected with reference to the recent ban on asbestos cement. The Communists' unchanging demand was countered with different examples of the government's determined policy, thereby arguing that a ban was not necessary.

Final analysis

The asbestos debate was heated at the beginning of the 1970s, and it grew more so after the alarm. However, our scheme of risk reactions has not brought out the differences between the actors. The category "Reduce the risk" proved to be very wide; it drew our attention to the principles where most actors agreed. We have been able to demonstrate points of consensus even between the bitterest of enemies. Let us now change our perspective and look at what it is that separates the actors. Which were the points of divergence? Which arguments were used?

If we collect all the reasons given *for* the continued use of asbestos, the following "ideal" defense for the material is obtained. The risks are not so great. They might even be nonexistent if asbestos were handled properly. Furthermore, the material has great advantages. In many areas no substitutes exist. Excessive interference will create unemployment, and might also lead to a worsened occupational environment. There is a danger that new and worse materials are substituted for asbestos. No actor had presented all these arguments at the same time. The view closest to this very clear-cut and uncomplicated position was that of the Association of Chemical Industries in their reply to the Committee for Social Policy in 1972.

The corresponding ideal argumentation *against* asbestos is the following. Asbestos is very dangerous. The problem is not only one of occupational environment: we can also expect an increase in asbestos-related diseases among common citizens. Moreover, substitutes can be found in all areas. There is, in other words, no danger of unemployment, etc. Only once has an actor spoken in such distinct terms. The arguments are found in the VPK's motion from 1972; the one where a "categorical ban" was advocated. Already in the subsequent protest against the Committee's treatment of the motion the Communist Party accepted that substitutes could be found in all areas, and they changed their demand to "a ban with possibilities of exemption".

An attempt to group the actors into three categories, those who mainly speak "against" asbestos, those who "balance" between the two ideal types, and those who are closer to the arguments "for", yields the following results. The Communists presented the above-mentioned motion against asbestos. When this was circulated for comments, the Party was backed by the Building Workers' Union. However, it should be noted that the Union restricted its remarks to conditions in the building sector. Representatives of industry reacted with a more positive view. They talked less of risks and more of the lack of substitutes. But differences can also be found between the sectors. The Association of Chemical Industries, for instance, stand for a more uncritical view than the contractors and housebuilders. The Board of Occupational Safety and Health, together with the political parties who opposed the ban, stand for a "balanced view". Asbestos was regarded as dangerous, but at the same time the lack of substitutes was underlined. From 1972 onward, the parliamentary debate is characterized by these ideas. The Communist Party emphasized the risks to health, and tried to show that the difficulties in connection with substitutes was not so great. The Social Democrats answered by claiming that both aspects were problematic.

After the alarm the VPK and the Building Workers' Union were joined by the Metal Workers in the critical group. The Trade Union Confederation backed the demand to forbid asbestos cement. The companies involved, including representatives from local trade unions, and Employers' representatives answered that the risks had been exaggerated, and that it was difficult to find substitutes. The ASV still argued for a "balanced" view. The Board emphasized both health and utility. The Factory Workers' Union represented a similar standpoint. Asbestos was viewed as an environmental problem at the same time as the Union pressed for consideration of the problem of substitutes.

The debate changed its character in parliament, and the question of the advantages or disadvantages of asbestos no longer dominated debates. The government defended its resistance against a ban with the argument that such action was not as effective as the majority strategy for fighting asbestos. The Center Party did likewise, but with even more emphasis. Goals were no longer discussed: the issue was put forward as a question of means. The Conservatives differed by claiming that health and utility have to be balanced.

This final analysis concludes our description of the debate. Most of the actors wanted to "reduce the risk", but within this frame there are tough confrontations concerning the trade-off between health and utility. Let us now try to explain the decision to forbid asbestos cement. The question we posed in the introduction can be reformulated as follows. What were the motives behind the ASV's decision to ban asbestos cement? Was the Board led by *substantive* consideration – a conviction in the matter – or was the decision based on *strategic* consideration – in other words an objective to reach advantageous relations with other actors?[27] We see how the Board's awareness of the risks gradually grew during the 1960s and 1970s. The first instructions contained a very incomplete description of the risks. Only in 1975 did a complete description appear, and then there was still a certain hesitation concerning the connection between asbestos and mesothelioma.

Apart from pointing to actual cases of death in Sweden, the asbestos alarm did not offer the ASV any radically new information. The discoveries did possibly lead to a dropping of the question mark concerning mesothelioma. What turned them into an alarm was that knowledge of the risks for the first time reached the general public. The media saw to it that people were informed of the dangers of asbestos. It was, in other words, mainly the strategic situation that changed. The decision makers now had a large public opinion to be concerned about. This put the ASV in a difficult position. New instructions were being printed after a long process of negotiations. The Board was, at the same time, severely criticized by the media (Stråby 1977, p. 74).

In this situation, the ASV was forced to act. A group was formed containing representatives from affected parties. We have seen how the Board occupied a middle position during the debate. Now we see how it manifested its will to compromise in action, too. It did not let itself be pressed by public opinion into promising a ban and radical action. Instead, it chose to form a representative group. Whenever topics came up demanding more representation, the issue was shelved until additional parties could participate. The question of asbestos cement was not discussed until people from the plants were present.

The Board tried, as far as possible, to find a solution that could create consensus. A draft proposal for new instructions still permitting asbestos cement was presented as late as December 1975. A compromise between the ASV and the companies can be perceived behind this document. The plants had earlier claimed that they faced great problems in finding substitutes. The draft for new instructions nevertheless reported that they were developing asbestos-free products. In other words, the Board first tests an approach where the companies voluntarily agree to abolish asbestos as an alternative to a ban. But the draft was not accepted by such actors as the Trade Union Confederation, the Building Workers' Union and the Metal Workers' Union. The Board's next move was to forbid asbestos cement from January 1, 1979. This measure was not enough to satisfy the critics. Finally, a decision was made to forbid the material from June 1976. The "hard-liners" had won.

The decision to forbid asbestos cement was thus prompted by considerations of a strategic character. The Board was forced to capitulate in the face of insistent demands for a ban. This interpretation is supported by other accounts of the events. Arne Stråby, himself an executive officer at the Board of Occupational Safety and Health, writes in his book "Riskmiljö": "It has been claimed that the ASV's restrictions on asbestos products are based on political reasons, not medical ones... our society is (normally) governed by political decisions that are based on medical, social and economic considerations as well as purely political ones. It cannot be a breach of duty if the Board in its decisions pays attention to a broad opinion among Swedish workers."

Swedish political culture has often been described as one of consensus and compromise. It has been said that no other democracy in the world can parallel Sweden in this respect (Tomasson 1970, Hancock 1972, Kelman 1980). The system has been compared to a tortoise that carefully plans every step and sees to it that all four legs – cabinet, parliament, administration and organized interests – move in the same direction (Lundqvist 1980). In the case of asbestos, we have witnessed how the tortoise got its legs tangled and as a result took a longer step than was originally intended.

Acknowledgments

I wish to thank Lennart J. Lundqvist, the National Swedish Institute for Building Research, Gävle, for great help in the creation of the original version of this essay. I also owe thanks to Evert Vedung, Department of Government, Uppsala University, for many good ideas when writing this final version. Last, but not least, I wish to thank my mother, Marianne Nordfors, MA, for great patience and tremendous efforts when aiding me with the translation of the manuscript. If the essay, in spite of these persons' help, is marred by mistakes and unclear thought the responsibility is, needless to say, mine.

Explanatory notes

1 See Stråby 1977 *Riskmiljö*, 111–112, where the knowledge of existing risks is discussed. A general discussion can be found in Sanne (ed.): *Kemisamhället och hälsan* (see the reference list for details).

2 A systematic interpretation is built on the assumption that the actors are consistent. Karl Popper (1962) describes it as follows: "wherever there are two interpretations, one of which will make (him) consistent and the other inconsistent, prefer the former to the latter, if reasonably possible."

3 The figure can be found in Lundqvist 1977 and in Vedung 1979. A large number of accounts can be found concerning these questions. Three examples are: Rowe (1977), Goodman and Rowe (1979), and Lowrance (1976) (see the reference list for details).

4 Today the Occupational Health Department of the ASV.

5 This was the so-called asbestosis project, concluded in 1974 (cf. Stråby 1977, p. 70).

6 Report from the Committee for Social Policy 1972/40.

7 Parliamentary records December 12, 1972.

8 Interpellation 1973/142, Parliamentary records November 1, 1973.

9 Motion 1974/1337.

10 Parliamentary records March 27, 1974.

11 Parliamentary records October 12, 1973.

12 Parliamentary records March 27, 1974.

13 Skandinaviska Eternit's comments to instructions, draft number 4. The Employers' Federation (Svenska arbetsgivarföreningen 1975) agreed with this company's ideas, and referred to it in their own response. The asbestos cement industry seem to have played a great part for the Employers' standpoints (cf. Kelman 1980, pp. 77–80).

14 The minutes of the asbestos group no. 1–5.

15 The minutes of the asbestos group September 24, 1975.

16 The minutes of the asbestos group October 9, 1975.

17 The minutes of the asbestos group November 10, 1975.

LENNART NORDFORS 193

18 ASV's proposal for new instructions December 4, 1975. Appendix to the minutes of the asbestos group December 8, 1975.
19 ASV's proposal for new instructions December 28, 1975.
20 Interpellation 1975–76/33, parliamentary records October 21, 1975.
21 Parliamentary records November 20, 1975.
22 Cf. motion 1975–76/755.
23 Minutes from the Committee for Social Policy 1975–76/9, December 2, 1975, appendix 2, appendix 3.
24 Motion 1975–76/755.
25 Motion 1975–76/1296.
26 The Committee for Social Policy 1975–76/40.
27 This distinction is central in the project "Politics as rational action" at the Department of Government, Uppsala University. It is developed in Lewin (1979) and in Lewin and Vedung (1980).

References

Arbetarskyddsstyrelsen (ASV) 1964–1976. *Documents and communiqués in the asbestos issue*. Stockholm: ASV

Björklund, S. 1968. *Politisk teori*. Stockholm: Bonniers.

Boglind, A. and K. Eriksson 1976. Arbete med asbestcement. In *Asbestcement-industrin – en förstudie*. Göteborg: Centrum för tvärvetenskap.

Byggnadsarbetarförbundet (The Building Workers' Union) 1972. *Comment to motion 1972/48*. Swedish Parliamentary records: Stockholm.

Goodman, G. T. and W. D. Rowe (eds) 1979. *Energy risk management*. London: Academic Press.

Grimvall, G. 1976. *Asbest som material. Några egenskaper*. In Centrum för tvärvetenskap Göteborg.

Hancock, M. D. 1972. *Sweden. The Politics of Postindustrial Change*. Hinsdale: The Dryden Press.

Industriförbundet (The Federation of Swedish Industries) 1972. *Comment to motion 1972/480*. Swedish Parliamentary records: Stockholm.

Kelman, S. 1980. *Regulating America, regulating Sweden: a comparative study of occupational safety and health policy*. Cambridge, Ma: The MIT Press.

Leijon, S. and L E. Norbäck 1976. *Kommersiell användning av asbestcement*. In Centrum för tvärvetenskap, Göteborg.

Levine, R. A. 1963. *The arms debate*. Cambridge, Ma: Harvard University Press.

Lewin, L. 1979. *Det politiska spelet*. Stockholm: Rabén & Sjögren.

Lewin, L. and E. Vedung (eds) 1980. *Politics as rational action*. Dordrecht D. Reidel.

Lowrance, W. W. 1976. *Of acceptable risk: science and the determination of safety*. Los Altos, Calif.: William Kaufmann.

Lundqvist, L. J. 1977. *The politics of determining socially acceptable levels of risk*. Stockholm : Samarbetskommittén för långsiktsmotiverad forskning.

Lundqvist, L. J 1980. *The hare and the tortoise. Clean air policies in the United States and Sweden*. Ann Arbor: Michigan University Press.

Metallarbetarförbundet (The Metal Workers' Union) 1975. *Letter to ASV's asbestos group*. Stockholm, 11 Sept. 1975. Stockholm: ASV.

Popper, K. R. 1962. *The open society and its enemies. I. the spell of Plato*. London: Routledge & Kegan Paul.

Rowe, W. D. 1977. *An anatomy of risk*. New York: Wiley.

Sanne, C. (ed.) 1981. *Kemisamhället och hälsan*. Stockholm: Sekretariatet för framtidsstudier.

Stråby, A. 1977. *Riskmiljö*. Stockholm: Bonniers.

Svenska Arbetsgivarföreningen (Federation of Swedish Employers) 1975. *Comment to ASV's draft for new instruction − version 4*. Stockholm: ASV.

Thiringer, G. 1976. *Biologiska effekter av asbest*. In Centrum för tvärvetenskap Göteborg.

Tomasson, R. F. 1970. *Sweden: prototype of modern society*. New York: Random House.

Vedung, E. 1979. Politically acceptable risks from energy technologies: some concepts and hypothesis. In *Energy Risk Management*, G. T. Goodman and W. D. Rowe (eds). London: Academic Press.

12 *The spruce budworm and Nova Scotia forest industries*

HOLLIS ROUTLEDGE AND
RON AURELL

Introduction

The story we are telling here takes place in Nova Scotia, a small "have not" province on Canada's eastern shore. It deals with the problems presented by a massive insect infestation, which is threatening a major portion of the raw material supply for one of the few viable industries in the province, the forest product industry. It involves many of the elements that are becoming typical in issues that face society in most Western countries; difficulties in formulating the alternatives available and evaluating them by some kind of cost–benefit analysis; problems in appraising the risks involved, which will always include an element of uncertainty; emotional public involvement fuelled by intense media coverage, often more interested in creating controversy than in facts; actions of pressure groups of various kinds, involved in various types of game plans, often inaccessible for rational discussions; and for the politicians, attempting to stay out of it all and normally favoring nonaction, but who ultimately are forced into a decision which they perceive is based on the "popular" view, although rationalized in other terms.

The situation in Nova Scotia is, of course, special in many ways being a small province regarded to be very "political", but this may only make the story more illustrative. It is not a happy story and it clearly shows the dilemma faced by society in trying to make rational decisions on controversial issues.

The story is told from a company point of view, a company that is located in the middle of the area affected by the insect attack, now seeing its future very much in jeopardy. Undoubtedly it will convey some of the frustration we felt as company employees, when we saw our motives questioned and facts readily misrepresented. The story is admittedly biased because of our interest, but we believe that most of the knowledge of the facts and consequences of various actions were available through our company, and the specialized knowledge in the forestry field that it has acquired over the years. Of course we are asking ourselves what we did wrong and what our integrity as individuals, as well as that of the company, would require us to do in a situation like this. How can a company with a vast amount of knowledge in a particular area make an input that could be regarded as acceptable; another dilemma.

The numerous aspects of the problem covered in this paper could be extended to any degree by the authors, who have been working on this problem for more than two years. We have not attempted to cover it in every regard, but rather to let the reader know our feelings on the subject.

Nova Scotia Forest Industries

In 1961, Stora Kopparberg (the Company) started up a bleached sulfite pulpmill at the Strait of Canso on beautiful Cape Breton Island, Nova Scotia. The major advantages in location here were the excellent harbor on the Canadian east coast and an adequate supply of softwood timber. The province of Nova Scotia leased more than 500 000 hectares of provincial crown land to the Company which was calculated to supply about 50% of pulpwood requirements. An additional 1 million hectares of privately owned woodland in the operating area would permit the Company to purchase the additional wood requirement from the private landowners. In 1971, a newsprint mill was added to the complex and the total wood requirement of 1.3 million m^3 stacked per year just about equaled the allowable harvest for the operating area. To secure the wood supply over the long term, a forest improvement program was implemented for the leased lands which were under Company management. The original sulfite pulpmill was not a financial success but after the newsprint expansion the Company, known as Nova Scotia Forest Industries, started to show better results beginning in 1974 and the future looked reasonably secure.

It is ironic that 1974 was also the year when the current spruce budworm infestation was detected in the northern part of Cape Breton Island. Indications are that the infestation was started by spruce budworm moths windborne from Prince Edward Island or New Brunswick, Canadian provinces to the west of Nova Scotia.

What is the spruce budworm?

The spruce budworm is a native of the northern evergreen forests of North America. When fir-spruce forests mature over large areas, and if spring weather is warm and dry, populations may explode to epidemic proportions within a few years. Such an epidemic, if left uncontrolled, will result in extensive tree mortality after three to four years. We are now in the midst of such an outbreak that covers more than 50 million hectares of fir-spruce forest in Ontario, Quebec, the Maritime Provinces and Newfoundland, as well as in the northeastern part of the USA, particularly in the state of Maine.

The spruce budworm overwinters in hibernation as a very small larva. In the spring this very tiny larva comes to life as tree growth begins, and it makes its way to the buds at the branch tips to begin feeding inside the bud. As the weather warms, the buds open and the larva continues to grow and feed on the needles developing from the bud. This feeding period lasts five to six weeks and the larva eventually grows to be about 2 cm long. The larvae feed continuously and, as the population on one mature tree can be as high as 20 000 insects, they are capable of eating all the new foliage and part of the older foliage in one feeding season.

After the larval development is complete, the insect goes into a pupa stage which lasts about ten days. From the pupa a small brownish-gray moth emerges and this is the stage when migration takes place and the infestation spreads. When the moths emerge, mating takes place and the fertile female lays part of her egg supply in that area. After depositing part of the egg load, the female can become airborne, and on warm evenings great swarms of these fertile moths rise into the air and can be carried by the wind many miles from their place of origin, to find new host trees where they deposit their remaining eggs. The eggs develop into the overwintering larvae and start the cycle again.

The budworm larvae are very well adapted to the Canadian climate and while cold, wet summer weather will slow down the feeding and eventually reduce populations, they appear to be unaffected by winter storms, late spring frosts or similar dramatic weather changes.

The present budworm attack

The spruce budworm has been harvesting the fir-spruce forest in eastern Canada for many thousands of years, and until man started competing with the budworm for the softwood timber there was no conflict between man and the budworm. Conflict has developed, however, because the budworm "harvests" very large areas every 30 to 70 years, whereas industrial forest managers must harvest small areas on an annual basis.

The first recorded budworm infestation affecting a forest industry occurred in the province of New Brunswick from 1912 to 1920. The insect destroyed the softwood timber on millions of hectares of woodland and made a shambles of the sawmill industry of that time. When the budworm attacked the forests again in New Brunswick beginning in 1951, the provincial forestry department and the wood-using industries began an insecticide spraying program based on a crop-insurance philosophy. The New Brunswick program had been successful to the degree that it had allowed the forest industry not only to continue to operate, but to increase greatly in capacity. In the early years of its program, New Brunswick used DDT as an insecticide and later switched to an organophosphate insecticide known as fenitrothion. In Ontario, Quebec and Prince Edward Island, other Canadian provinces, insecticide spraying is carried out to protect woodlands or park areas. The total area sprayed in 1976 in all of eastern Canada was 7 million hectares which is 1.4 times the total area of the province of Nova Scotia.

SURVEYS, ESTIMATES AND FORECASTS

The Canadian Forestry Service which is a branch of Environment Canada, under the federal government, surveys insect and disease conditions in Canadian forests on a regular basis. When insect populations are at normal low levels, the survey results are published in regular reports but when something unusual turns up, the provincial forestry officials and others involved with forest management are advised at once. The provinces are responsible for natural resources including forest protection.

In the current spruce budworm outbreak on Cape Breton Island, forest managers were supplied with aerial mapping showing the location and degree of defoliation, egg-count data, overwintering larvae data and a degree of severity forecast for the following year. The entomologists involved proved to be able to predict population levels and severity of defoliation with surprisingly good accuracy.

A CHRONOLOGY OF FRUSTRATION

With the appearance of heavy budworm populations in northern Cape Breton Island in 1974, the Company quickly arranged consultations with the provincial forestry department and the Canadian Forestry Service to see what could be done about the infestation. Because the threatened area was provincial crown land leased to the Company, provincial approval was needed for whatever action was to be taken.

Following discussions based on the insect survey data, it was concluded that 8000 hectares of mature forest land was seriously threatened and the Company suggested insecticide spraying in the summer of 1975 to protect the timber stands. The provincial forestry officials did not feel that spraying was necessary and it was finally agreed that the Company should build additional roads and start an emergency harvesting program for the timber that was expected to die if it were not protected. The Company proceeded with the program and all concerned waited anxiously to see what would develop in 1975.

In the early summer of 1975, it became evident that the infestation had spread over a much larger area and the egg-count surveys in late summer indicated that a dramatic population explosion could be experienced in 1976. With this development, the Company again consulted with the government people and suggested that the provincial forestry department and the Company jointly develop a plan involving the protection of certain key forest areas by insecticide spraying and accelerated harvesting of other areas. Even though the surveys clearly indicated that the forests would be devastated in 1976 if nothing were done, the provincial forestry people continued to resist any suggestion of protection and said that the population build-up might collapse the next year due to natural causes. They did not present any comparative information but cited past records which indicated that the spruce budworm had caused some damage between 1955 and 1960 without causing major losses of timber. To the Company managers and Canadian Forest Service managers, it was evident that the insect populations in the 1950s were not comparable to the 1975 situation, and it was concluded that the Company could not risk waiting another year without taking action to protect the forests.

The Company prepared an application for permission to spray 40 000 hectares of prime forest land on the Cape Breton highlands more than 8 km from areas with any population. This area contained about 2.4 million m^3 stacked of standing timber. The Company also said that it would proceed immediately to salvage-harvest 1.2 million m^3 stacked of timber surrounding the area to be protected, which would be left to die due to the insect feeding. Although the provincial forestry department would not agree to this plan, in early 1976 the Nova Scotia Government in Cabinet did approve the plan and the Company started arrangements to have the work carried out for spraying the following summer.

While all this was going on, six urban environmental associations in the provincial capital of Halifax started up a strong anti-spray lobby and received considerable media support in their campaign.

In the early part of 1976, the environmental groups released a report by a medical research group working in a children's hospital in Halifax on the cause and treatment of a rare but sometimes lethal children's disease known as Reye's Syndrome. The report indicated that there may be a connection between Reye's Syndrome and emulsifiers used in forest spraying. Within 24 hours, the Provincial Cabinet, through the Minister of Health, cancelled the approval for an insecticide spraying program. The Company accelerated its harvesting as promised and started clearing what is now expected to be the largest clear-cut area in North America. The province of New Brunswick, alarmed by this same report, empowered a panel of scientists from outside the province to investigate the Reye's Syndrome research work. This panel reported its findings and, after this report, the neighboring province decided that there was no reason not to go ahead with its spraying program. New Brunswick then sprayed an area of about 4 million hectares in 1976.

The State of Maine in the USA carried out a budworm spraying program in 1976 involving more than 1 million hectares. The State Forestry Service took the initiative and provided information to the public and environmental groups well in advance of the operation. A carbamate insecticide "Sevin" widely used in agriculture was used with good results.

In the summer of 1976, the budworm populations exploded as predicted, devasted the Highlands area which was earlier designated for protection and spread over an area of 800 000 hectares of forest land, both Crown lands and privately owned, covering most of Cape Breton Island and part of the Nova Scotia mainland. Late in the summer of 1976, the Company again mounted a campaign to promote insecticide spraying to protect areas that were not too seriously damaged at this time. It became evident that many of the provincial forestry people had changed their minds and would support some protection.

The environmentalists, however, quickly developed a saturation campaign against spraying and technical truths were swamped in a sea of emotions and politics. The Company changed its tactics in publicly suggesting the use of a less potent, well-known agricultural insecticide, "Sevin", which had already been used for budworm control in Maine and which could be used without emulsifiers. Sevin is used extensively in Nova Scotia for protection of commercial vegetable crops such as corn and blueberries and is readily available and commonly used in household gardening. The cause was lost when the executive of the Nova Scotia Medical Society came out publicly against spraying. The executive released an emotional statement containing several factual errors, the essence of which was that spraying with insecticides might cause some unknown long-term dangers to public health. This very emotional dialog, which rated newspaper headlines and special television programs, finally came to an end in the early winter of 1977 when the Premier of the province made a special television appearance to announce that there would be no spraying in the forests of Nova Scotia.

During the summer of 1977 the budworm population levels continued to be extreme and the softwood forests deteriorated as predicted. Survey results indicated that unless some natural control miraculously developed, 1978 would be as bad as 1977. The only conclusion the Company could make was that its predictions would be proven correct, that 50% of the softwood inventory on Cape Breton Island or 24 million m^3 stacked of softwood timber would be killed by the budworm and that 90% of this wood would be wasted due to market constraints and wood deterioration.

CONSEQUENCES

The pulpwood supply problem for the Company will not become serious for a few years since it will be possible to use the dead trees for three or four years after mortality takes place. Other effects will be noticed earlier and some of the serious consequences are as follows.

(a)   Timber value losses.
(b)   Employment losses.
(c)   Impairment of esthetic quality which will affect the tourist industry.
(d)   Damage to the environment which will affect recreational forest users.
(e)   Forest management costs will increase.
(f)   Damage to the Company's ability to compete due to increased wood costs.
(g)   Forest fire danger will increase due to the extreme hazard caused by vast areas of dead trees.

DECISION MAKING

The decision process in dealing with the spruce budworm problem in Nova Scotia is baffling and the way it developed has to be unsatisfactory to everyone irrespective of stand; but there must be some underlying reason for things working out the way they did. It is interesting to separate the positions of the various agencies or sectors involved and try to rationalize why they reacted as they did.

The Company   The Company based its position on economics, technology and experience in other parts of Canada, and once a decision was reached it set out to implement that decision. Except for other business people in the public sector, this straightforward cost–benefit approach was not understood or appreciated.

The Provincial Government Departments   The provincial Departments of Lands and Forests were not prepared and had no policy regarding the protection of the forests from large-scale insect damage. The closest thing to a policy was a statement by one senior civil servant to the effect that there would not be any forest spraying carried out in Nova Scotia so long as he had anything to say about it.

  At the time the Company made its first application for permission to spray insecticides on a selected area, most of the provincial forestry officials had a negative attitude toward protection through aerial spraying. This position was made known to the public and used as a major weapon by environmentalists in their anti-spray campaigns. This situation badly damaged the Company's credibility with the general public. (The position of most officials of the provincial Department of Lands and Forests has since reversed.)

The provincial Department of the Environment and the Department of Health, which were also involved in the government decision making, did not appear to have any sympathy or concern for the consequences of the budworm attack and were more interested in rebutting the Company position than in finding a solution to the budworm problem. It is indicative that no written report or submission covering the reasons for their anti-spray position has been made public.

The Canadian Forestry Service The Canadian Forestry Service is mainly involved with forest research and, since it is a federal government agency, has branches all across Canada. In eastern Canada, the Canadian Forestry Service has worked on spruce budworm research and control for many years and must be recognized as the expert in the field.

The Canadian Forestry Service, well informed and because of its experience in other parts of Canada, was convinced that protection through spraying could and should be carried out. Its influence, however, was restricted due to a lack of jurisdiction in the forest-management field, which is a provincial responsibility.

The provincial politicians When the provincial civil servants were pressed by the Company for permission to spray insecticides in 1976, they apparently were unable or unwilling to make a decision and the problem was transferred to the Provincial Cabinet for a decision. At that point, the budworm problem became a political problem and it remained that way. The politicians, after an initial flurry of good intentions, eventually sat back to see how the public was going to react. Then, like true politicians, they made a short-term political decision against spraying even though it was recognized that this decision would cause serious long-term social problems for the people of Cape Breton Island.

The environmentalists Nova Scotia has its share of environmental activists usually belonging to one or more associations dedicated to the preservation of something which they regard as most important and not subject to any kind of benefit analysis. When the budworm situation developed and the government was debating the pros and cons of aerial spraying, the environmentalists finally has an important "cause" and an opportunity to unite and demonstrate their strength and political "clout". The environmentalists concentrated on scare tactics such as comparing insecticides to Nazi nerve gas, and as the media are very receptive to controversial issues of this nature, they were successful beyond all expectations. The environmentalists exploited public emotions and appeared to have considerable financial resources to carry out their campaign.

The media Off and on for a two-year period various media agencies had a tremendous campaign exploiting the budworm issue. The issue was controversial and nothing makes better news than a controversial subject. Hundreds of columns were printed in daily and weekly newspapers, television stations interviewed anyone who would take a stand, and radio open-line shows exploited the story as long as it could be used.

The Company participated actively in the media battle and tried to reason with the public regarding the advantages and disadvantages of spraying, but the Company's voice was eventually buried under an avalanche of opinion from environmentalists and sympathizers.

The medical doctors Although the environmentalists were conducting a very active campaign against spraying, for many months during the debate in 1975 and again in 1976, the politicians seemed to be trying to keep an open mind and weigh the pros and cons. In both instances, however, the political decision was probably influenced most by medical developments and doubts about public health.

The debate started in the fall of 1975 and ended with the release of research information hinting at a possible relationship between spraying and Reye's Syndrome. In 1976, the politicians seemed to have overcome the Reye's Syndrome scare and were holding firm until the executive of the Nova Scotia Medical Society took a public stand against spraying. They expressed doubts about the long-term implications in using insecticides, the same doubts that are expressed regarding the use of many products in modern society. Many individual doctors privately and publicly supported spraying.

In environmental debates, medical opinion has a tremendous affect on public opinion. This is quite different from their influence on dangerous personal habits involving cigarette smoking, drinking alcohol or driving cars without using seat belts.

The public at large There is little doubt that after two years of debate, the majority of the people were against the Company's proposal to spray chemical insecticides to control the spruce budworm. The reason why an individual comes to a certain conclusion is complex, and partly specific to that individual; however, some general conclusions can be drawn regarding the public at large.

(a) The mystique of the forest. Although people know that insecticides are used in agriculture and they do not object, the forest seems to be different. Farming is food, but the forest is nature. One must not interfere with nature.

(b) Apathy and fatalism. The rural landowners on Cape Breton Island while watching the budworm destroying their forests have not taken any initiatives to protect their valuable timber. This seems difficult to comprehend, but is a fact. The forest does not have a high priority.

(c) Regard for industry. In Canada, and probably in many other countries, it has become fashionable to take a stand against large industries. In Canada as a whole the problem is further complicated by a high degree of foreign ownership and the foreign-owned company becomes a target for criticism. In Nova Scotia, the regard for industry is further eroded by the tremendous government presence in society. Nova Scotia is a "have not" province in Canada and government subsidies and involvement have spread through all levels of activity. Most people in Nova Scotia work directly or indirectly for government or its services. Relatively few work in independent, unsubsidized industry. The result of this tremendous government presence is that the public does not attach much importance to private industry. If Nova Scotia Forest Industries should fail as a private industry, the government would take over and look after the people.

(d) Chemical spraying and public health. The effect of uncertainties regarding public health had a very strong effect on public opinion. The doubts of medical doctors regarding the safety of spraying helped the environmentalists tremendously in their campaign.

(e) Information through the media. Information on the spruce budworm situation was made available to the public mainly through the media. This information originated from two main sources, the Company and the environmentalists. Both sources could be considered to be biased in supporting their own positions, and no neutral sources such as provincial government agencies entered the debate. This was unfortunate for the Company, because its information in many instances was based on material such as government forest inventory statistics and could have been verified by government. The environmentalists purposely underestimated the damage to the forest caused by the infestation, and provincial forestry officials remained silent. The other main point about information to the public is the accuracy of media reporting. In neighboring New Brunswick an analysis was made by a government-appointed task force of 200 newspaper reports with headlines purporting to inform the public about budworm/forest behavior. In 54% of the reports, there was one or more factual errors and in 34% of the cases, the facts were correctly stated but were misinterpreted. The accuracy level of 12%, as found in New Brunswick, would probably be similar if such an analysis were made in Nova Scotia and explains some of the problem with public opinion.

Conclusion

The spruce budworm problem involving Nova Scotia Forest Industries developed into a classic confrontation between environmentalists and industry.

The long-term effect of the decision taken will be devastation of a valuable resource and very severe socioeconomic problems in an area already hampered by high unemployment and with a poor prospect for the future.

The Company's efforts were complicated by public apathy, bureaucratic indecision and other factors which may be peculiar to Nova Scotia. However, this whole exercise does show how a decision can be made without proper evaluation of the risks involved, the benefits or disadvantages involved or social consequences because an emotional approach is allowed to override a more rational basis for decision.

Part III
COMMUNICATION ABOUT RISKS

13 Risk and accident reports in the mass media

ANNA-CRISTINA BLOMKVIST AND
LENNART SJÖBERG

Introduction

In the mid-1960s, a large number of people were killed in Indonesia. Little attention was paid to these events in the mass media. According to Hellmark *et al.* (1969), the reason for the comparative lack of attention was that the massacres were performed over a rather long period of time and that it took a long time for the news to reach the West. But we all heard of the Mau-Mau, the Kenyan liberation movement that struck at night, and everyone has seen pictures from the burning Zeppelin Hindenburg: 37 out of the 97 passengers died and that was the end of the Zeppelins. We have all read about the Titanic disaster.

Some events concern and fascinate us and have an influence on our plans for the future; we become definitely frightened. Other events do not concern us. Does the difference depend on the events themselves, or is it hypothetically possible to describe almost any event so as to make us feel involved and so catch our attention? How is the accident news in the mass media selected and what are the effects of news reporting? The purpose of this chapter is to discuss those questions that arise in connection with accident reports in the mass media. We will perform the discussion with reference to a few concrete cases, but initially we present some more general points of view.

Why are accidents so frequently reported in the media? Our press must make a living out of its sales so, in choosing news, the attractiveness or degree of interest must be considered. The same is true, of course, for radio and television which are also quite dependent on public reactions even in a country which does not have commercial television and radio, such as Sweden. A simple answer to the question of why accidents are reported is, thus, that they arouse curiosity. A more sophisticated answer may be the following. According to Hadenius and Weibull (1972), it is commonly held that the mass media in Scandinavia are characterized by social reponsibility and reports should not be confined to sensational news items which have a high immediate level of interest. Mass media also have a responsibility for social development and they must be prepared to report news items of lesser interest. People in powerful positions often state that the press should exert some control on the establishment. Now the question arises whether the notion about responsibility is compatible with the very extensive attention which is sometimes given to accidents. In Swedish newspapers, accidents and crimes are the most commonly reported news items on the front pages (20%) and one of the largest topics in the total content (10%) (SOU 1975:78).

Social responsibility is clearly insufficient to explain the degree of attention given to accidents. According to Hadenius and Weibull (1972), citing Östgaard, news items which are unusually sudden or with an uncertain outcome and also significant and culturally close to the reader, are particularly likely to be reported. The event should be about people from the establishment, and all references that provide a personal and concrete angle are likely to increase its news value. Accidents fulfill most of these demands. The description of an accident can also be carried out in such a way as to strengthen the important aspects that constitute its news value.

Policemen and firemen are often cited as authorities by the newspapers. They and other interviewed persons are freely allowed to criticize the authorities, organizations or corporations without any sceptical comments in the newspapers. The general attitude of an article can also be communicated by headings, quotation marks and, of course, the selection of a person to interview. For example, in a debate on margarine, discussed below, the subheading "Do not eat with a spoon" was used. The source of the subheading was a statement from an expert who has calculated that one had to eat margarine by the spoonful in order to consume as much as was needed to produce a dangerous effect, but, used as a subheading, the expression seemed ambiguous and ridiculous.

In the following discussion we refer to four events that were given considerable publicity in the mass media, and which have been chosen here in order to cover different kinds of risks. We discuss mainly the mass-media contents rather than the realities of the mass-media reports.

Case 1: erucic acid in margarine

On September 3 1970, there was an article in a Stockholm daily newspaper stating that erucic acid from rape oil was found in margarine. The acid was said to counteract normal weight increase and to bring about changes in certain organs. It was also stated that there had been discussions between the producers and the Swedish Board of Health and Welfare, and the welfare board had appointed a group of experts to probe the issue. No further reactions to the information were reported at the time.

On November 17, 1975, more than five years later, a report was released to TT (the Central News Agency of Sweden) from the Swedish National Food Administration announcing that the lowest limit for the amount of erucic acid which brings about changes in organs (the heart musculature in rats) corresponds to 4% of the energy intake, and that the average Swede consumes eruric acid corresponding to 0.4% of the total energy intake. In the same report, it was stated that research into the effects of fatty acids on the organism was being carried out and that industry and agriculture were both continuing work to decrease the amount of erucic acid in food. This announcement was published in several newspapers.

On the same day, the news item was published in a news program on television. A summary of the television statement is as follows: "Today a research group appointed by the Swedish Board of Health and Welfare and the Medical Research Council present a report which shows that most of the margarine which is on sale contains a fatty acid E which has been shown to bring about heart damage in animals. This was known earlier, but the new finding shows that the damage already occurs at rather low levels of the acid. In an interview with Professor Ernstner, the Head of the Swedish National Food Administration, tonight, he said that the amount of erucic acid in margarine will be decreased but, at the same time, he said that he does not believe that anyone who eats margarine today is exposed to any risk. Arne Engström, Head of the Swedish National Food Administration was also interviewed."

Some headings in newspapers on the following day were: "Mice contract heart damage from acid in margarine." "The Swedish National Food Administration confesses: Risk in margarine was silenced." "Anxious not to frighten people." "Did you also find it hard to eat your sandwich last night?" "Here is the truth about The Great Margarine Scandal." "Margarine danger to the heart." "'Non-dangerous' heart poison in margarine." In one evening newspaper, there was a column headed "Confused television alarm: No danger in eating margarine. Continue using it on your sandwiches." Another evening newspaper wrote: "Have another sandwich, margarine is not dangerous."

The "confused" news items on television consisted of one of the reporters giving a list of margarine brands that did not contain erucic acid, but it was necessary to repeat it twice during the transmission in order to correct it.

On September 19, the television news program brought the question up again but only with a brief statement. It was stated that many people had become anxious and that the Swedish Food Administration had been inundated with telephone enquiries. The Head of Information stated that the enquirers were told that the situation was under full and safe control when it comes to erucic acid in margarine. Again, a number of margarine brands were mentioned that did not contain eruric acid.

Some newspaper headings on the same day were as follows: "Alarm about poison in margarine: wrong way of cooking is worse than the criticized acid." "Swedish margarine below the risk level." "In these packages you find the discussed acid. The acid in margarine: normal use not dangerous." An evening newspaper gave a short history of margarine and a brief note with the heading "Not dangerous" and then listed the names of certain margarine brands. "Today one can eat margarine without being anxious." "New alarm about rape poison in margarine: an unnecessary shock." "This is where the non-poisonous margarine is grown" was the caption of a picture of a farm. "Dangerous acid in margarine but too little to be poisonous. Swedish regulations are much stricter than those within the EEC countries."

Television gave a confused statement but so did the newspaper reporters. Some newspapers simply presented the material from TT or the material they got from other news bureaus. Some newspapers we investigated here presented the report from the working group as a scandal, and some thought that the other newspapers had made too much of a scandal out of the report. The "scandalmongers" argued that the authorities knew that the margarine was dangerous but kept silent about it. The original TT telegram about changes in heart musculature at 4% energy intake of eruric acid was, in one major evening newspaper, reported as "Rats contract serious heart damage due to very small amounts of erucic acid."

It was never stated who had silenced the question of danger, but a major daily newspaper stated that "Within the margarine industry and agricultural organizations, anxiety was great that the matter would be publicized ... The authorities acted that time without making any noise about it." It seems that the newspapers wanted to say that the margarine industry, the farmers and the authorities were guilty of silencing the affair. Another newspaper said that there must be greater demands on keeping the public informed, although the same newspaper had taken the first television announcement in a very cool manner and encouraged their readers to go on using margarine on their sandwiches.

One morning newspaper argued that although erucic acid was not dangerous to the average person, there may be people who ate quite a lot of it, but to cook in the wrong way was still worse. That comparison was apparently used to calm the readers, the same calming strategy as was used by the agricultural organization which pointed out that the requirements in Sweden are much stricter than those in the EEC countries. A further way of calming readers was to call this new alarm an old alarm.

A news magazine representing agricultural organizations wrote that there were no unequivocally useful or dangerous foods, and that the report about eruric acid should be seen as a dangerous piece of information. They argued that the information about the dangers to the heart from alcohol, tobacco and even coffee, seem not to give rise to as much attention and excitement as cyclamate, erucic acid, glutamate, etc.

The people who were used as sources by the newspapers were mostly experts, university professors, the Swedish National Food Administration and industrial or agricultural organizations. Few newspapers had reporters that specialized in scientific journalism with sufficient knowledge of technical details. This means that newspapers could not, even if they wanted to, criticize or clarify the contents of an original news item. The rather weak substantial contents of the margarine scare, as well as a certain monotony in the face of many contemporary alarms, may account for the fact that the margarine scare finally became the target of jokes.

It is remarkable how quickly the mass media changed their minds in the case of margarine. In the first phase, the risks were not reacted to at all, then they were given inconceivably large attention, but assurances from experts and the Swedish National Food Administration made the news media drop the item. Even the fact that the issue was ignored for five years (1970–5) was finally only given very brief attention. Columnists were, in the end, vigilant about the dangers and made jokes about them.

Case 2: the Mjölby accident

This case concerns a railway accident in southern Sweden which occurred on March 31, 1975. The Swedish Railroads gave the following official account of the accident:

> At the Norra Berga level crossing, a car hit the second carriage of express train 105. The car's engine and rear axle were accidentally caught under the carriage causing a set of wheels to leave the track. About 70 metres further

along from the point of derailment, the coupling between carriages 1 and 2 broke. The twelve carriages behind pushed the derailed carriage down a slope onto a field with tremendous force. As a result, eight further carriages were derailed and several of them overturned. Thirteen passengers were killed as well as the driver, and 29 people were injured. One badly injured passenger later died.

The speed of the train at the moment of impact was about 125 km/hour. The automatic lights and alarm signals at the level crossing functioned normally when the accident occurred (SJ Security 1976).

The accident was given a great deal of coverage in the mass media and was reported on television the same day, and the following day. The major evening newspapers devoted about seven full pages each to the accident. Pictures from the scene of the accident were shown on television together with interviews with an ambulance driver, a chief physician, the Safety Expert of the Swedish Railroads, an engineer and the Swedish Minister of Communications. Examples of other persons who were cited in the press were people living close to the scene of the accident, physicians in a hospital to where the victims were taken, the parents of the car driver who caused the accident, railroad personnel clearing up after the accident and train passengers. In one of the evening newspapers, 11 eye witnesses were interviewed even on the first day of presentation.

Some headings on the first day were: "14 dead and 40 wounded. How did it happen? Car insurance to pay." "I never saw the car." "The most serious accidents (followed by a list of train accidents)." "The scene of disaster (followed by a description of the alarm system and plans for rescue operations)." On the following day, the headings were "Norling (the Minister of Communications) promises more level crossing gates." "Many level crossings are similar. Unique accident does not change plans of the railroads." "Parliamentary debate to be held on the train accident." "Insurance company pays 40 millions."

The road accident statistics for the month of March were published at the same time as the accident became known, and the two pieces of information were often commented upon simultaneously. In a major morning newspaper, it was pointed out that the extraordinary publicity about the Mjölby accident in itself was an indirect sign that serious train accidents are extremely rare. Fourteen people killed in car accidents during a weekend is a tragedy of similar proportions, which is an average consequence for normal traffic during a weekend, but this is given very little attention in the mass media. The same reasoning was taken by a socialist evening newspaper as an indication of capitalist indoctrination. Collective means of transportation are given a lot of negative publicity when a rare accident happens, they argued, but the drawbacks of the allegedly capitalist system of private automobiles are not mentioned.

The media also discussed the amount of money allocated to safety improvements suggested by the Department of Communication. The Minister of Communications was criticized for not allocating more money for safety measures also in road traffic. It was pointed out that the budget for safety improvements for the following fiscal year was suggested to be only 7.5 million Kr. The Head of the Safety Department of the Swedish Railroads stated that the only risk-free railroad crossing is a crossing on different levels: since, at that time there were about 26 000 crossings and only 1000 of them were on different levels, the cost of completely eliminating the risk would be "astronomical." The costs for erecting level crossing gates where necessary would be about 50 million Kr, compared with the 7.5 million Kr allocated for all safety improvement measures the following fiscal year. The media, however, devoted more attention to comparing the 50 million Kr to the sum that the insurance company was expected to pay: 30 million Kr. It was pointed out that this sum, taken together with all the costs for rescue operations, was probably so large that it was comparable with the whole cost of increasing safety so as to make an accident of this type completely impossible. The 50 million Kr was considered in many newspapers to be a very small sum for eliminating the risk and it was considered almost a scandal that the measures had not been taken a long time ago. The railroad company was criticized for having too cynical and frugal views on safety. However, it was clear to some writers that goal structuring and areas of responsibility must be taken into account. The railroad company was simply not responsible for hospital expenses for the victims and, on the other hand, given the sum of 50 million Kr for safety improvements, they were not quite sure that the best thing would be to assign that amount of money to increasing safety on the railroads, since accidents were much more common in other types of traffic. Many newspapers, however, believed that in the future, with the increased speed of trains, accidents such as the present one would be more common and more serious and that, therefore, it would still be important to increase railroad safety and to try to build crossings on different levels. Many newspapers also stressed that it was important not to discourage people from using trains.

There was a wealth of speculations about the cause of the accident and suggestions for safety improvements. Various ways of reducing the speed of approaching vehicles were suggested and one evening newspaper proposed that there should be a law requiring automobile winter tires to be kept in good condition. The newspaper assumed that the accident was caused by worn-out tires on the automobile.

On May 15, 1975, there was a new accident involving the railroad: two trains collided and ten people were killed, five of whom were children. Newspapers were alarmed about the new accident and concerned about the risk that confidence in the railroads might be negatively affected. Parliament decided to invest 15 million Kr in improving the safety of level crossings.

The coverage of the Mjölby accident is interesting for several reasons. Why was the accident given such extensive coverage by the media? Train accidents are infrequent and perhaps attract interest therefore. The year before, there had been no train accidents involving multiple deaths. One had to go back ten years in time to find accidents comparable in severity. Still, the number of people killed was lower than is common in an airplane accident.

Perhaps the cause of events also was of importance. The circumstances of an accident like this are well known from everyday life and journalists did not have to suffer from their lack of expertise in this special case. We can easily understand the events and the serious consequences of a trivial human mistake. There are simple and, seemingly, efficient ways of stopping such accidents, viz. to use gates or have crossings on different levels. Still another large accident occurred within six weeks and public opinion demanded drastic measures to be taken. Some measures were also taken by the responsible authorities. Probably part of this action was caused by a wish to improve confidence in public transportation. There was a further accident a whole year later, in June 1976, with as many dead victims as the Mjölby accident, but it was given much less attention; only about half of the coverage in the mass media. Part of the lack of attention may have been due to the fact that it occurred during manual guidance of the train at the time when the railroad company was in the process of changing to a computerized system and, because of this, the accident perhaps was not as interesting.

On June 2, 1980, SJ had a severe accident which again received extensive coverage in the mass media, even more than the accidents reported above. Only 11 people died, as compared to the 14 victims in the Mjölby accident, but 61 people were injured. The accident was caused by a misunderstanding of a detected failure in the alarm system. The system failure probably brought forth more worries than a mishap due to the so-called "human factor." Never before during the 25 years in use had such a failure occurred and as the consequences of system failure might be far reaching, an extensive technical investigation was initiated and several new rules were issued about personnel action in cases of failure.

Case 3: carcinogenic substances

The newspapers nowadays often carry articles about carcinogenic substances. Headings in such cases frequently refer to specific individuals, especially in the evening newspapers. von Hedenberg (1975) investigated four weekly magazines and found that they carried between two and three medical articles per issue. Out of 103 investigated cancer articles, 56% were evaluated as informative and 35% as "tragic accounts" where a victim or his/her family related their experiences.

The newspapers' treatment of occupational risks has increased successively. In November 1975, one major evening newspaper wrote about the Stigen factory outside the town of Borås with the query: "Is a dyeworks dangerous? Nine cancer deaths in factory." The Safety Officer said in the article that after having read about health risks due to asbestos (see further, Ch. 11), a count was made of the number of employees who had died of cancer at this particular factory. Other interviewed people were a physician and management representatives. The topic was immediately taken up both by the local and national press. The headings were "9 died of cancer." The articles were based mainly on statements made by the shop steward. The local union had carried their suspicions further to the National Union which demanded an investigation by the Swedish Board of Health and Welfare. Both the shop steward and the secretary of the National Union pointed out that there had been attempts to subdue the information in order not to cause alarm among the employees. The shop steward further said in the newspapers that many chemicals are being used, among other things industrial solvents, and that it is impossible for anyone who is not a specialist to know what happens with chemical mixtures.

A local morning newspaper in Gothenburg criticized the Labor Inspector in Borås who had stated that there must be a proven connection between the cancer deaths and environmental factors before some action could be taken. The newspaper argued that the experiences and suspicions of people are among the most important sources when it comes to finding out what constitutes a health risk.

After about a month, the Labor Inspector had completed a report which concluded that the number of cancer cases was rather normal and that the disease was spread over different organs. The manager of the corporation stated in the press that he was satisfied with this investigation and that there was no further need to be anxious.

A long and complicated story was brought to light in 1975 concerning the corporation BT-Kemi in southern Sweden. According to a national newspaper, the corporation had dumped herbicides at night (similar to those used in the Vietnam war). Inhabitants of the local community had, for the past ten years, been complaining about first the smell and then about the allergic reactions, dying tomato plants, dead fish and revolting drinking water. They had the support of experts but gained no hearing. During 1975 and 1976 the mass media finally took notice of the production complication. This occurred because of an official meeting, arranged by the local body of the Swedish Social Democratic Party after which the director of BT-Kemi was described as arrogant and untrustworthy, and because the herbicides were suspected of causing cancer. Until then all reports had been successfully denied by the director.

Gradually, local opinion and the attention from the mass media made local government force the corporation to dig up cans containing refuse and submit the contents for chemical analysis. During 1975, opinion formed against the activities of the corporation and questioned the renewal of provisional permits to continue the production. It also became clear that the corporation had actually acted against agreements made with the provincial government. The head of the corporation now stated, according to two newspapers, that the production would be moved to Denmark.

The employees at the factory called a press conference in February 1976, to say that they did not feel that the production process involved any danger for them and that, thus, they did not understand how people outside the factory could get sick from pollution. They now felt threatened by the possibility of losing their jobs. Besides, as the most dangerous parts of the production were going to be transferred to Denmark, why not "leave us alone." The conference was probably planned to contradict the headlines of an evening newspaper edition saying: "They discharged pollutants in panic. New proofs today. The corporation lied. Facts were withheld." Emotions were intense.

In March 1976, the Concession Board had a meeting and new reports appeared about the corporation. Employees earlier involved in the BT-Kemi production in another area reported cancer cases among fellow workers. The television interviewed a retired employee suffering from cancer, the local manager of BT-Kemi and a professor who confirmed that the chemical substances were carcinogenic. Several newspapers had then supplied news on the risk for cancer. A head physician of a department of occupational medicine confirmed that the number of suspected cancer victims among previous employees in the other area was too high a proportion to be random. According to the media, the regional manager of BT-Kemi still did not feel it was justified to make such a fuss about the topic. It was all about unsupported assumptions, he argued. But the corporation agreed to an investigation into the matter. In March 1976, the demand to investigate was supported by the National Nature Conservancy Board at the request of the Provincial Governor.

The dumped material was judged as so dangerous and so voluminous that this contributed to the Government's decision to forbid further production in 1977. How to get rid of the refuse is still a problem. One person in the National Nature Conservancy Board and one from the Local Public Health Board were found guilty of having accepted substantial gifts from the corporation. The sentences came in 1979, the same year as the factory was demolished. The case of unsatisfactory handling of toxic material by the director has still not been concluded (Autumn 1981).

The two cases of alarm were, from a factual point of view, quite different. The case of Stigen was a false alarm. It points to the fact, we think, that normal cancer frequencies are highly underestimated. When people count up the number of fellow workers who have died through cancer, they get a shock. There was no cause for anxiety on the information at hand, but anxiety was probably caused by the mass media's reporting of it.

The latter case was tragic. The factory was deliberately deceiving local and national authorities (von Krogh & Nowotny 1981). When the trouble started in 1965, pollution, conservation and dangers of herbicides did not make the news headlines. The journalists did not react to facts about the effects of discharge into the water supplies in the neighborhood. When the news finally leaked out, it was the "facts withheld," the "lies" and later the surmised cancer that attracted attention, not really the dangers or inconveniences caused to people. Once the director was mistrusted, the employees did not win much sympathy either, but lies and cancer made the mass media argue against the corporation and demand appropriate steps from the authorities.

Case 4: dangerous transports

During 1975, major truck accidents were published every month in the local morning newspaper in Gothenburg. One of the major truck accidents happened in the town of Helsingborg. The great potential risks of the accident made it a national news item and it was also reported on television. A summary of the television news statements is as follows: "A truck fully loaded with liquified petroleum gas tubes overturned and exploded in Helsingborg today. The truck overturned close to an apartment house which caught fire. All the tenants were evacuated." Police and the head of the fire brigade in Helsingborg were interviewed. According to the City Fire Engineer in Helsingborg, the accident caused a certain local debate in the town. The apartment house in question had, due to its position, earlier been considered a traffic danger and, since it was completely destroyed by the fire, the house was to be demolished.

The day after the accident, the newspapers referred to its sensation value.

The number of liquified petrol gas tubes, the number of shocked people, the extent of damaged material, the number of curious onlookers and the fact that the driver had consumed alcohol, were the main ingredients in the description of the accident. The descriptions tended to give rise to images associated with a war: tens of thousands of liquified petrol gas tubes became dangerous missiles. There was the sound of machine-gun fire and grenades. The street became a minefield, thousands of liquified petrol gas tubes bombarded houses and thousands of onlookers were lured by smoke which in height and shape was reminiscent of a nuclear bomb.

One of the tenants said he had been waiting for this to happen for a long time. The chief of the fire brigade said that transport of dangerous chemicals in a densely populated area must be considered to be irresponsible, but there was no prohibition against it. The owner of the house made a statement on the insurance question and the manager of a nearby factory made a statement about the risks that arose when the tubes were hurled into the factory, which happened to be empty at the time as the accident happened on Midsummer Eve. Many people who had been tenants in the block found themselves homeless.

A heading in an evening newspaper seems to be guided by a need for uncertainty: "It can happen again – nobody can stop the dangerous transports." The contents of the article did not deal with the event. But surely it cannot be a goal to stop transportation of dangerous goods. A few days after the accident there was a new piece of information published about it. Apparently the goods had entered the country illegally and it was pointed out that if the accident had happened on board the ferry, a real disaster could have resulted. The captain of the ferry was interviewed and he, of course, stated that the truck would not have been permitted on board had it been known what its contents were. In future there would be stricter investigation of any goods carried on board.

Since nobody was killed or even wounded in the accident, it was considered mainly a sensational piece of news. No authority or organization could be blamed. The driver had been drunk and the goods had entered the country illegally. Previous accidents of a similar nature had received attention in the mass media a few years earlier, but no further effects or discussions had appeared. It seems likely that there is a rather small effect of near-accidents, partly because the mass media coverage is short-lived and briefer where there are no casualties. The fact that dangerous goods were quite common on the roads in Sweden was not given much attention.

Discussion

Reports about life and death, illness and health take up a large part of the space in the mass media. Reports about accidents seem to be rather simple descriptions of events. There is often verbatim reports of criticism of authorities from people who have been involved in accidents. It is obvious that the mass media do not usually have direct access to the expertise which is necessary to decide what is a false alarm and what is a serious case that deserves attention and follow-up. It is also typical that investigation of an accident takes rather a long time. It is not unusual that the mass media draw public attention in a rather inarticulate way at the beginning of an event, but when a reassuring expert explanation is given, they will deny their previous standpoint. The question is, however, what is the degree of attention given to denials and in what way has public opinion meanwhile been affected by the sensational reports? Part of the answer to the question is, of course, dependent upon the credibility of the mass media. A series of cases, some of which have been exemplified above, could well lead to a sceptical attitude towards mass-media reports.

In certain cases, the causal sequence of events is quite clear, and seemingly also the measures that need to be taken. Editors may then point to such necessary measures. The priorities and the attention given by authorities and politicians to various safety problems are in this way easily influenced by mass-media coverage.

In order to attract wide publicity and to cause political debates, it seems as if an accident must exceed a certain boundary in terms of the number of killed or wounded. Potentially serious accidents that, by a happy turn of events, do not lead to serious consequences, receive much less attention too and seldom lead to extensive discussions. The truck accident in Helsingborg referred to above is an example of this.

What is the effect of accident reports on the perception of the readers about the risks that they themselves are exposed to? It has been shown (Lichstenstein et al. 1978) that the experience of risk for the average person is rather closely related to the amount of mass-media coverage of different types of accidents, illnesses, etc. It should be noted in this connection that accidents and disasters after all are rare events in the life of the individual and that his notions about the probability for this reason must be based on indirect information, for example, of the type that reaches him via the mass media. An interesting possibility is that the total experienced risk level is increased by a large frequency of accident reports.

The debate in the mass media is partly concerned with "new" risks and dangers. Consider, for example, the intense discussions about carcinogenic substances in the work environment, or the risks of nuclear power! It is conceivable that the conception of the ability and will of society to create secure and safe conditions for its citizens is affected by mass-media debates on these issues. The common observation that there is a growing distrust in the establishment and political leaders, and the feeling that the world is becoming more and more dangerous may be partly due to such biased mass-media coverage.

There is also an effect of the mass media on the decision makers in society. In the case of an accident or a disaster given much attention, it creates a reason for, and the possibility of, political action. The government may be afraid that the opposition parties will take the initiative in some critical question like this and criticize the government and administration and make suggestions that are temporarily unpopular. Therefore everyone wants to take the initiative and quickly start investigations, make certain moves to improve conditions or implement stricter requirements of some kind. This mechanism can create a gloomy mood among administrators who are experts and responsible for certain sectors, and who lack a consequential overall plan for priority discussions about how resources should be allocated in order to decrease risks in the best possible way. There is even less of a discussion of the total risk panorama which each individual is exposed to.

When it comes to the three components: cause, responsibility and action, it seems as if the most interesting aspect to some mass-media sectors is the cause, possibly coupled with responsibility. The media are quite quick to come up with their own hypotheses as to the accidents and they may be quite erroneous. The tendency towards speculation is probably inhibited by ethics and laws when it comes to pointing to the people responsible, as well as acts by those who do not hold any public office, and well-defined responsibility may rather be subsumed under the heading of the human factor.

Discussions of measures to be taken against accidents are quite confusing because there is usually no attempt to discuss these measures within a wider framework of priorities. Because of this, and because of the lack of more profound expertise, the mass media may not contribute much towards rational action against risks in society.

The present discussion has been concerned with conditions in Sweden. There may be interesting differences among different countries; especially interesting is the case of the socialist countries in Eastern Europe where accidents apparently receive much less attention in the mass media and may even be suppressed entirely. The net effect of such a policy can, of course, be that mass-media reporting is replaced by rumors which are even less accurate than some of the mass-media contents.

References

Hadenius, S. and L. Weibull 1972. *Press radio TV* (revised edition) Stockholm: Aldus.
Hellmark, C., B. Lindberg and K. -O. Nilsson 1969. *Ni har väl läst tidningen i dag?* Stockholm: W & W.

Lichstenstein, S., P. Slovic, B. Fischhoff, M. Layman and B. Combs 1978. Judged frequency of lethal events. *J. Exp. Psychol. Human Learn. Memory* 4, 551–758.

SJ Security 1976. *SJ Security Service 1975*. Stockholm: Central Traffic Department's Security Section.
SOU 1975:78 1978. *Svensk Press III. Pressfunktioner i samhället*. 1972 års pressutredning. Stockholm: Allmänna Förlaget.

von Hedenberg, C. 1975. *Det medicinska reportaget*. Unpublished paper. Stockholm: The University School of Journalism.
von Krogh, T. and C. Nowotny 1981. *Varför fick vi inget veta?* Stockholm: Tiden.

14 *Scientific information –*
a review of research

MARGARETA CRONHOLM AND ROLF
SANDELL

Introduction

This survey of research on how scientific information is spread to the general
public tries to give an account of answers offered by the research literature to
a number of important questions.

(1) The journalist and the mass media: how much scientific information is
    published by the press and by television? What importance does scientific
    information have as news matter? How does the scientific journalist work
    and how is he educated?
(2) The scientist: what is the rôle and responsibility of the scientist in the
    process of spreading scientific information? What are the opinions of
    scientists about scientific journalism? How do scientists themselves use
    the mass media for acquiring information in scientific matters?
(3) The audience: who reads scientific information in the press and who looks
    at television for it? What scientific topics are considered most interesting?
    Do journalists and the public differ in their interests and in their views
    about scientific information? What categories of people prefer mass
    media to acquire scientific information?
(4) Design of scientific information: what methods have been employed to
    measure accuracy of scientific information and what results have come
    up? What kinds of inaccuracies are most common? How important is the
    personal relationship between the scientist and the journalist? How
    readable is scientific information? How important is readability to pro-
    duce interest and knowledge among the public?
(5) The effects of scientific information: what categories of people acquire
    most knowledge from scientific information in the mass media? What is
    the quality of this knowledge? What makes a campaign, based on scien-
    tific information, succeed or fail? What indirect effects may scientific
    information have?
(6) Environmental information: what issues have been given most attention
    by the mass media? How do local mass media cover local issues? What
    is the relationship between interest in environmental issues and exposure
    to environmental information in the mass media?

Information about scientific research intended for the general public
(hereafter referred to as "scientific information" to be distinguished from

"scientific communication" among scientists) is becoming increasingly important in the light of two current trends. One is the ever-growing demand for deeper and wider participation in societal decision making. The second is the, at least apparently, ever-growing technical complexity of the issues to be decided on. Thus, results from scientific research are becoming more important to the development and evaluation of policies. But, as a consequence of increased participation, information about such research must be accessible and comprehensible to a greater number of persons who are also less qualified in this respect.

Scientific information comes in various forms. Some are distributed under such rigorous control as to become means of manipulation and propaganda, as Alexander's (1966) account of NASAs information activities implies. Some spread out of control, like rumors, to provoke irrational scare and action (Allport & Postman 1947). In neither case is the scientific information functional to society and its members. This raises an important problem which is fundamental to the study of scientific information: to what extent do the various forms of scientific information produce an unbiased knowledge among the general public, unbiased as well in the distribution among the public as to veracity? In the ideal case, information about a scientific fact or controversy should be a truthful account of that fact or controversy *and* it should be available and comprehensible to all members of society.

Many factors contribute to the effect of scientific information: the scientists, the mass media and the journalists, interests and habits of the audience, and content and design of the information are among the most important. In the following chapter, we shall review research on the rôle of these various factors in scientific information. In view of the considerable political importance, special emphasis is given to environmental issues.

The volume of scientific information in the mass media

In relation to other kinds of editorial matter, the volume of scientific information in the mass media is generally small. As an example Althoff *et al.* (1973) found environmental news being ranked lowest, with respect to actual coverage, among the news areas, politics, education, economy, crime and environment, by a majority of mass-media managers. Statistics from the Swedish Broadcasting Corporation (Berg *et al.* 1975, Berg & Höijer 1976) also support this generalization: in the early 1970s only 2.5% of the total time in Swedish television could be classified as scientific information. Roughly ten years earlier, American data from the San Francisco area (Sherburne Jr. 1963) indicate a larger output, if the data are at all comparable: 6% of prime time on television was devoted to scientific information, albeit with a very liberal definition (including e.g. Dr Kildare).

Naturally, there is a large variation among the different mass media in the volume of scientific information published. In relation to total space or time, Althoff *et al.* (1973) found the largest volume of environmental news reported by radio managers, whereas weekly and daily newspapers reported the smallest. Irrespective of medium and country, the volume of scientific information seems to be increasing. In actual time, the output in Swedish television has increased by about 100% during the 1970s, while Cole (1975) found a

100% increase between 1951 and 1971 in the number of science items per issue in four large American daily newspapers. The largest increase occurred between 1951 and 1961.

This may be an effect of scientific news having become more dramatic and spectacular as such, with the space programs as an example. Furthermore, it may be that the daily lives of people are possibly more concerned with, and affected by, scientific advancement and news (e.g. in the environmental movement). These two examples are probably among the most significant in increasing the volume of scientific information. However, it seems that medicine is the scientific subarea given most space in the news media. Sorenson and Sorenson (1973), when studying science content in eight magazines from the mid-1960s, found medicine to be the subject devoted most space, and Nunn (1979) noticed medicine, or rather public health and welfare, to be the scientific subarea which had the largest volume in daily newspapers in 1971 as well as in 1977. Natural sciences, like physics, chemistry, biology, etc., are probably getting an increasing share. The social sciences have probably still a quite small share, while the "space sciences" may be declining from an original top level boosted by the novelty of the space programs.

The science journalist

Obviously economic factors determine to what extent mass media have specialized scientific journalists on their payroll. Perlman (1974) has compared commercial and noncommercial television from this point of view, finding, for example, that the entirely tax-financed BBC has scientific reporting of high quality. The economic factors of course lead to the fact that specialized science writers are more common on large papers than on small ones.

The person who writes about science is also determined by the nature of the news. Finding that an increasing share of scientific news was about controversies among scientists, Cole (1975) noted that this kind of news was reported more often by general journalists than by science journalists. This may also be true of scientific events of a dramatic or sensational kind, like the launching of space ships, discoveries of unhealthy ingredients in food stuff, etc.

Becoming a science journalist may not be a matter of one's own decision, however. Reporting the results of an investigation among specialist science journalists in 1957, Fraley (1963) noted that as many as one-fifth of the journalists interviewed had turned to their speciality after a decision by their editor-in-chief. In view of that finding, it is not surprising to learn that less than 5% in Fraley's sample considered themselves specially trained for scientific writing. This differs with age, however, and a third of those under 30 reported that they had intentionally chosen their training to become science journalists.

This training is mostly academic. Fraley reports that 70% of his sample had four to seven years at college and that over 80% had at least one year at college. More recently, Ryan and Dunwoody (1975) reported that only 13% of science writers lacked an academic degree. Some 35 years earlier, when Krieghbaum (1940) made the first study of science journalists, this figure was over 25%.

Still, an increasing number of journalists seem to recommend more scientific training. In Fraley's (1963) investigation, almost 50% did not consider special training for science writers necessary and less than 10% felt it important to have knowledge or training in the sciences. On the other hand, Small (1964) found that at the same time almost 50% of the American science journalists whom he interviewed considered it desirable for their future colleagues to have training in the sciences as well as in journalism. At the beginning of the 1970s, Ryan and Dunwoody (1975) found that science journalists as a rule recommended future science writers to take more courses than they had themselves.

The value of formal academic training may be disputable, however. One may learn to write about science, but can one ever be taught? To answer this and other questions, Broberg (1973) compared science journalists with high and low "communication accuracy". She studied how scientists had made alterations and corrections in journalists' manuscripts for press releases about their research. As a common feature among those journalists who were often corrected, she found that they lacked formal scientific training. The journalists with high communication accuracy mostly had academic courses in English, journalism and biology. In contrast, the two categories did not differ with respect to professional practice and experience but according to Broberg, that was not enough. The importance of training, particularly various kinds of vocationally oriented courses, has also long been acknowledged by the National Association of Science Writers (NASW) and the Council for Advancement of Science Writing (CASW) (Troan 1960). Another contribution to professional advancement may be a growing professional conciousness and pride, as evidenced in the increasing number of science writers' associations founded in different countries.

The information sources of the science journalist are, however, the backbone of their professional skill and quality. In two BBC series about scientific research, Jones and Meadows (1976) found that the journalists, when using journals for their information, most often consulted those that were general in coverage, like the *New Scientist* etc. From the point of view of accuracy, this may be unfortunate, since it often means that the information chosen by the journalist is one step further removed from its original source, the scientist himself. Jones and Meadows also noted that, as these journals have a tendency to be more speculative than average, there is a risk that the picture of science as shown in mass media will be atypical.

There are things we still do not know about the science journalist. Among the most important ones are his views about science and scientific information. Although these attitudes probably are not verbalized, and possibly are not even consciously recognized, they will certainly determine how the journalist goes about his task of informing the public. It would be interesting to approach them from two points simultaneously, by attitude questionnaires and text analysis.

The scientist

Several writers (e.g. Perlman 1974, Troan 1960) have noted the tendency of many scientists to view their work as an exclusive rite for a few initiated, not taking any responsibility or initiative in informing the public. Quite the opposite problem is represented by those scientists who act and publish freely, *as scientists*, in areas far removed from their own areas of competence (Mayer 1971/72). This is most troublesome in subjects where public opinion is involved and there is dispute among more or less competent scientists, in particular since scientists tend to be most easily tempted to act in the mass media in this case (Mazur 1973).

Unfortunately, no research has been done on the experiences and motives behind these individual differences among scientists. Is overactivity a way of channeling frustration over withdrawn grants? Is it a tactic for preparing ground for grant application? Is it vanity, publicity hunger and other "low" interests that drive overpublishing scientists? Or is it a purely unselfish belief in the value and importance of one's own area of research? Is it a matter of political and societal concern? Maybe an endeavor to serve democratic values by keeping the public informed? This is apparently not known, but Cronbach (1975) has given an interesting review of the inability of scientists to cope efficiently with the demands of the media and the public. When analyzing five decades of continuing controversy over mental testing, he described a scientist who easily falls into a polemic style leaving the real matter aside.

The opposite tendency, to neglect the public, may of course also have its personal causes. But it may as well be explained by some of the conditions under which scientists typically work. Promotion in the academic career is generally dependent on scientific communication, i.e. publishing activity in scientific journals, rather than on scientific information to the public. Popular science has no value as a "formal" merit as far as academic careers are concerned, nor does it produce much informal approval from scientific colleagues. To publish results twice, once in the general mass media and once in the professional media is not generally possible, as Krieghbaum (1967) notes, on account of the policies of the professional media. Some scientists have even had to renounce their right to publish their research findings altogether, according to Ravets (1976), in order to survive on grants from industry, the military complex, etc.

In addition to these complications, many scientists are apparently rather negative about scientific information in general. Tichenor, Olien, Harrison and Donohue (1970) asked a number of scientists to obtain feedback from readers of scientific information about their own research. They also asked their respondents for their opinions about scientific information in general. They discovered an interesting contradiction. While as many as 95% considered readers' accounts of their own research as satisfactorily correct, only slightly more than 50% felt scientific information in general to be correct. Reading a correct article about one's own research produced strong confidence for, and willingness to help and cooperate with, that particular writer, but apparently it did not affect one's opinion about scientific writers in general.

Nevertheless, many scientists seem to use the general mass media for their own scientific information, even within their own field of research. Shaw and Van Nevel (1967) found that 60% of the members of a medical faculty, and O'Keefe (1970) that almost 90% of a sample of university or private physicians, admitted getting professional news through the mass media now and then (more often through the press than through the broadcast media). As a rule they considered this information reliable (in contrast to the results of Tichenor, Olien, Harrison & Donohue 1970), but only 25% (O'Keefe 1970) regarded the information to be of any particular importance to them. The most important and useful source was still the scientific or professional journals, and roughly 70% of the respondents were completely satisfied with the professional information system, except for the generally long publication lags.

There are still some things one would like to know about the scientist and scientific information, most of all, whether he thinks scientific information to the lay audience is important and good *in principal* or not, and his reasons for feeling what he feels about this. This is probably related to his attitudes about society in general, in terms of democracy versus autocracy, populism versus elitism, etc., and what he feels about science in general and his work in particular and their rôle in his particular life and in society.

The audience

The audience as a variable of scientific information has occasioned much research interest. Estimates of audience size vary appreciably. Krieghbaum (1959), in the USA, found in a survey that 40% of people reported that they regularly read all information about medicine and health in the daily newspapers and that about 30% read all other kinds of scientific information as well. A surprising finding was that as many as roughly two-thirds of the respondents declared themselves prepared to sacrifice other kinds of information (regrettably unspecified) for more scientific information.

This may be due to national differences or to the different media, but Swedish investigations of television viewing come out with much lower audience estimates. Data from the Swedish Broadcasting Corporation (Berg & Grahlin 1977) showed that the average audience of a program about nature, natural science or medicine was only 13% of the population 9–79 years of age. The average viewer looked at 14% of the total output of programs with this kind of content. Contrary to what some people may believe, the data also showed that the audience was not composed of viewers with specialized scientific interest, but of generally heavy consumers of television fare. This may be interpreted, positively, as a token of the wide reach of scientific information in Swedish television, but also, negatively, as indicative of undiscriminating, passive viewing.

Evidently, several cultural factors interact to determine the audience size for all kinds of programs. Tichenor *et al.* (1976) compared two different communities with respect to the interest in scientific information, both among the general public and among the leadership. Whereas the leaders in both communities were generally more interested than the general public and did not differ between the communities in this respect, the general public was more interested in scientific information in the larger and more heterogeneous community with many schools and places of work and various religious groupings than in the smaller and more homogeneous one. However, the research design did not allow any conclusions regarding the responsible cultural factors. A corollary of the findings that may have some importance is that the difference in attitudes towards scientific information between the leaders and the general public was larger in the smaller community.

There may be no general interest in scientific information as such, the interest may depend on the kinds and contents of the information. As already noted, Krieghbaum (1959) found a more widespread interest in medical and health information than for other kinds of scientific information. Patterson *et al.* (1969) in a more sophisticated analysis tried to detect different kinds of interest patterns on the basis of interest ratings of articles by different categories of respondents. Three such patterns emerged, one characteristic of readers with academic training and a general scientific interest, another of young people with a not so good education but with research-associated occupations and with more special interests, like medicine, and a third of journalists with even more special interests: space and space flights.

Differences between journalists and other categories have been noted by others as well (e.g. Johnson 1963) and are quite intriguing. What are the consequences of divergent interests between journalists and their readers: that the audience does not get what it wants and gradually turns away in disappointment, or that its interest is aroused for timely and important issues to the benefit of a democratic society? But maybe the differences are more a matter of what journalists believe is the opinion of the general public than of their own true opinion. Data collected by Tannenbaum (1963) suggests that this may be the case. He found general consonance between journalists, expert scientists and the general public in their opinions about mental health and mental illness, but low accuracy among journalists in predicting the opinions of the general public – and it was on the basis of those erroneous predictions that they produced their prejudiced programs on the topic.

Some research has been done to study which of the mass media people turn to for the scientific information which they seek. Several investigators (Wade & Schramm 1969/70, Wright 1975) have found preferences for print media compared to broadcast media for scientific information and information on health problems, but reversed preferences for political information. This preference for print media is particularly pronounced among the well-educated and well-off citizens (Swinehart & McLeod 1960, Wade & Schramm 1969/70, Williams *et al.* 1977). There is also a tendency for the well-educated to utilize more and different media and to do this purposefully for information rather than for sheer entertainment. There also appears to be a positive correlation between use of print media and topical knowledge (Wade & Schramm 1969/70).

The objectivity of scientific information

One of the most heated discussions currently in the scientific community is about the possibility and/or desirability of objectivity in science. Objectivity is also one of the most controversial issues in discussions about, and research in, mass communication. This should make objectivity one of the core problems in the field of scientific information. Some research has indeed been undertaken but much remains to be done. Problems of balance, collectively or in each individual medium or even in each issue or program, have not been studied, nor have problems of representativeness in the selection of topics and news, nor problems of scope in covering scientific trends as well as single events. The effects on social, cultural, moral, political and other aspects of scientific discoveries, as well as their purely scientific meaning, background and evolution and their consequences and implications have not been researched. Rather, studies of objectivity in scientific information have been restricted to studies in Charnley's (1936) sense, that is, the accuracy of single news stories in the judgment of the news sources.

It appears that scientific information is not as accurate, in this sense, as regular news reporting. Tankard and Ryan (1974) and Pulford (1976) found between 10 and 30% error-free articles in their sampling of scientific articles. For regular news, earlier as well as later investigators (Charnley 1936, Berry 1967, Blankenburg 1970, Marshall 1977) have reported corresponding findings of between 40 and 60%. Pulford's (1976) supposition that the number of erroneous articles found in a study correlates positively with the length of the list of errors offered to the judges is probably correct, but his results were obtained with a much shorter list, and Tankard and Ryan's with a much longer list, than those employed by the other investigators. Thus, 10–30% seems to be a representative range for correct scientific information. With a principally similar method, Broberg (1973) studied the corrections scientists made to manuscripts about their research that had been written by professional writers. It is not possible to deduce from Broberg's report how many manuscripts passed the review without any changes at all, but the average change rate appears to have been around four corrections per paper.

A sound development of Charnley's method was made by Tichenor, Olien, Harrison and Donohue (1970), who asked source scientists to read, not articles about their research, but readers' summaries of such articles. Seventy-three scientists participated, and each article had around 25 readers, on average, each with one summary. The scientists rated each summary of "his" article for accuracy on a 7-step scale, and the operational definition of the accuracy of an article was the proportion of summaries of "his" article that the scientists rated in the accurate half of the scale. The range of accuracy for the different articles was 30–95% with an average of 65%. It is somewhat risky to compare these figures with those of Tankard and Ryan, and Pulford, but they do seem more positive for the accuracy of scientific information. It is indeed interesting to note how generally positive the respondent scientists were to scientific information (about their own research) when they knew what readers got out of it – and how negative they were when they did not – both in general opinion, according to Tichenor, Olien, Harrison and Donohue's (1970) own data, and specifically, according to Tankard and Ryan, and Pulford.

Attempts to classify the errors which scientists find in scientific information have not been tied to the research on communicative distortion in rumors (Allport & Postman 1945), serial communication (Pace & Boren 1973) or memory (Bartlett 1932), which might have been theoretically advantageous. In both Tankard and Ryan's study and in Broberg's, one finds deletions of various kinds of the most common error. These occurred also in Pulford's data, together with obvious inaccuracies like erroneous statements and even incorrect citations. Ryan (1975) carried out factor analysis on Tankard and Ryan's data, but the degree of data reduction was not great: the three first factors accounted for only slightly more than 30% of the total variance. Exaggeration, overemphasis and deletion together characterize the first factor, whereas under-emphasis seems to be the theme of the second. The third factor is clearly a spelling factor. To find that deletion correlates more with over-emphasis than underemphasis may surprise the reader who considers it the extreme of underemphasis. The correlation may be more comprehensible as a matter of exaggeration by black-and-white writing, where some details are strongly emphasized and others completely left out.

Attempts to "explain" the inaccuracies by cross-tabulations against various background factors have been made by Tichenor, Olien, Harrison and Donohue (1970) and Tankard and Ryan (1974). One of the most important factors found in studies of the accuracy of regular news is the amount and quality of contact between the source and the journalist, but this factor did not exhibit any strong correlations with accuracy in Tichenor, Olien, Harrison and Donohue's (1970) or Tankard and Ryan's (1974) investigations; neither did the topic, classified according to scientific discipline, the degree of educa-tion of the scientists, the circulation of the paper, whether the article was syndicated or produced by the paper on its own, or whether the article was by-lined or not. However, established and particular routines for handling scientific information seem to be important, either as a matter of responsibility and experience of the individual scientist or as a matter of organizational routines at the scientific institute. A possible step in such routines might be for the scientist to have an opportunity to review and correct information before publication, and that was found by Tankard and Ryan (1974) to be the only factor to have any significant effect on error rates. Findings about accuracy factors by Tichenor, Olien, Harrison and Donohue (1970) imply, surprisingly, that articles originating from a journalist on his own initiative, are below average in accuracy. The hypothesis was, naturally, that the journalist who discovers his own story would do a proud and better job.

Charnley used mainly three classes of errors: mechanical or typographical, writers errors, and errors in meaning. In evaluating the findings on causes of Charnley-type errors, it is necessary to consider, however, that the definition of error is the source's completely. It is then only natural that any factors that increase the influence of the source will also increase accuracy. It is possible to find several arguments for this conception of accuracy but also several against: the importance of a free press and its possibilities and responsibilities to present scientific news from an extra-scientific point of view may be the strongest. That journalists may consider these responsibilities is indicated in a study by Oates (1973) on the amount of social and ethical comments about Dr Barnard's first heart transplantation.

Counts, Jr. (1975), Donohew (1967), Flegel and Chaffee (1971), Grew (1975), Gerbner (1964), Kerrick et al. (1964) all undertook very interesting work on the influence of attitudinal factors of the journalist, the editor and the public on news reporting. There is a tendency for journalists to over-emphasize the other side if reporting on matters that do not correspond with their own attitudes. None of these researchers, however, dealt with the heated problems of today, for example nuclear power or genetic engineering, but rather with political issues. However, an investigation in that direction was done by Andersson and Hertzman (1977), who studied the representativeness of attitudes to security matters in the nuclear power debate on editorial pages in Swedish daily newspapers. They found few papers giving a true account of the official reviews. From many positive reviews and a few negative ones, many daily papers selected the negative ones and they did not always report correctly upon the contents of the reviews.

The language of scientific information

The scientific style of language is often ridiculed by journalists and laymen, as if their difficulties in understanding were wholly a matter of language and not at all a consequence of the fact that science, by definition, deals with things that are difficult and not yet completely known. Research on the readability of scientific information has been reported by Gruning (1974), Kwolek (1973), Witt (1976) and others, but the most ambitious project has been conducted by Funkhouser and Maccoby (1971, 1973, 1974, Funkhouser 1969). Funkhouser (1969) has found a strong correlation between linguistic styling and the proportion of readers with university degrees in the audience of magazines ranging from *Reader's Digest*, over *Life, Time, Scientific American*, etc. to *Physical Review*. In all magazines the texts analyzed were scientific information, and the style employed would therefore seem to be conditioned more by the expected audience than by the topic or "scientificness." Maybe scientific information does not necessarily have to be hard to read? Or have scientists and other qualified readers forgotten to write and understand plain English, or do they for some other reason prefer difficult texts to easy texts on the same topic? No, not according to a later investigation by Funkhouser and Maccoby (1971). They found that articles written for unqualified readers did not repel qualified and interested readers, whereas more demanding articles repelled all but the qualified. They also found that various kinds of effects like knowledge, attitudes, interest, etc. correlated with each other and exhibited large variations, despite the fact that all articles were written by experienced and established writers.

Their attempt to find any correlations between style variables and effects of the texts was not very successful due to their small sample of texts, but in a later study (Funkhouser & Maccoby 1973, 1974) they developed an intricate design of experimental manipulations with this purpose in mind. Three categories of subjects were tested: junior college students, university students and professional scientists. The findings of their 1971 study concerning the intercorrelations between various effects and the interaction between qualifications and difficulty of style were replicated. Generally, they also found students more influenced by style variables than scientists. Among the latter none of the style variables produced any significant effect, whereas the junior college students were most influenced by style, in terms of number of manipulated style variables with significant effect. (This may also be taken as indirect evidence for the idea that scientific education directs attention to matter rather than manner.)

The effects of the style manipulations generally appear rather irregular. However, several of the manipulations that had an effect have to do with the frequency, position and emphasis of "filler items", that is practical applications. However, general principles, with possible exceptions combined with an example, is a more effective form of presentation than mere examples and instances of the general principle. On the basis of their studies, Funkhouser and Maccoby (1973) concluded with a number of rules for writing in which they recommend a varied vocabulary and lots of examples and general rules. They end up: "Just because some people who are well versed in your topic may read what you write, don't let yourself be bluffed into trying to impress them with big words and complicated sentences."

The effects of scientific information

It is probably difficult to design studies to yield meaningful general conclusions on the effects of scientific information. Some scientific information probably produces effects whereas some does not, and the important thing is rather to find out in what way they differ. Effective research in scientific information has largely been of a casuistic character, with little chance for generalizations. It appears, however, that the effects are mostly rather superficial. Swinehart and McLeod (1960) found that almost 50% had not heard of "man-made moons" 6 months before Sputnik 1 but only 10% had not heard 6 months after. Almost 90%, however, could not give more detailed, accurate information on the scientific purpose of the satellites, whether 6 months before or after the Soviet launching.

Along the same lines, a study by Robinson (1963) indicated that readers may not internalize scientific information to the degree of affecting their ways of living. Half of his respondents felt that the general scientific development had influenced their personal habits but very few could say in what ways. Although they might have been aware of such consequences of technical science as being able to fly to foreign countries and having their work made easier by various machinery etc., few had stopped smoking, taken polio vaccine, or started using seat belts in their cars, despite all the information in the mass media about scientific findings concerning lung cancer, polio and traffic accidents.

Another, possibly general, finding is that scientific information primarily reaches those who already have some knowledge on the topic, or those who are used to studying. Swinehart and McLeod (1960), Tichenor, Donohue and Olien (1970) and Krieghbaum (1967) all present positive correlations between exposure, knowledge increments, etc. on the one hand, and prior knowledge, education and socioeconomic status, on the other. Thus scientific information may increase the knowledge gap in society, which of course is against the idea of democracy. The solution certainly is not to abolish scientific information to make all equally ignorant, but rather to adapt its format so that it can be understood by those who are not reached by it at present.

Among the casuistic material, the big debates about fluoridation during the 1950s and nuclear power during the 1970s are particularly interesting from the effects point of view. Both situations seem to have been like this, in principle: a series of scientific discoveries was believed to offer solutions to important societal problems. The information, not about the discoveries *per se* but about their practical implementations on a large scale, produced a vehement reaction. Still, in terms of formal power, the pro side was superior, for example with greater information resources, while the contra side was more of a guerilla-type movement. Despite these power differences, the information from the contra side seems to have had a considerable impact, in some ways superior to that from the pro side: more ardent proselytizing, deeper internalization and, in some places and at some times, even more votes totally. Several writers have analyzed these debates, most of them mainly to explain the phenomenon of popular opposition, but also with some glances towards the information aspect of the problem.

One of the most persistent explanations of the failure of the fluoridation campaigns has been called the alienation hypothesis. It locates the opposition to those who are, or feel themselves to be, lacking power and who are socially unintegrated. For them, the opposition means to attack those in power. Mausner and Mausner (1955) found suspicions and prejudice against science and the scientific establishment among the opponents on the fluoridation issue. Those people would accept a scientist only on the grounds that he had the courage to oppose the rest of the scientific community. The failure of campaigning, according to Mausner and Mausner, is a matter of relying too much on the prestige of the sources and too little on preparing the public for the campaign by way of public meetings, discussions and exhibitions, etc. *before* any decisions are taken.

Sapolsky (1969/70) suggests that the opposition is a consequence of the confusion created among the general public by the debates started by dissident scientists. Although the public may have been quite positive originally, the confusion and uncertainty and the anxiety they may provoke causes protective responses which lead to maintainance of the *status quo*, at least until further and unanimous information is gathered. Sapolsky claims to support his speculations by citing positive correlations between negative attitudes towards changes and factual knowledge about the subject.

Mazur (1975) rather views the contra opinions as the result of complicated interactions among the opposition leaders, the mass media and the general public. Both during the fluoridation debate and the nuclear power debate, there was, according to Mazur, a correlation between the coverage of the mass media and the size of the opposition (with a certain time lag, of course).

Since it is probable that the position of the mass media on the issues varied from medium to medium and from time to time, the correlation reported by Mazur is probably not due to any direct effects of the mass media, as if the audience directly adopts the views of their medium. Rather, the effect of the mass media may be to make people aware of, think about, and discuss an issue before forming opinions of their own, based on various influences. That the mass media may not be very effective in forming and changing opinions among the public as direct copies of their own is, of course, well known since the opinion leader and personal influence studies of Katz and Lazarsfeld (1955). In the area of scientific information, Maccoby and Farquhar (1975) have touched on this question in a field experiment where they found that mass communication has some effect but a much smaller one than mass communication plus personal, almost therapeutic, advice on changing attitudes and habits of smoking, diet and body exercise.

The interpretation of Mazur's correlation, which was proposed above, is in line with what has become known as the agenda-setting function of the mass media (McCombs & Shaw, 1972). This concept has not stimulated any research on scientific information, to our knowledge, but may prove quite fertile. What rôle do the mass media play in making certain scientific areas and issues salient and what are the consequences for the contribution and distribution of grants, the recruitment of students and scientists-to-be (Jones & Meadows, 1976), not to speak of the public's opinion about what areas of research are urgent and valuable?

Scientific information and the environmental movement

A salient area in the scientific information of the mass media during the 1970s has been the ecological sciences. It is rather difficult to distinguish between scientific information and general information about environmental problems – and it may not be important for any practical purposes. This trend has brought some attention from mass-media researchers. Its rate has been documented by McEvoy (1972), who found that the number of articles within this area in American magazines has increased by 500% between 1952 and 1969, and the rate of increase during the 1970s is probably even higher. At the same time, there has been a redistribution among topics within the area. McEvoy reports that attention has shifted from problems in the rural, agricultural environment to the environment of the urban society. Bowman and Hanaford (1977) and Rubin and Sachs (1973) have found a shift from the population explosion to resource problems (energy, raw material, food, etc.) and water problems (supply and pollution) between the 1960s and the 1970s. Local attachments of the media appear to play no important rôle in their gate-keeping, according to Murch (1971). Although one might expect to find national papers dominated by national and global problems and the local press dominated by local problems, only 10% of the articles analyzed in the local press in Murch's sample dealt with local problems.

That the attention of the mass media has had effects on the public awareness of the ecological problems seems quite clear from data reported by Erskine (1972), although Simon (1971) indicates that the apparent level of awareness depends quite a lot on the wording of the questions in the survey. An interesting finding by Murch is that the general public seems less aware of, or less concerned with, local problems than with national and global ones. (This, says Murch, may be an effect of the alleged negligence of the local press to cover local problems.) Despite awareness of the problems, optimism was quite widespread, according to Murch. Almost three-quarters believed that the environmental problems could be solved or much reduced.

According to the same study, the mass media were by far the most important way of keeping the public informed. Only 12% mentioned other sources as being more important. But this may well be a matter of education. Among college students, Novic and Sandman (1974) found 55% preferred sources other than the conventional mass media (radio, television, daily newspapers, nonspecialized magazines but *not* ITV, internal radio, students' magazines, newsletters within the environmental movement, etc.). Novic and Sandman also made the interesting observation that those who for some reasons were dependent on the mass media for their information felt themselves worse informed and also felt that the environmental problems were less serious than other categories. As Novic and Sandman point out, the interpretation of this is not clear. The mass media may not be as effective in producing problem awareness, or the unaware people may prefer the conventional mass media. Be that as it may, Wiebe (1973) points out that problem awareness is not enough: what is also required is a sense of being able to do something about the problem and a determination to do so. What the mass media have done, according to Wiebe, is to create among the general public a sense of "well-informed futility", a nonconstructive apathy.

Scientific information outside the mass media

So far, scientific information has almost exclusively been conceived of as a mass-communication phenomenon, that is, as information spread through the mass media. Obviously, however, information about scientific facts and discoveries may be disseminated to the general public through other channels, particularly by personal face-to-face transmission. As noted above, it is well established since the early 1940s that personal communication may be more effective than mass communication from various points of view, and this might be particularly true about things that are not easily grasped, like scientific news. Despite this, there are few studies of scientific information by word-of-mouth. Anecdotal data are available, for example an account by Hirsch (1976) of the Austrian discussion about nuclear energy. There was an ambitious program instituted over the entire country with panel discussions among expert proponents and opponents. While the purpose of the program was not to argue for nuclear energy, the most spectacular effect was to create suspicions among the public that it indeed was. The discussions often ended in open conflicts with opponent parts of the audience. Now, It appears that the Austrian campaign was more of a mass-communication character, without the flexibility, adaptability and feedback that characterizes personal communication, despite the fact that it employed living humans on location. The audience was indeed allowed to put questions to the panel but only in advance and in writing. The possibility of a dialog was effectively prevented.

Particularly on such scientific–political issues as nuclear power, fluoridation, etc., where the safety of many living and still unborn is at stake, the possibility of a dialog seems essential, however. On such issues, people are concerned and worried, with or without reason. Lots of thoughts, and questions, are pressing for answers, not in terms of reassurance but rather in terms of "getting to know what it is all about." Insofar as these thoughts and questions vary among people, the mass media may not be the most effective vehicle for informing the audience. What may be required is rather information that may be adopted itself. Attractive alternatives are the use of school and the regular education system. The disadvantage, however, is that it is mainly children who have access to schools and that knowledge can be too old-fashioned when they come to use it. Another alternative could be the popular "Open University" projects. Some sort of consultant expert at the university could be another way to communicate science. If using culture as a medium, we have to mention science fiction in literature. The disadvantage of these models is the knowledge we have about the selective behavior of people, for example the probability of a non-book reader reading science fiction is low. Ideally, except for the costs, the information about science should be adapted to the individual audience member, to his unique and changing states of knowledge and anxiety. As science is becoming involved more and more with issues of policy that concern the individual citizen, perhaps scientific information has to become less and less sophisticated technologically, maybe to the point of the two-person face-to-face talk?

Acknowledgments

This work was supported by grants from the National Swedish Environment Protection Board and the Committee for Science Policy Studies at the Swedish Council for Planning and Coordination of Research, by the Audience and Program Research Department at the Swedish Broadcasting Corporation and by the Risk Project sponsored by the Committee for Future Research.

References

Alexander, L. 1966. Space flight news: NASA's press relations and media reaction. *Journalism Q.* **43**, 722–8.

Allport, G. W. and L. J. Postman 1947. *The psychology of rumor*. New York: Holt.

Allport, W. W. and L. J. Postman 1945. The basic psychology of rumor. *Trans. NY Acad. Sci.* **8**, 61–81.

Althoff, P., W. H. Grieg and F. Stuckey 1973. Environmental pollution control attitudes of media managers in Kansas. *Journalism Q.* **50**, 666–72.

Anderson. P. Å. and P. Hertzman 1977. *Tidningsbevakningen av remissvaren till AKA-utredningen*. Risk Project Report, 5–77.

Bartlett, F. C. 1932. *Remembering*. Cambridge: Cambridge University Press.

Berg, U and A. Gahlin 1977. *Hur vi tittade säsongen 1976/77*. Report from the audience and Program Research Department. Swedish Broadcasting Corporation: No 22–1977.

Berg, U. and B. Höijer 1976. *Hur programvalet sker*. Report from the Audience and Program Research Department. Swedish Broadcasting Corporation: No 4–76/77.

Berg, U., K. Hallberg and B. Höijer 1975. *Hur valde tv-publiken?* Report from the Audience and Program Research Department. Swedish Broadcasting Corporation: No 113/73.

Berry, F. C. Jr. 1967. A study of accuracy in local news stories of three dailies. *Journalism Q.* **44**, 482–90.

Blankenburg, W. B. 1970. News accuracy: some findings on the meaning of errors. *J. Comm.* **20**, 375–86.

Bowman, J. S. and K. Hanaford 1977. Mass media and the environment since earth day. *Journalism Q.* **54**, 160–5.

Broberg, K. 1973. Scientists' stopping behavior as indicator of writer's skill. *Journalism Q.* **50**, 763–7.

Charnley, M. V. 1936. Preliminary notes on a study of newspaper accuracy. *Journalism Q.* **13**, 394–401.

Cole, B. J. 1975. Trends in science and conflict coverage in four metropolitan newspapers. *Journalism Q.* **52**, 465–71.

Counts, T. M. Jr. 1975. The influence of messsage and source on selection of statements by reporters. *Journalism Q.* **52**, 443–9.
Cronbach, L. J. 1975. Five decades of public controversy over mental testing. *Am. Psychol.* **30**, 1–14.

Donohew, L. 1967. Newspaper gate-keepers and forces in the news channel. *Public Opinion Q.* **31**, 61–8.

Erskine, H. 1972. The polls: pollution and its costs. *Public Opinion Q.* **36**, 120–36.

Flegel, R. C. and S. H. Chaffee 1971. Influences of editors, readers and personal opinions on reporters. *Journalism Q.* **48**, 645–51.
Fraley, P. C. 1963. The education and training of science writers. *Journalism Q.* **40**, 323–8.
Funkhouser, R. 1969. Levels of science writing in public information sources. *Journalism Q.* **46**, 721–6.
Funkhouser, G. R. and N. Maccoby 1971. Communicating specialized science information to a lay audience. *J. Comm.* **21**, 58–71.
Funkhouser, G. R. and N. Maccoby 1973. Tailoring science writing to the general audience. *Journalism Q.* **50**, 220–6.
Funkhouser, G. R. and N. Maccoby 1974. An experimental study on communicating specialized science information to a lay audience. *Comm. Res.* **1**, 110–128.

Gerbner, G. 1964. Ideological perspectives and political tendencies in news reporting. *Journalism Q.* **41**, 495–508.
Grew, D. G. 1975. Reporters' attitudes. Expected meetings with source and journalistic objectivity. *Journalism Q.* **52**, 219–24, 271.
Gruning, J. E. 1974. Three stopping experiments on the communication of science. *Journalism Q.* **51**, 387–99.

Hirsch, H. 1976. Austria's nuclear debate. *Austria Today* **3/4–76**, 19–20.

Johnson, K. G. 1963. Dimensions of judgement of science news stories. *Journalism Q.* **40**, 315–22.
Jones, G. and J. Meadows 1976. Public understanding of science – British experience. *Sci. Public Pol.* **3**, 433–6.

Katz, E. and P. F. Lazarsfeld 1955. *Personal influence.* New York: The Free Press.
Kerrick, J. S., T. E. Anderson and L. B. Swales 1964. Balance and the writer's attitude in news stories and editorials. *Journalism Q.* **41**, 203–15.
Krieghbaum, H. 1940. The background and training of science writers. *Journalism Q.* **17**, 15–18.
Krieghbaum, H. 1959. Public interest in science news. *Science* **129**, 1092–5.
Krieghbaum, H. 1967. *Science and the Mass Media.* New York: New York University Press.
Kwolek, W. F. 1973. A readability survey of technical and popular literature. *Journalism Q.* **50**, 255–64.

Maccoby, N. and J. W. Farquhar 1975. Communication for health: unselling heart disease. *J. Comm.* **25**, 114–26.
McCombs, M. and D. Shaw 1972. The agenda-setting function of mass media. *Public Opinion Q.* **36**, 176–87.
McEvoy, J. III 1972. The American concern with environment. In *Social Behavior, Natural Resources and the Environment*, W. R. Burch, Jr., N. H. Cheek, Jr. and L. Taylor (eds) 214–36. New York: Harper and Row.
Marshall, H. 1977. Newspaper accuracy in Tucson. *Journalism Q.* **54**, 165–8.
Mausner, B. and J. Mausner 1955. A study of the anti-scientific attitude. *Sci. Am.* **192**, 35–9.

Mayer, J. 1971/72. Science without conscience. *Am. Scholar* **41**, 265–8.

Mazur, A. 1973. Disputes between experts. *Minerva* **11**, 243–62.

Mazur, A. 1975. Opposition to technological innovation. *Minerva* **13**, 58–81.

Murch, A. W. 1971. Public concern for environmental pollution. *Public Opinion Q.* **35**, 100–6.

Novic, K. and P. M. Sandman 1974. How use of mass media affects views on solutions to environmental problems. *Journalism Q.* **51**, 448–52.

Nunn, C. Z. 1979. Readership and coverage of science and technology in newspapers. *Journalism Q.* **56**, 27–31.

O'Keefe, M. T. 1970. The mass media as sources of medical information for doctors. *Journalism Q.* **47**, 95–100.

Oates, W. R. 1973. Social and ethical content in science coverage by newsmagazines. *Journalism Q.* **50**, 680–4.

Pace, R. W. and R. R. Boren 1973. *The human transaction: facets, functions and forms of interpersonal communication.* Glenview, Ill.: Scott, Foresman.

Patterson, J., L. Booth and R. Smith 1969. Who reads about science. *Journalism Q.* **46**, 599–602.

Perlman, D. 1974. Science and the mass media. *Daedalus*, **103**, 207–22.

Pulford, L. 1976. Follow-up of a study of science news accuracy. *Journalism Q.* **53**, 119–21.

Ravets, J. R. 1976. Barriers to communication: knowledge, property and power. *Sci. Public Policy* **3**, 440–1.

Robinson, E. J. 1963. Analyzing the impact of science reporting. *Journalism Q.* **40**, 306–14.

Rubin, D. M. and D. P. Sachs 1973. *Mass media and the environment: water, resources, land-use and atomic energy in California.* New York: Praeger.

Ryan, M. A. 1975. Factor analytic study of scientists' responses to errors. *Journalism Q.* **52**, 333–6.

Ryan, M. and S. L. Dunwoody 1975. Academic and professional training patterns of science writers. *Journalism Q.* **52**, 239–46, 290.

Sapolsky, H. M. 1969/70. The fluoridation controversy. An alternative explanation. *Pub. Op. Q.* **33**, 241–8.

Shaw, D. L. and P. Van Nevel 1967. The informative value of medical science news. *Journalism Q.* **44**, 548.

Sherburne, E. G. Jr. 1963. Science on television: a challenge to creativity. *Journalism Q.* **40**, 300–5.

Simon. J. 1971. Public attitudes toward population and pollution. *Journalism Q.* **35**, 93–9.

Small, W. E. 1964. The science writer survey. *Nat. Assoc. Sci. Writers Newsletters* **11**, 1–13.

Sorenson, J. S. and D. D. Sorenson 1971. A comparison of science content in magazines in 1964–65 and 1969–70. *Journalism Q.* **50**, 97–101.

Swinehart, J. W. and J. M. McLeod 1960. News about science: channels, audiences and effects. *Pub. Opinion Q.* **24**, 583–9.

Tankard, J. and M. Ryan 1974. News source perceptions of accuracy of science coverage. *Journalism Q.* **51**, 219–25, 334.

Tannenbaum, R. 1963. Communication of science information. *Science* **140**, 579–83.

Tichenor, P. J., G. A. Donohue and C. N. Olien 1970. Mass media flow and differential growth in knowledge. *Public Opinion Q.* **34**, 159–70.

Tichenor, P., C. Olien and G. Donohue 1976. Community control and care of scientific information. *Comm. Res.* **3**, 403–24.

Tichenor, P. J., C. N. Olien, A. Harrison and G. Donohue 1970. Mass communication systems and communication accuracy in science news reporting. *Journalism Q.* **47**, 673–83.

Troan, J. 1960. Science reporting – today and tomorrow. *Science* **131**, 1193–6.

Wade. S. and W. Schramm 1969/70. The mass media as sources of public affairs, science and health knowledge. *Pub. Opinion Q.* **33**, 197–209.

Wiebe, G. D. 1973. Mass media and man's relationship to his environment. *Journalism Q.* **50**, 426–32, 446.

Williams, F., H. S. Dordick and F. Horstman 1977. Where citizens go for information. *J. Comm.* **27**, 95–100.

Witt, W. 1976. Effects of quantification in scientific writing. *J. Comm.* **26**, 67–9.

Wright, W. R. 1975. Mass media as sources of medical information. *J. Commun.* **25**, 171–3.

Part IV

CONCLUSION

15 Risk, power and rationality: conclusions of a research project on risk generation and risk assessment in a societal perspective

LENNART SJÖBERG

Introduction

Risk research has been sponsored by industry and government in many countries, largely because public opposition to some technological development has created powerful constraints on further expansion in, for example, the nuclear power industry. It has been found that large segments of the public are easily aroused over risks. Some of the factors responsible for risk reactions have been delineated by risk researchers: moral indignation and the existence of credible experts who support the alarm signals may be among the most potent factors. Psychologists, being perhaps less sensitive to the power games played in research funding than their colleagues in, for example, sociology, have been successful in demonstrating the lack of rationality in common sense thinking.

Bias

The work on heuristics and biases by Kahneman and Tversky (e.g. Kahneman *et al.* 1982) is also well known. However, the Kahneman–Tversky type of inferential tasks have no established ecological validity. They mainly resemble exam questions in undergraduate statistics courses. Several authors (e.g. Hogarth 1981, Edwards 1983, Berkeley & Humphreys 1982) have questioned the Kahneman–Tversky findings; see also the special issue of *The Behavioral and Brain Sciences* issued in 1981 and devoted to this topic. It is a little shocking to read in the paper by Berkeley and Humphreys (1982) that *none* of the citations of Tversky and Kahneman (1974) in sources other than core psychology journals was critical to the conclusions that people's thinking is severely deficient due to the use of simplifying heuristics. It seems not to be generally known that the work on heuristics has usually not attempted to describe the psychological processes leading to the judgments, nor has it tried to depict the phenomenology of how the judgment problems are interpreted. It is often quite dubious if the allegation of cognitive deficiency is justified. Furthermore, as stressed by Hogarth (1981), what looks like a bias may, in dynamic situations, be an efficient way of approaching a goal if action is continuous and allows for repeated adjustment on the basis of feedback. One may accept with some tranquility the existence of bias factors in single judgments.

There has been much less work on risk indifference than on risk exaggeration. The reason is probably that those sponsoring risk research see exaggeration as a problem, not indifference. The funding agencies are rooted in the power structure and it is only natural that they basically accept the premises of technological and social development which are being questioned by those in opposition. The rationality of the informed experts is rarely questioned by those in power, but the general public is assumed to be less than rational. Still, the indifference to the very real risks in such strategic sectors as that of nuclear power is just as irrational as the emotional exaggeration of risks, and just as emotional. The Three Mile Island accident in 1979 exposed an ill-prepared organization which had neglected its responsibilities for human lives and large economic investments. The factors responsible for the neglect of risks constitute an important problem for further research on risks.

Cognitive perspectives

Risk reactions have usually been treated within a cognitive framework. The cognitive perspective is very natural for contemporary psychologists and cognitive models have come to dominate theoretical psychology. However, it is unclear just how well an exclusive cognitive approach will generalize to real-world problems with their typical mixture of cognitive, motivational and emotional factors. A broader approach would seem to be required in obtaining a better description of risk reactions in real-life settings.

One type of question is the linguistic one. Politicians, of course, have to be sensitive to the choice of right words so as to create the desired connotations and avoid unwanted ones. The term accident is a case in point. Calling something an accident probably tends to mitigate the burden of responsibility which otherwise should have been adopted by one or several agents. The concept of an accident seems to imply that an event was random and could not have been foreseen. In the traffic sector, for example, road accidents occur with fairly constant frequencies but each one is the outcome of a number of at least partly random factors. So who is responsible for each one of them? Accidents involve in a concrete way a few individuals, whereas the planners are only involved in a very abstract and detached manner. Children are taught to be careful and to be concerned about their own safety. It is therefore likely that the responsibility for an accident is mainly put on those directly involved in the chain of events, not on the people who made decisions about the environment in which the accident took place.

Linguistic habits tie in with moral dimensions and the area of risk surely brings in some of the most central moral values. Respect for human life is demanded of decision makers and moral indignation is a powerful political force. If a risk is accepted or not probably depends partly on how it is labeled and where the label fits in the system of moral dimensions that is applied. The linguistic and ethical aspects of risk reactions deserve further investigation.

Emotional perpectives

The emotional reactions to risk have been little investigated. Risk reactions concern life-threatening events, however, and therefore it is likely that they are closely connected to emotions and imagery. The reactions to risks may well be heavily influenced by strongly salient events which give rise to powerful imagery, the rôle of which has not been thoroughly examined. Some of the emotionality may be neurotic, of course, and only loosely tied to reality. It should also be stressed that emotionality is usually present in *both* sides of a technology debate (cf. Sjöberg 1980) and not a phenomenon exclusively to be found among technology opponents.

Debates tend to bring about black and white pictures of the issues. Montgomery (1983) has suggested that decisions are antedated by an elaborate process of editing the information so as to produce one dominating alternative. Such an alternative can then be easily defended. Beliefs and values should correlate strongly and positively for an "edited" and preferred option (cf. Sjöberg 1982), and negatively for a rejected alternative. It is typically found that many strong belief-value correlations exist in a group of subjects. They apparently prevail even if there is no acute emotional arousal (Sjöberg & Biel 1983). It may be the case that people act defensively in distorting information so as to avoid any unpleasant emotional experience; but this hypothesis cannot explain prevalent tendencies towards "hyper vigilance" (Janis & Mann 1977), i.e. exaggeration of risk.

There are indications that experts play a crucial part in affecting the risk reactions of the public. What makes some experts sound the alarm and under which conditions will they be heard? Case studies of several risk topics might be of value in answering these questions.

Social conflicts over risks arise because some parties see risks where others see opportunities. Take, again, nuclear power as an example. Many people are mainly concerned with the threat of an accident and subsequent dangerous radiation. For them, electric power has always been available in other ways and they see little or no benefit in getting it from a nuclear power plant. Others, who are in favor of nuclear power, consider mainly its economic benefits in producing cheap power. The risk is considered to be an unpleasant side effect to the major purpose and rôle of a power plant. Thus, the entire cognitive orientations of the two sides differ. They do not have the same decision problem. Opponents to nuclear power are mainly concerned with promoting safety and avoiding risks; proponents with economic benefits.[1] Conflict between parties which structure a decision problem differently is an important area for further study.

Risk reactions and risk generation are partly overlapping topics. Risks are typically produced as side effects to some industrial programs. Risks are often produced when dangers are overlooked or underestimated. If risks are paid attention to only rather late in the process, the chances are great that there will be much opposition towards the cost involved in backing up and trying other solutions. The risk perceptions of responsible decision makers, and their evaluation of the risk perceptions prevalent in the public at large, therefore constitute another important problem.

Rationality and decision making

Finally, rational decision making in the area of risk should also be considered. Rationality requires knowledge. Risk problems often involve complicated technical and statistical aspects, and democratic influence on decisions demands that the public be sufficiently well informed about them. Mass media nowadays do carry more scientific information than previously, but chances are that it is not too widely read or understood. Also, experts typically disagree on crucial issues when the topic becomes hot enough, and the public is left with inconsistent messages. The media seem many times to exploit controversy for commercial reasons; the concept of "expert" may at times appear to be very widely stretched in order to give some credibility and respectability to more or less alerting viewpoints. The general education in scientific matters provided by primary and secondary schools could play an important rôle in promoting rationality in the field of risk; it would be of interest to investigate to what extent schools give information about risks. But even if schools score fairly well here, it is still necessary that mass media assume the major responsibility for informing the public. Risk research should obviously be concerned with the media, and with their effect on the rationality of decision making.

Rationality is not only a question of having valid and sufficient information, but also of utilizing that information in the right way. Choice alternatives are typically in conflict with each other; no one alternative is dominating. (If it were, there would be no decision problem.) When it comes to risk, one usually has to evaluate options with small probabilities of large negative consequences. The normative and descriptive analysis of how such options should be, and are, evaluated constitutes an important topic for further research.

Explanatory note

1 I believe this to be true in spite of the presumably valid argument that fossil sources of energy are at least as dangerous as nuclear power. This is an argument added *post hoc* by the nuclear power proponents; while factually well supported, it does not explain why the decision was once taken to develop nuclear power.

References

Berkeley, D. and P. Humphreys 1982. Structuring decision problems and the bias heuristic. *Acta Psychol.* **50**, 20–52.

Edwards, W. 1983. Human cognitive capacities, representativeness and ground rules for research. In *Analyzing and aiding decision making*. P. C. Humphreys, O. Svenson and A. Vari (eds), pp. 507–17. Amsterdam: North-Holland.

Hogarth, R. 1981. Beyond discrete biases: Functional and dysfunctional aspects of judgmental heuristics. *Psychol. Bull.* **90**, 197–217.

Janis, I. L. and L. Mann 1977. *Decision making*. New York: The Free Press.

Kahneman, D., P. Slovic and A. Tversky (eds) 1982. *Judgment under uncertainty: heuristics and biases*. New York: Cambridge University Press.

Montgomery, H. 1983. Decision rules and the search for a dominance structure. Towards a process model of decision making. In *Analyzing and aiding decision processes*. P. C. Humphreys, O. Svenson and A. Vari (eds), pp. 343–70. Amsterdam: North-Holland, in press.

Sjöberg, L. 1980. The risk of risk analysis. *Acta Psychol.* **45**, 301–21.

Sjöberg, L. 1982. Beliefs and values as components of attitudes. In *Social psychophysics*, B. Wegener (ed.), pp. 199–218. Hillsdale, N.J.: Erlbaum.

Sjöberg, L. and A. Biel 1983. Mood and belief-value correlation. *Acta Psychol.* **53**, 253–70.

Index